Sandra Gregory was born in C
up in Kent. She ran a succ
travelling to Thailand aged 25
teacher. Jailed in 1993 for sm
seven years of a 25-year sentence.

Since her release she has worked with prison reform groups and has given talks about her experiences in schools. In 2002 she began studying geography at Oxford University.

Michael Tierney is an award-winning writer with *The Herald*, where he most recently won Feature Writer of the Year at the 2003 British Press Awards. He was born in Glasgow in 1968 and now lives there with his wife, daughter and son.

Praise for *Forget You Had A Daughter*:

'I believe that Sandra Gregory's book should be required reading everywhere… through her experience, and her most eloquent account of it, she surely has saved and will save many others from the same ordeal' MARTIN BELL, OBE

'Her time in Bangkok is vividly described, full of the colour and liveliness of Thailand… The description of life inside the jail is horrifying… This is an extraordinary story, and Sandra Gregory's resilience and spirit make her book oddly uplifting at times, even though the circumstances she describes are about as dark as it gets' waterstones.co.uk

'[Sandra Gregory] was jailed for 25 years in Thailand's infamous "Bangkok Hilton". It seemed that, for the sake of foolish greed, she betrayed everything her safe middle-class upbringing had promised. But as her extraordinary biography reveals, amid the degradation she found redemption, and the strength to rebuild the life she had thrown away' *Mail on Sunday*

'[A] salutary story of a convicted drug smuggler' *The Times*

'What a startling, challenging, disturbing book. Anyone who cares about prison conditions will find the worst here; anyone who cares about making prisons better must read it. This is not a comfortable book – that is why it matters'

ANDREW RC McLELLAN,
HM CHIEF INSPECTOR OF PRISONS FOR SCOTLAND

'Writing about one's experiences and opening up one's life and emotions in such a public way is a very brave act – what Sandra went through and what many prisoners still go through has a devastating effect not only on the person in prison but also their family and friends' PRISONERS ABROAD

'She covers her ordeal, in gory detail, in *Forget You Had A Daughter*. The book is not a cry about Thai justice. Instead, it bristles with horror – directed at young travellers, their parents, and anyone who cares for them'

The South Australia Advertiser

'Sandra Gregory deeply regrets her crime. She accepts that it was a serious offence and she deserved to be punished. Her book is a warning to others not to take the risk that she did and to recognise how one serious mistake can change your life' MALCOLM BRUCE MP

'Will serve as a powerful warning to anyone who thinks smuggling drugs could be a good way to make a fast buck'

Daily Post

'A tragic story... there were some wonderful moments'

TAMZIN OUTHWAITE, *Red*

'The incredible story of Sandra Gregory' *The Booklover*

Forget You Had A Daughter

Doing Time in the 'Bangkok Hilton'

SANDRA GREGORY
WITH MICHAEL TIERNEY

VISION

First published in Great Britain in 2002 by Vision,
a division of Satin Publications Ltd.
101 Southwark Street
London SE1 0JF
UK
info@visionpaperbacks.co.uk
www.visionpaperbacks.co.uk
Publisher: Sheena Dewan

This edition published 2006.

A catalogue record for this book is available from the British Library.

ISBN: 1-904132-01-4

2 4 6 8 10 9 7 5 3 1

Printed and bound in Great Britain by
Cox & Wyman Ltd, Reading, Berkshire.

For parents everywhere.

For all those who remain behind bars.
For those who will never leave.

And for Pippy.

I never saw a man who looked
With such a wistful eye
Upon that little tent of blue
Which prisoners call the sky.

OSCAR WILDE, *The Ballad of Reading Gaol*

Contents

Introduction

Sandra Gregory has a story to tell. It is the story of an ordeal that would have broken most people and came close to breaking her. Its redeeming features are her courage and resilience, and the enduring love and loyalty of her family. On the face of it, it is a story about a young woman imprisoned for drug trafficking in Thailand. It is also – and this is how she herself sees it – a story about love and the things people don't say when they should.

In 1993 she was arrested at Bangkok airport, with her companion Robert Lock, about to board a flight for Japan. She was found to be carrying 89 grams of heroin for him. Her pay-off, had they not been intercepted, would have been the £1,000 which would have bought her air ticket back to Britain with plenty to spare. It wasn't the easy money that it seemed. Instead, she was sentenced by the court in Thailand to 25 years in prison. Robert Lock, already known to the police, was acquitted; he was released and had already re-offended while she was still in jail.

The title of Sandra Gregory's book, *Forget You Had A Daughter*, comes from the letter that she wrote to her parents after her arrest. It is a story told without self-pity or self-justification. 'What I have done is not excusable,' she writes, 'and above all else I knew better than to do what I did.' Nor does she reproach the Thai authorities and their system of justice, except to allow herself the wry reflection that their prison sentences are perhaps a touch on the long side.

She served four years in Bangkok before being transferred to British prisons including Holloway and Durham. She found them no better, and in some respects worse, than Lard Yao, the women's section of the notorious 'Bangkok Hilton'. Back in Britain she was spared no brutality, partly as a consequence of the length of her sentence, which led to her being classified – along with Myra Hindley and Rosemary West – as a high security risk. Anyone who thinks that we operate a prison system which, for all its faults, is fundamentally humane and decent, should read her personal account of it and think again. In Durham especially she found herself living in hell and surrounded by evil. And as for Holloway, it was 'home to the biggest bunch of nutcases, psychos, robbers, thieves, druggies, gang members, whackos and dysfunctional lunatics I had come across'.

The irony was that, although detained in British prisons, she was outside the British justice system. She could be released only through a pardon by the King of Thailand. As her ordeal entered its eighth year, the prospect of the pardon still seemed remote. Her parents wrote to me, as to many other MPs, about her plight and the disproportionate length of her sentence. Sympathy for drug-smugglers was not a popular cause; but I am proud to have supported her own MP, the Liberal Democrat Malcolm Bruce, in his campaign for her release. The King's pardon was eventually granted, following an adjournment debate initiated by Mr Bruce. Contrary to popular belief, MPs are sometimes able to play a part in making good things happen.

The chapter that Sandra Gregory wrote about her release, into a foreign country known as freedom, is one of the most eloquent in the book. She was still unsure of herself, and almost in a state of exploration, when she came to meet us in the House of Commons. The more I learned of what had happened to her, the more I felt that she should write it down, for the benefit of others; and I urged her to do so.

The road from Thailand to Oxford University does not regularly run through Holloway, Durham and Cookham Wood prison in Kent. Sandra's acceptance by the University delighted her and helped to restore her confidence. But before going there she took a year out, not only to write the book, but to talk to high school students all over the country about the drug dangers awaiting the unsuspecting, especially young travellers in their gap years, not only in Thailand. I have spoken to some of the kids who listened to her. They could not have found a more credible witness. Without intending to, she had been to hell and back on their behalf. They were deeply moved and impressed.

I believe that Sandra Gregory's book should be required reading everywhere, not just in our schools. Through her experience, and her most eloquent account of it, she surely has saved and will save many others from the same ordeal.

Blessings don't come in harsher disguises than this; but at the end of her story, and most remarkably of all, she describes what happened to her as 'actually some kind of privilege'. The privilege is ours, that she has shared it with us.

Martin Bell

ONE

'Boom, in Thai, You Die'

6 February 1993

To my dearest parents, grandparents and brother

I am going to ask the hardest and very last thing from you all. I do not want you to forgive me, what I have done is not excusable and above all else I knew better than to do what I did… I have not been wise and I am asking you all to please forget that you ever had a daughter, granddaughter or sister. I know that this will come as a shock. I am so very sorry for the shame I have brought on you all.

I needed to come home with my pride and this seemed the easiest and quickest way to do it. I have not been well for months now and have been so terribly homesick. I love you all and God I do miss you, but please never mention my name again, try to do as I say and act as though you never knew me and throw any photographs of me away. I cannot do five, ten or twenty years like this. You produced a wonderful human being who wanted to change the world, but has instead messed it up.

I am so very, very sorry.

Sandra

Every few minutes the evening trains slip in and out of the darkness in Hualumphong Railway Station in Bangkok and I watch them roll on their tracks, bursting with commuters. Masses of dark faces emerge, like spectres, from the carriages and they stare at me as they amble through the station. Except for the grind of metal and iron the only thing I can hear is the sound of my own heartbeat. I am sticky, wet and very tired.

It is rush hour and the effort of standing here alone, while waiting for Robert Lock, is unbearably painful. My thoughts stray to home, in West Yorkshire, and to my mother and father and grandparents, in Scotland, and how I will be seeing them all soon. I run my fingers across my new travel bag. The bag and also my new clothes – a white cotton shirt with tiny blue, purple and green flowers on it, a pair of baggy cotton trousers and a pair of green suede court shoes – help disguise the way I am feeling. In a way they have turned me into someone else, someone innocent.

I pace up and down the small stretch of platform, flexing my legs, feeling the light bead of perspiration on my upper lip. Does anyone have any idea what I am planning? Can they see it in me? Does every glance I make, searching for Robert, give me away?

'It's not really you carrying the drugs,' I repeat over and over like a mantra. 'Just a few more days and you will be home.' I am 27 years old and I almost believe it.

Where is Robert? He is late. For an hour I have stood here at the express train ticket point, where we have arranged to meet. Ruth Billingham, his girlfriend, is coming with him and we will all fly to Tokyo together. What will I do if they don't appear? One thing's for sure: I won't go to the airport by myself.

The light is fading as the last express train pulls away. It is well after 6.00 pm and we should have been on it. A knot, the size of a small child's fist, appears again in my stomach and I sigh nervously. A man walks by me, staring. I'm sure he knows.

On the platform, next to where the trains are leaving, I feel completely alone and I want to abandon the plans I have made. It would be simple. All I need to do is walk away from the station, and return to my apartment. I still have time to throw this terrible stuff away, out of my mind and out of my life for good.

Suddenly, frantically, Ruth is running towards me, waving her arms. My stomach heaves again. Ruth, with her bleached-blonde hair and rugged features, is wearing a pair of very tight jeans and a T-shirt, and she looks more frightened than me.

'Where have you been?' she demands, as she gets closer, her face contorting with mild fury.

'I've been here for over an hour waiting for you and Robert,' I reply, slightly annoyed by her tone.

It turns out that there are two express train ticket offices and we have been standing at different ones. Robert, meanwhile, is frantic and angry, his face like an exit wound. He virtually ignores me when we catch up and I sense he blames me for the mix-up. Things are not going well but I'm in too deep to back out now so I suggest we get a taxi to the airport.

'No,' he snaps, picking up his bags, 'we'll get a train.' Robert dashes around the station, across the rails and up the tracks while Ruth and I trail behind, like useless acolytes. Eventually he finds a train that is going to the airport area of Bangkok. The three of us, hardly saying a word, clamber aboard. Faces, heads, hands, elbows are hanging out of the windows and there is little in the way of air.

Again, I wonder if anyone suspects anything. Have they any idea what I am attempting? Do these people – who are brushing against my legs, touching my hands, breathing on me, breathing on windows – do they have any idea I am carrying heroin? Would they care?

Chunks of metal grate against the tracks, and the train crawls onwards, stopping at each station; perhaps, more hopefully than anything else, I think we will miss the plane. I still have time to walk away and my family will never know. No one will ever know.

Leave them, Sandra. Leave them.

Weeks earlier I developed acute pains in my abdomen, which were excruciating, and now they are intensifying. It is a monster pain, like nails splitting through my flesh, and it's getting worse as the train rattles to its destination. It had been high in my stomach but now it has travelled down my right-hand side towards the bottom of my ribcage. I lean over the back of a seat with one of my bags rammed into my ribs because the pain is so bad and I barely have the strength to make a fist. I can hardly stand up straight.

The train might slow down, Sandra, it might even break down.

The heat inside the train rolls back and forth across my face while the number of passengers multiplies at every stop; they become my co-conspirators. They do nothing to stop me.

'Get off the train,' I whisper to myself. 'Take a taxi, a motorbike, a tuk-tuk, anything, but just go.' I want to be braver than I have ever thought possible, but I can't.

A scuffle breaks out halfway to the airport and the train comes to an unscheduled halt. A group of men jump off, grabbing a young man who is fleeing and he is dragged back to the carriage. They sit him in a window seat, while one man from the group sits next to him and the others surround him. It is a citizen's arrest.

Eyes popping and scared, the young man is very agitated. I look at Robert, but he just stares through the grimy windows so I shut my eyes, and try to forget the thoughts I am having. What will happen if one of the packages bursts? Will it kill me? The thought of death doesn't concern me. I wipe another bead of sweat from the top of my lip.

It feels like I'm watching an old movie where I already know the ending, where I can actually see it, even feel it; it is swimming inside me, but I pretend it's all new and that I'll still be surprised by the outcome. I know what is going to happen. I pretend and imagine it will all work out – although I have a strange foreboding that it won't. If I can just do this, get to Japan, and take the money that Robert has promised me, then travel back to Bangkok. After that I will have enough money to buy a plane ticket and return home. I have even made a list of all the presents I will buy my family and friends and their children.

I think of my dad. Whenever he went away on a business trip he always returned with presents for my mum, my brother and myself. I want to do the same. Everyone will be amazed that I have stayed away so long, but they will welcome me back with open arms, and there will be no questions. Then I'll regale them with stories of my adventures over the previous two years, about my life in a tropical paradise, with beaches on numerous islands too beautiful to describe – it almost hurts to imagine them again. The only difficult questions I will face will be my own. And I can dream away the bad bits.

Eventually we reach our station. We get off. Robert and I begin arguing over the direction we should go. Finally, for some reason, my logic prevails and we skip over a bridge, and arrive in the airport terminal. Our flight is leaving in 20 minutes but we are so late getting there that all the other passengers have already checked in and are sitting on the plane.

'We'll check in, then separate,' Robert says.

'OK,' I reply. 'Fine.'

We reach the check-in counter and just as we are about to present our tickets, three or four men arrive.

'Mr Lock,' says one man, 'you've come already. Please come this way.'

All of them are wearing casual shirts and trousers. Each of them hides behind rather ominous-looking, gold-rimmed mirrored glasses; they possess an efficiency and urgency that is immediately unsettling. Who are they?

'Are you with him?' one man asks.

'Yes,' I reply, 'I am.' I bite my lip and nod.

For some stupid reason I think they have a list of all the passengers who have booked on our flight and who are late in arriving at the terminal. I imagine they are going to expedite our journey to the plane. Robert's face doesn't see it my way and he has the vacant look of a child who has been caught doing something wrong.

'Come this way.'

We follow them, walking at pace through the airport, past people checking in, past people milling around and past others waiting for the arrival of recent flights. No one pays much attention to our group. As we walk, the moment seems to be increasing into something more spectacular; the officials are walking with the confident air of men whose purpose is a great deal grander than that of airport check-in staff. We are walking way too far and not in the direction of the gates at all.

Finally we come to a door and find ourselves in a hallway with a pale green and yellow linoleum floor, smelling of disinfectant and cigarette smoke. The familiarity of the airport has gone, and we are now in a small room further away again from any terminal activity. There are more linoleum tiles on the floor. It is a seedy little space, sheathed in regularity and dirty convention; a real sense of foreboding chokes the air.

No sooner have we stopped walking than more people descend upon us and both Robert and Ruth find themselves surrounded. The contents of their bags are quickly, and abruptly, strewn across the floor. The Thai officials look like vultures fighting over a dead carcass. Robert is suddenly barefoot.

To my left there is a large pinboard and above it a sign – Customs Seizures. On the grubby pinboard there are many large, glossy photographs, mainly of African men holding small black boards, with a number of packages containing drugs placed in front of them.

Oh my God! Oh shit, Sandra.

We are in the customs room. My heart booms; it is beating out of my chest.

None of this is making sense. Robert assured me there would be no hitches. Everything was supposed to have been cleared with customs officials; there would be no searches and no one would be caught. That's what he had told me. That's what I had been promised.

'I need to go to the loo,' I blurt out. By now I really do need to go, but I also want to flush away all the evidence.

'In a minute you go.'

They begin conducting a serious and diligent search of Robert and Ruth while I stand by the door, vacant, and a little grotesque, doing nothing at all, except staring. Slowly, I am going into shock. My eyes dart around the room. I have never really intended to smuggle heroin, and they will understand this. Of course they will. I am just a mule. I'm just carrying it – it's not mine.

The men remove Robert's belt; Ruth is also barefoot. No one is paying me or my bags any attention. Minutes pass and I think again about the presents I will buy for everyone at home.

'Here,' someone barks, 'come here.'

Robert is taken behind what looks like a hospital screen, and then quickly reappears. He makes a dark sound in his throat, which he directs at Ruth, quickly explaining that he has just been X-rayed.

Oh shit!

The word explodes in my head. They can't X-ray me. One official shoots an occasional glance in my direction as I look at Ruth, who is shaking. I don't know much about her. I have met her only once before and she seemed pleasant enough. Ruth is taken behind the screen. Like Robert, a few minutes earlier, she quickly reappears and I presume she has also been X-rayed. Quietly, without much fuss, the customs men begin replacing the contents of Robert and Ruth's bags. I look at Robert. He stares blankly in my direction.

'Come this way, please,' says a woman I have not even noticed standing there.

My breathing gets massively heavier and I can hear myself trembling.

Be polite, I tell myself.

'Come here,' the woman says again, and I am led behind the screen. The X-ray looks like a torture chamber.

'We need to X-ray you,' she says.

Slowly, I raise myself up onto the table, like some shapeless vegetable. Suddenly, and enormously, I am involved in something that has lost all sense of proportion. My head is spinning and, for an instant, I am back in my apartment staring at the black packages of heroin that Robert gave to me only hours earlier. Why have I done this? I want to throw up.

'OK,' says one of the men, 'you can go now.'

'What?'

'You can go now.'

His words explode in my face. 'You can go now.' I hear it again.

Oh my God! I scream to myself. *Oh my God.*

Did I hear him correctly? The heroin couldn't have shown up. I am bursting with relief. Nothing has shown up.

Christ, I've made it.

Was it right that they didn't see it? I don't know, and I don't care. Immediately I feel guilty but stay quiet. Back in the customs search room, Robert, his face cold-set like a statue, and Ruth, more animated than before, are kicking up a fuss about how they have missed their plane and doesn't anyone realise how inconvenient all this is?

The customs men assure us the plane is waiting; the pilot has been told to wait. Robert and Ruth continue...

'Don't you realise we are British citizens?'

Shut up, Robert, you prat, I think to myself.

We move quickly from the room while Robert and Ruth quietly mumble to each other. At the bureau de change we pick up some Japanese currency and are joined by a woman from the airport authority who begins talking, via a walkie-talkie, to the pilot on the plane. We have made it.

Our escort points to the toilet 30 metres away from where we are standing, and asks if we still need to go. I look up. If I really want I can get rid of this stuff, I can flush it all down the toilet and there will be no more worries. But what is the point? I have made it this far. I have earned £1,000.

'No, it doesn't matter,' I say to her. 'I'll go on the plane.'

She smiles; then, through the walkie-talkie, reassures the pilot we are almost there and I can hear the sound of the plane's engines gunning. Robert and Ruth walk ahead. Time to gather my thoughts.

Then I hear the sound of rushing footsteps behind me and suddenly someone grabs my shoulder while another hand grabs vigorously at the handle of my brown leather bag. I look around in a panic, complaining, half-heartedly, that he is making a mistake.

'What's all this about?' I ask, looking for Robert.

'I don't know,' replies the woman with the walkie-talkie, sounding a little upset. 'I'm very sorry. I think they want you to go back.'

They march me briskly back to the customs room and the official who appeared to be in charge, who had been waiting for Robert at the check-in counter, looks straight at me.

'We know you are trying to leave my country with heroin.'

The man looks up at one of the walls where an X-ray has been attached to a light box. I know instantly that the X-ray belongs to me. I shake my head. I take a step backwards and my heart sinks. Transparent, endlessly relevant and guilty, it is a picture of my lower abdomen. He points and I look up. There are four packages containing heroin and they are identical – it is the heroin Robert brought to my apartment. Robert, his face a mask of beetroot anger, and a panicked Ruth are hauled into the room and Robert is screaming the place down.

'I've got a plane to catch,' he snarls. 'What the hell's going on? It's disgraceful.' His voice is fighting, almost in pain.

Can't he see? Can't he see the X-ray on the wall?

'Count the packages, Robert, and you'll see why they're making all this fuss.' My head is spinning around the room, and all I can hear are the shouts from the customs men. My body feels like it has been wedged under something heavy, something unpleasant. I look at Robert, and point at the evidence on the wall.

'Robert,' I whisper, almost crying, 'they know. They *know*.'

When Robert sees the X-ray his face buckles, and he turns away from me.

'I don't know this woman,' he shouts. 'What's going on? I don't know her. This is disgraceful. Will someone please tell me why I am here?'

I stare at Robert. What did he just say? *What did he just say?*

My God! No, Robert, you can't say that. Please, don't say that, it's not true.

My heart pounds almost to the point where it might explode inside me. I feel tired, like an old woman who is suddenly lost and confused. For a while I just stare at the X-ray. The customs men are still screaming in Thai. One of them looks at me and puts two fingers to his temple.

'Boom, in Thai, you die.'

I can see my pitiful reflection in the gold rim of his sunglasses.

'You bad. You heroin. You die. Ha ha.'

'Robert, tell them the truth. You've got to tell them.'

He is cuffed behind his back, shackled at the ankles and led away. As he is taken out the door, one of the customs men turns to one side, jumps high into the air and kicks him in the small of his back. As he shuffles screaming down the hallway, in chains, over and over I hear the sound of kicking. Ruth is led away to another room.

The officials leave me in the search room with an officer who tells me to sit down while a set of heavy handcuffs is brought out for me. This is no dream, and no amount of dreaming will take this away.

My God, Sandra, what have you done, what have you done? Emotionally I shrink to my childhood self.

The customs man is laughing; the acoustics of the room echo. 'Boom,' he says, 'in Thai, you die.'

I don't cry. I am in such a state of shock that I am just numb and I sit there quietly, staring.

The man, his fingers at his temples, repeats himself again. 'Boom, in Thai, you die.'

I wonder if it will hurt.

TWO

Class Act

School Report, 1978
Sandra's unfortunate desire to always have the last word will, I fear, lead her into trouble for some time yet...
Swadelands School, Lenham

I close my eyes. We are together, my brother and I, riding on bicycles next to our house and there is a cartoon sticker on the red frame of mine. It is warm and breezy, the summer of 1971 and I am happy for sure. Moments earlier – or moments later, I can't quite recall – we are whizzing around the cul-de-sac street and in the distance I can hear the distinct sounds of family. It might be our family or it might be someone else's, I don't know, but the sounds retain that shiny-haired, clear-eyed warmth of a relationship from years gone by, that somehow seems missing now.

Here I am again, Sandra Mary Gregory, two years old, with curly, yellow hair, and a crinkle in my eyes. I am wearing my new, pink nightgown and gazing at the camera as if it might whisk me away somewhere magical. Beside me again is my brother, ordinary yet sparkling; he is five years older than me, though sometimes it seems like a lifetime.

I picture another scene, this time with John, my first and best friend for a decade of my early life; he is giving me a piggyback ride on the grass. As recollections go they are nothing much, just little snapshots of childhood, but they are precious and my memory is littered with them. In yet another I am 12 years old, riding across the grass on Goldie, my beautiful pony. For years I imagined him as mine, something special, not a riding-school pony at all. I was a distant child, caught up in my own little dreams, some happy, some sad, and others mostly selfish. At 12 I wanted everything.

I was born on 30 May 1965, in a place called Minchinhampton, Gloucestershire, but grew up in Hollingbourne, five miles outside Maidstone in Kent, after my parents moved there when I was six months old. Hollingbourne looks as quaint as the name might suggest; it is quintessential Middle England and everywhere there is a nascent image of well-bred people imagining themselves as humble folk of the soil. The people who lived there spent their time making jams and pies, while swapping recipes with neighbours, and attending the village fete. Everyone took great pride in their gardens. Perhaps the most memorable aspect of Hollingbourne is Eyehorn House, where a famous poltergeist has, for years, wreaked havoc upon its residents.

Typically, it was a middle-class upbringing, although both my parents, Stan and Doreen Gregory, grew up in working class districts of Stockport and Dundee, respectively. They met in London and married there soon after meeting, breaking the hearts of my maternal grandparents with the knowledge that their daughter had been stolen, by an Englishman no less, from them and, of course, Scotland. My mum was concussed with love while completing her nursing training.

Hollingbourne really was the most wonderful place to be young. John and my brother and myself built fantastic tree houses and dens, and we roamed the vast expanse of open fields and splashed around in rivers and streams. I attended Hollingbourne Primary School, a wonderful little place, which never had more than around 70 pupils.

When I was aged four my mum took me to ballet lessons at the local village hall, but even then the quiescent life of running around in a pink tutu didn't suit my nature at all.

'She runs like a baby elephant,' the teacher told my mum, 'and will not pirouette. She's also a little *boisterous*.'

It was true. I possessed none of the delicate co-ordination that my classmates displayed, preferring, instead, to thrash around wildly when instructed to point my toes. My mum tells me she was slightly shocked by the teacher's stinging comments, and asked whether it was worth bringing me back to the class.

'No, it probably isn't,' replied the teacher before turning her nose away. I doubt I mourned very long.

Thinking back I know my mum thoroughly enjoyed her daughter, but I suspect she always carried with her the weight of fear and loss that comes with something coveted. My litany of betrayals was not too far off. She was a family planning nurse who really was the most liberal of mums and whatever I wanted to do she always seemed to find a way. Feigned little tantrums would see to it that she sometimes skipped work, opting instead to spend an evening with me, regaling me with stories of fairies in blue dresses. She was good for tales.

I hated school from my first day and could never seem to engage in learning, nor adapt to being told what to do, whether this involved running, singing, dancing or reciting silly numbers. It was nothing to do with school itself, or my parents, but it had everything to do with me.

When I was aged about eight or nine my childhood existed as a kind of hazy dream where I found normal things difficult to comprehend. Television bored and baffled me. While my friends all raved about *Dr Who*, *Star Trek* and, later, *Happy Days*, I just couldn't see the point and I became mischievous and introverted.

I suspect I was also demanding, clingy and rather obnoxious.

By contrast, with enormous vitality and enthusiasm my mum would make most of my clothes, carefully choosing patterns and materials. She would also bake and make wonderful sweets. One Saturday I arrived home from the shops, with a small bag of sweets that had cost all my pocket money, and Doreen, her eyes grey and neutral, was horrified. The following week she made treacle toffee, peppermint creams, tablet and toffee; it was a feast and all the children in the area came along to buy them.

It was wonderful and quickly I learned her famous recipes and was making them myself. I can see her now: her fiery hair, the grey in her eyes and the sweetness of her sugary delights.

There are many photographs of my dad, scattered between my mum, my brother and myself. In all of them he is elegant, but always slightly out of reach, as if he did not want to be captured by the pokey nose of the camera lens. As if being caught would somehow render some part of him redundant, or at least make him belong to someone else. He couldn't. He wouldn't. He belonged – he *belongs* – to my mum.

My dad is aware of the camera, as much as he is aware of himself. He is self-contained, suspicious and, in photographs, especially family ones, his posture rarely gives any clue as to his relationship to those with whom he shares the lens.

Stan Gregory is a wonderful man, with kind eyes, but he rarely enjoys being the centre of attention, to the point that it is almost disfiguring. He fears, as I do, examination and this was true of our relationship most of my early life. He was never much of a talker, rarely speaking to me about much, if anything, until I was an unruly teenager, intolerant or unable to listen. I'm not sure what other adults made of him because he was, and is still, a very serious, strong and remote figure, rarely provoked to smile. Every morning, wearing a fresh suit, he would leave for work after kissing us all goodbye, before returning late in the evening. He worked as an engineer and, perhaps, the ingenuity and secretiveness that went into his planning at least partly explains his nature.

It is strange writing about him, even slightly improbable, because my mum is constantly reminding me how much alike we are and only now, when the events of the last few years have finally put their stamp on my personality, can I see how right she is. He will probably smile at this, he may even agree, but no doubt with a kind of sadness. I'd like to think that in all our little fall-outs throughout my troublesome teenage years he was preparing me for something beyond childhood, building up a bank of resilience that could be debited whenever a desperate situation required it.

I suppose I had always imagined myself as the second-class child. It was always Sandra who was never quite good enough. My brother was the academic achiever, the pride and joy of his teachers; he was creative and clever, and only ever politely and discreetly rebellious. He was practical, sensible and, of course, he is a boy. And yet he was always my hero, whom I looked up to for almost everything.

Like my dad, he turned out to be an engineer; I suppose it was inevitable given that they were always together in the garage making and fixing things. I was never invited to join in. Every weekend the two of them would go sailing together, competing at Sheerness and often returning home with trophies, plaques and silver-plated cups.

One Sunday, when I was about 11, I discovered what it meant to be scared. My brother was unable to go sailing and my dad asked if I'd like to accompany him in his small yacht, *Chaos*. I was almost levitating with excitement as we set off on that gorgeous morning in Kent. He had never asked before.

The sea was calm and, after getting the hang of water, boat and sails, I loved being there with him. He showed me how to strap on the harness and stand on the side of the boat to stop it capsizing. I trembled and learned.

Towards the end of the afternoon, after stopping at another bay, we suddenly headed back to the initial beach after the weather had changed and the sea became choppy. My face, by now, was the colour of grey meat. The storm started to build and my dad's eyes filled with apprehension and his voice changed its pitch; I quickly suspected that he regretted bringing me on that trip.

'Sandra,' he said, his voice rising, 'we're going to have to move a bit quick to get the boat back to the clubhouse.'

We were no longer practising as the sea rolled and the boat jogged into the wind while the rain lashed against us. I was frightened. I strapped on the harness and stood on the side of the boat again, but the harness snapped and I was thrown over the side into the water. It's impossible to simply stop and turn a boat round, like a driver would a car, so I watched my dad sailing way off into the distance, believing he was leaving me for good. He was, of course, doing no such thing, but floating there felt like I was watching myself dying.

Eventually, he turned the boat around and came back for me. Cold and exhausted, I scrambled into the boat. We said little to each other. Despite my terror and humiliation, I did not want to let him see how I was feeling, so I stayed outwardly calm, while he concentrated on other things. Returning to the clubhouse I showered and changed then found him amongst his sailing friends. They were all in fine spirits. They were laughing and he was laughing. And I thought they were laughing at me. They were actually laughing with me rather than at me but it was the first time I remember not getting sympathy, because my mum wasn't there. I couldn't wait to get home, away from all those men. I was never taken sailing again.

I had almost everything as a child: gymnastic classes, followed by swimming and, later, private French lessons. But what I loved most of all was animals.

'Sandra,' said my mum, 'would you like riding lessons?'

'Oh, yes,' I shrieked, 'yes, I would.'

Unable to believe my luck, I spent all my spare time down at the riding stables, regularly coming home covered in mud and hair from the horses.

My mum would take me along to the stables half an hour early so that I could groom and saddle up the pony I would be riding that day. On most days she would have to pull the car over before we arrived at the stables, so that I could dash for a wee in the bushes because I couldn't wait to get there. After learning to ride I would go on hacks with other young riders.

As the months went by I became the sort of unofficial stable manager for the woman who had started up a riding school, getting other girls to organise and help. One day a new, feisty little pony, which had just been shod, was probably feeling a little tender when I decided to show off to one of the girls, while most of the others were out on a hack. I decided to try lungeing him on the end of a four-foot rope in an open area.

Lungeing is supposed to be done with a familiar horse, on a long rope and always in an enclosed arena. Showing off my lack of skills, the pony decided he would go and explore the new field and, as I stood right behind him, tugging on the rope, he lashed out at me. His left hoof caught me straight in the face. The girl came running towards me looking shocked; as I took my hand away from my face a spurt of blood shot out, covering us both in bright red.

It took 17 stitches to fix the cuts around my right eye and the scar, which is still very visible, runs from my eye to the curve of my cheekbone. After that I grew depressed. I didn't go out and for weeks I was not allowed to look in a mirror; at school I was nicknamed Scarface. I looked and felt like a monster. My love affair with horses ended and, after the age of 13, my selfish little world became less than perfect.

Who gives parents the right to move home when their children are settled? When I was 14 we moved to King Alfred's ancient capital of Winchester and I was devastated. After living in a place where everyone knew me I found the upheaval of moving to a new place difficult to cope with – like most teenagers do. Occasionally, I attended Westgate High School.

Gradually the communication between my dad and I deteriorated; he understood me no better than I understood him. Meanwhile my mum tried to understand us both. Not entirely unexpectedly my academic reports fell below par, and they became the subject of his increasing annoyance. In keeping with the liberal times, I suppose, my parents granted me control of the family allowance money and I was told that I now had to buy anything I required for myself – except school books and uniform. In this way I would be taught the difference between what I wanted and what I needed.

The jeans were on sale, at half their normal price. My dad listened intently as I explained about how, if he lent me £10 to buy the jeans, I would pay him back over the coming weeks from my allowance.

'I'll give you the money,' he agreed, 'on the condition that you give me 50 per cent of the overall saving on top of the return.'

'That's not worth it.'

'Exactly. If you want a pair of jeans you should save your money to buy a pair.'

It was a moot point, but I didn't particularly care for moot points. From his point of view, teaching me to be a little more careful with money wasn't a bad idea. I certainly never went without, but was brought up to respect money, almost fear it. When it was there you certainly shouldn't waste it on frivolous things.

I don't blame my parents for being the way they were with me, but I resented their lessons, and rebelled in any way I could.

School was a waste of time and I grew accomplished at bunking off. I began to hate everything conventional. Although I was always impatient for learning, I never had the patience to sit and to be told. My preference was to learn by living, not studying in claustrophobic classrooms with teachers who, I imagined, had no idea of real life. I wanted to know, but I wanted to know now. I wanted to experience. Now.

Claudio was 18 and I was 14. Desperate to fulfil the cliché of our teenage infatuation we decided we were head over heels in love. My parents hated him. Claudio spoke little English and he worked in an Italian restaurant. And he had a motorbike and he smoked and he was different.

Claudio finished work around midnight. I was supposed to be sleeping. My hormones had kicked in. I felt like an adult in a kid's body.

After a bath and my mum had plaited my hair into pigtails, I would pretend to go to sleep but once my parents had gone to bed I'd climb out the window and be gone until four or five in the morning. This went on for ages and I loved the excitement and freedom.

Oh my God, I was petrified. I had arrived home one morning, to find the kitchen door locked and the front door bolted. My parents had done this on purpose. I rang the bell. I prayed it would be my mum.

Please, please let it be Mum.

A figure in a black dressing gown walked casually across the hall landing, and slowly down the stairs. I stood outside the door, shaking. The door opened.

'You've always got to have the last laugh, Sandra,' he said, with all the wrath of a biblical patriarch, 'haven't you?'

What happened next, I think, was done more in sadness than anger. He grabbed hold of me and punched me straight in the face. I'd never been hit before and the strength of the punch together with the shock of being hit sent me crashing back, and I sunk down the wall, collapsing in a heap. It was a strange moment. I was hurt, shocked, embarrassed and humiliated. Although I thought him the most stubborn person I had ever known – even his pauses could last an hour – he was right; I always did have to have the last laugh. Not surprisingly, our falling-out period continued.

*

'How would you feel about living in America?' my mum asked me one day, after my dad had been offered a transfer.

'America? Yeah!' I was 15 years old. It sounded great. I'd love to live there.

A short time later we were living in a wholesome little place called Sewickley Heights, just outside Pittsburgh, in Pennsylvania. *How wonderful*, I thought, *this is where Dracula lived*.

Sewickley smelled like giant hot-dogs and ketchup. For my parents it was a breath of apple-pie family values and we stayed here for two years. I loved it as well, though for entirely different reasons. There was beer, boyfriends, a strange school and those new things that my mum had always warned me about: drugs. All of these provided distractions that fitted perfectly with the way this wayward teenager felt; I wreaked havoc at Quaker Valley High School. Before long I was as familiar with the American detention system as anyone else on campus.

Quaker Valley was my first real introduction to drugs, although I managed to resist initially. It was seen as kind of quaint that the little English girl refused them. I wanted to fit in. Physically it was impossible because all these amazing looking Americans, with their tanned skin and luminous hair, surrounded me. Slowly, I came round. I wanted to try the new things that others were doing. When I was 16, I smoked a marijuana joint with a girl from school.

I knew my parents wouldn't approve but what did they know? How could they understand any of this? From smoking a joint I graduated to a little speed and later to acid. Everybody around me was doing it and, to be honest, I didn't dislike what I was doing. I was amazed at the reaction these drugs produced; I loved the novelty and loved the fact that I knew it was unconventional. It was my secret.

Despite my promising Sewickley debut, two years after we moved to America we returned to the UK and to the same house we had lived in before. Again, my fragile, teenage world took a hammering. My brother had not gone abroad with us because he was away at university, so I bore the brunt of my disappointment alone. It rained on our return. I was 17.

Having missed my O level examinations by moving to America and then leaving there before I got the chance to finish high school meant that I had no academic qualifications. Sixth form college appeared and disappeared in a fit of my academic rejection. Who needed qualifications anyway? And I wanted to prove it. Following six months of studying for exams I should have taken two years earlier the head of the college called me to his office and asked if I was happy.

'No,' I replied, 'as it happens, I'm not.'

Politely he asked me if I'd rather leave. I did and the sense of relief was wonderful. I was free. I was an adult.

Shortly before leaving the college I started going out with Spike, a wild-looking, unconventional and rugged 37-year-old father of a four-year-old daughter. He was perfect.

'How old did you say he was?' asked my dad, his eyes squinting as I spat out yet another lie.

It was a terrible time for my parents, especially my dad, and I can see now that it wasn't right. They couldn't stand Spike but I didn't care.

Once again my parents moved house, this time to Aberdeen in Scotland, and I decided I couldn't cope with another move. Winchester, then America, then Winchester again. Now Aberdeen. Where the hell was Aberdeen anyway?

So my parents left for Scotland and I rented a room in the house of an old lady whose son was a transvestite. I would like to say it was great, I really would like to, but we never hit it off and I decided to leave. After moving out I lived with Spike for two and a half years and we shared his passion for antiques. Before long we set up our own business stripping pine furniture and, later, once I realised that Spike was not the man of my dreams, I promptly left him. For a while I lived a peripatetic lifestyle moving to Salford, then Halifax before settling in the house I live in now, where I set up on my own buying and selling antiques and bric-à-brac. It is a small, two-up and two-down terraced house facing south onto the Calder Valley. I bought it from the landlord after renting it briefly and set about fixing it up. Before long I was living happily alongside my beautiful border collie, Kara, two cats and a parrot. I doubt I was ever so happy.

Around November 1990 I was working at home, not particularly looking forward to another inevitable freezing winter standing at markets and fairs, hoping for a decent sale. A black sports car pulled up outside and one of my friends, Shanty, jumped out of the passenger side. A rather dashing looking man, with jet-black hair, stepped out the driver's side. Who was he?

Shanty brought him into the house, introduced him as John, and promptly drove off in his car. It was a rather strange introduction but given my lack of convention I was curious to find out what this was all about. John explained. His girlfriend of two years had just left him and, in a fit of desperation, he had promptly bought a flight ticket to Thailand with the intention of drowning his sorrows on a tropical island in the sun.

In a few days he would be travelling there but he had got cold feet about going alone and wanted a companion; none of his friends could travel at such short notice. Shanty couldn't go either; however, she knew someone who might be interested in going.

'Travelling companions,' said John, matter-of-factly. 'No strings attached. I'll even lend you the ticket money.'

In that moment my life began mapping itself out for me. I was lured by the magnetism of curiosity. Within two days I had my visa, enough spending money for a few months, and someone to rent my house. My best friend, Holroyde, would take care of the dog. Shanty would take care of the cats and collect the rent from the house to keep up the mortgage repayments. I began dreaming of tigers, elephants, rain forests and sandy beaches. It seemed like such a wild thing to do; I didn't even know the man I was going with.

Most of my friends thought my trip was a fantastic idea. Holroyde had some reservations. 'Please don't go, Sandra,' he said. 'I've got a strange feeling about this.'

The trick about premonitions is knowing when to listen to them and when to ignore them. They happen all the time. Yet even the most hideous premonition would not have prevented me going. I said all my goodbyes.

'Be careful,' said my mum. 'See you soon.'

Two hours into the flight and John was driving me crazy. While he spent the entire journey in his seat, I spent the flight sitting next to the toilet looking out of the little window at the back of the plane.

Two middle-aged men on the plane told me they were going to Bangkok for the girls. 'Best women in the world, Thai women,' said one. 'They'll do anything for a few baht.'

I told them I was going to Thailand to see tigers and elephants and the jungle. 'You'll see them,' they said, 'or at least parts of them, in tourist shops in Bangkok.'

Suddenly I had a feeling I was travelling with the wrong person, to the wrong country, and for the wrong reasons. I took a drink.

It'll be fine, Sandra.

Two months was a long time to be away. I would cope.

THREE

Opium Mountain

I have only been away for two months but it feels like a lifetime. Life here is wonderful and I am enjoying Thailand far more than I ever imagined. I have decided to stay on and look for a job. Thailand has taught me so much ... life is a gift and being here, in what is considered the drug centre of the world, I no longer need or want to smoke marijuana. I love the food, the people, their culture, the climate and everything about this lovely country. The mountains were wonderful and the beaches are more beautiful than I ever imagined possible. I love it here.

I love you both

Sandra

Letter home, late January 1991

Before long it was dark. No twilight, no warning, just pitch dark, as if someone had switched off a giant city light. Stupidly, we had decided to save the taxi fare and walk to Bangkok. An hour later and we didn't appear to be anywhere nearer the neon and gleaming, flickering city that lay up ahead. We had landed in the darkness of another planet.

A battered, white Toyota pulled up along side us. The driver, a squatting gargoyle with teeth like crumbling tombstones, beamed out and asked, 'Where you go?'

'Bangkok. We are going to Bangkok.'

The driver looked bemused. 'Bangkok very big, you walk long time. I take you. 150 baht?'

We hadn't actually given much thought to where we would stay. John and I both were totally unprepared and knew nothing about the place. My dreams were of jungles and tigers and a part of me had imagined they would both be waiting for me when I arrived. The last thing on my mind was urban chaos. Quickly, we threw our small bags into the back of the car and jumped in.

'*Wow!*' I squealed, 'This is amazing!' Giant, colourful billboards were everywhere, covered in pictures of smiling Thais looking clean and exotic. Shops were crammed full of television sets, ornaments, toys, clothes, shoes – anything and everything. There were children, so many beautiful children, in their school uniforms; blue and white for the girls and beige and white for the boys. In and out of the traffic we weaved.

With increasing degrees of weariness police, wearing skin-tight uniforms and mirrored sunglasses, attempted to direct vast queues of vehicles. The chainsaw-like drone of the traffic grew louder. The heat penetrated my skin.

An old man – his hands fat and plump, like overripe bananas – waddled under the weight of a heavy load. Steam erupted from pots cooking on charcoal fires and glass cases held noodles of all shapes and sizes. Bangkok was hot, mercilessly so, chaotic, exotic and slightly uneasy. I was drawn to it like a pretty pink moth.

John was still a problem. The doubts I had on the flight over seemed to multiply by the time we left the airport. He was loud, arrogant and self-centred. Like an oversized child he irritated me constantly throughout the journey. Was it simply nerves on his part? Somehow I doubted it. I decided not to stay in his company for much longer than I needed.

'No room, no room.' Because I was young and blonde, wearing tight trousers, no bra and a small T-shirt, most guesthouse owners, I later learned, saw me as competition for their own girls and, after about an hour of searching for accommodation, the two of us had almost given up.

John had been given the name of a hotel, but when we arrived it proved far too expensive so we tried to find somewhere else in the Soi Nam du Plee area of Bangkok; this was the 'old travellers' district where backpackers could find cheap rooms and even cheaper girls for the duration of their stay. We hadn't known at the time but this was one of the many red-light areas the city boasted.

The Thai woman sitting outside Anna's Guesthouse eyed me with suspicion, but looked at John and told him yes she had a room, but it was downstairs. The woman, who was swigging from a bottle of cheap whisky, was fat and wore a tight-fitting pair of shorts, plastic flip-flops and a Manchester United football shirt.

'You look at room? 100 baht a day.' Sitting alongside her was a very blonde, very suntanned European girl. Neither of them smiled, but the blonde sniggered as we accepted the offer to look around.

The light was on. It was nothing more than a square box but didn't look so bad for the money, so we took it. John immediately left to go for a beer and I paid the woman. The room was roughly two pounds a day.

I showered in the toilet that doubled as the shower area. The cold water was a welcome relief from the heat. Standing there naked over the drain in the floor, with cracked tiles all around me, I realised how pale my skin looked. Brown skin or white skin? In Thailand it said everything about you. I scrubbed my skin twice as vigorously in preparation for some colour.

While I stood scrubbing my body, massive, dark-brown insects scuttled around my feet. I was horrified. Back in the room, I switched on the light and was greeted by hundreds of these creatures from the shower, running off the bed, scurrying out of my bag and across the floor. No wonder the blonde woman outside had sniggered.

John was sitting in a bar with a middle-aged European man and a young Thai girl aged about 16 or 17, under an open-air canopy, in the car park of a brothel. A Chinese action movie was playing on a television screen. The girl sat next to the man, feeding him. Delicately, she nudged the food into neat piles on his plate as she prepared each mouthful, while speaking gently in Thai. Her words sounded pretty, like an Asian nursery rhyme.

We drank cold beer. John became more obnoxious and loud with each bottle.

A man rode by on a bicycle, carrying a mangle and a rack. He wore a floppy straw hat, grimy shorts and a pair of flip-flops. He smiled broadly as he stopped and put down the rack and started rolling what looked like thin cardboard through the mangle. What was he doing? After a few minutes he passed me a paper bag containing the mangled cardboard and a small bowl made from a banana leaf full of thick chilli sauce. 'Yes,' I thought, 'this is the real Thailand, at last.' The cycle man and the barman both looked bemused as I gazed into my bag of delights.

It was dried, hot squid, with the texture of leather. It was foul so I gave it to the young Thai girl who was feeding the oafish European. The girl smiled and munched happily. I really was a long way from home.

John and I had to share the bed. He slept on one side while I slept on the other. Eventually I nodded off only to be awakened by several hundred insects touring my body. Over coffee the following morning, I really did consider taking the next flight home. Why was I here? After all, I couldn't stand John and I didn't know a single soul. What on earth would I do next?

John wanted to go south to the islands and he went off to buy a plane ticket; I couldn't afford to fly down so I planned to travel elsewhere. Although I was relieved about leaving him, it took a deep breath to walk away. We said our 'goodbyes' and John disappeared into a crowd.

'Where are you going?' said a girl, as she was getting off the bus that would take me north.

'Chiang Mai,' I replied.

'No,' she said, 'go to Wisid's in Chiang Rai. It's a great place.'

Chiang Rai was roughly a 15-hour journey north of Bangkok and Wisid's is situated in the province of northern Thailand, bordering Laos and Burma. I was sure there would be elephants, jungles and tigers.

With a guy I had met briefly in Bangkok, who was travelling north, we eventually found ourselves in a place five miles west of Chiang Rai. The little town I was entering lurched precariously close to being ancient.

We had taken a ride in one of the multicoloured, two-seater rickshaws peddled by an old local man who looked barely able to muster the energy to walk. A flash of dirt slipped past as he hauled us along the bumpy roads and I felt guilty watching the muscles of the old man's neck and back rippling against his soaking T-shirt. He trundled on regardless.

When we reached the gates of a small wooden house on stilts our driver smiled, such a beautiful, charming smile, but his face was still puffing. His arms sweated and his stomach heaved. The fare was just 40 baht – about 70 pence – but I gave him 80 and his face burst. He put his hands together in the attitude of a prayer and raised his fingers to the tip of his nose. He thanked me, Thai style.

Wisid's guesthouse was a small, teak-wood building; open underneath for the simple reason that it is never a good idea to sleep at ground level because of scorpions and snakes. A family who spoke reasonable English ran the guesthouse.

It was stunning. There were raised wooden platforms covered in triangular cushions for resting on; there were plants blooming paper-thin, pink flowers. All around songbirds sang in large wooden cages suspended from the balconies, and friendly dogs flopped around in the shade. My room was large and airy with a bed big enough to sleep four people. For the first time since my arrival in Thailand I could relax.

A day or two later my friend moved on and, once again, I was alone.

At night I would light a bonfire with some of the other guests and sit around with the Thai workers chatting, strumming guitars and nibbling on some unusual Thai snacks. Deep fried crickets seemed to be one of the favourites.

Wisid, the guesthouse owner, organised a trip to the mountains for the weekend, and a few of us agreed to go. Three hours in the back of his jeep and still there were no elephants, or tigers; just hills, piercing sun, dust and bushes. At the time Thailand had not been too trammelled by tourists and when we finally came to a halt I found myself in the middle of what looked like a David Attenborough documentary. We had travelled high into the mountains and, amidst spectacular views of northern Thailand, we could look down upon those who had been here before. We entered one of the numerous hill tribe villages.

Children carried smiling infants on their backs while others, stopping in their tracks, looked vaguely horrified at who had just arrived. Even more children appeared, all with cute, dirty little faces, and arms like kindling sticks. They kept staring. Chickens ran around scratching in the dust and women ground huge piles of rice on a large millstone. The big flat stone had a large stick attached and the women walked around and around in a circular motion. It took hours for a small amount to be ground into a powder. I was awestruck.

'You want to go and see an opium field?' asked an old man who had stopped by to greet our group.

Surprisingly, no one did except for me. I followed this very old, broken-looking man as he trotted through the village. Past bamboo huts with grass roofs, huge black pigs and dust, so much dust, we ran through the village and around the side of a mountain for over an hour. Eventually, the old man stopped.

'Opium,' he said, in clipped English. 'Opium.' He pointed.

I looked down to the cultivated section of the mountain and

saw little plants that looked exactly like funny little cabbages. This is what we had come to see? I had imagined all these pretty little poppy flowers blowing around in the wind.

Just looking at them made me feel dizzy. All I could think of was the film *The Wizard of Oz*, when Dorothy lay down in a field and fell asleep amongst thousands of poppies. Up here in the mountains, surrounded by nothing but light and air, I wanted to lie down and go to sleep in the field like Dorothy.

Since 1959 opium growing has been illegal in Thailand but in 1990 it was still going on in many places. Rampant production and refining of the crop during the 1960s and 1970s became commonplace in the lawless regions on the border of Thailand, Burma and Laos, and the area soon earned the nickname Golden Triangle. I was standing amongst it all.

When the government decided to destroy huge areas of poppy fields it meant that the hill tribes had to find alternative livelihoods. So the Thai government were forced to introduce more legitimate cash crops, like corn, peaches and strawberries. In many parts of the north, vegetables are often grown at the same time in the same field to hide the crops. I could hardly believe that much of the heroin in Thailand came from places like the old man's secret field.

We turned and began trotting down again and in no time we arrived back at camp. A young German, with an agitated look on his face, kept asking for, 'The doctor. Where's the doctor?'

'Who needs a doctor?' I asked, scanning the village for someone sick, but the German ignored me.

Another old man and his son appeared and Wisid greeted them both with feigned solemnity. The venerable old gentleman unravelled a small roll of cloth and proceeded to set up an assortment of items contained within it on the bamboo platform. He lay down on his side and Wisid lay down facing him. In between them were a small metal bowl, a lit candle and a well-worn pipe. The old man melted something over the candle, kneaded it in his fingers and pushed it into the pipe. He passed one end over to Wisid and lit the bowl. They were smoking opium.

That's why we had come up to the mountains, I laughed to myself. Wisid and the others were all opium smokers. Each person took a turn on the pipe, and the whole procedure lasted about half an hour. They all lay on the platform with the old man and everyone got high.

There are seven rules to smoking opium, the group explained; a procedure that must be followed otherwise bad luck will follow. Most of them I forget but one of those curious rules are that you must smoke an odd number of pipes: three, and five, seven or more. One pipe, they said, has no effect. Two was simply bad luck. Wisid and the old man charged 15 baht per pipe.

'Go on,' they all said, 'try it.'

After the first one, trying two would have spelled bad luck and three would have been too much. So one pipe was more than enough. The opium made me ill for hours and I wanted to be sick; I huddled around a small fire that we had built praying my head would clear. The others sat for hours, each having another go on the old man's pipe, over and over again. That was my first experience of drugs in Thailand.

I lost interest in the people who were staying at Wisid's guesthouse. They were there for the opium, nothing else. It was time for a change of scene. Maria, a French girl at Wisid's, had travelled to northern Thailand before and she was going to 'Guesthouse Three', situated somewhere between Chiang Rai and Chiang Mai. She wanted her boyfriend to see it before they left for Australia. Did I want to go with them?

We took a bus a few days later and, after a few hours, it dropped us off at the edge of a local marketplace, on the side of a dusty road. Maria bought Thai sweets, fruits, bread and vegetables and suggested that I do the same. We waited for a ride up into the mountains.

A Toyota pick-up drew alongside us and Maria agreed a price

with the driver – ten baht each. In the back of the pick-up there were about eight Thais. Miles and miles through thick clouds of dust, we climbed the mountain. There was nothing to see through the dust except for more dust, which got everywhere and stung terribly. If only my parents could have seen me, they would have thought I was crazy.

We pulled up in the middle of thick forest and we got out, while Maria proceeded to plan our route to the guesthouse. Through miles of forest we walked and, in the trees around us, the sound of exotic birds echoed, announcing our presence. Lizards dashed from our path. Gradually, through the trees, I saw a clearing and what looked like a village.

Bamboo huts stood on tall wooden stilts covered by layers of thin grass that made thatched roofs; chickens and dogs ran around looking for scraps. A huddle of pigs scratched in the dust nearby, grunting. Children – some naked, others dressed in tatty rags, all barefoot – came running from all directions to greet Maria. She had been here before, and they all seemed to know her.

Of course, that's what the sweets were for! Maria picked up one child after another, and lowered them to pick up yet another. Her boyfriend and I were amazed. This was Guesthouse Three, a beautiful secret hidden way up in the mountains.

The children ran on, leading us through the village, shouting to others in a language that seemed unlike anything I had ever heard, even in Bangkok. I could tell by the tone of it, the way it carried itself from mouth to ear, that they were very excited at our arrival.

Three little children dominated the group and took great pride in holding our hands, walking us towards their family. They belonged to a woman called Annum and we were to stay with her. Ever so gently, Thailand began unfolding like the pages on a beautiful and ancient history book. We had arrived in San Jalo Mai. I was speechless.

Maria and her boyfriend stayed in the village only a few days, before leaving to catch planes to Australia. But I couldn't leave; I was seeing so many things that I had never even dreamed about. Why had I never come to this country before?

For the next five weeks, Guesthouse Three was my home and I began working with the women of the village up in the mountains. Whatever was happening at home or around the rest of the world I had no idea. Up in the mountains there were no radios, televisions, telephones or newspapers.

All over the UK people were getting up in the morning hating their work and their life. Not me. I was in heaven.

Unless we were out in the forest my diet consisted of mounds of heavy rice, a few leaves sprinkled on top and a thick, red-hot chilli paste, three times a day. In the forest the children would pluck fat insects and caterpillars from tree bark and pop them in their mouths. Standing there, with their fat little stomachs, they would point out to me which were good to eat and which ones best avoided. I never did manage to swallow a squirming bug, despite repeated and hilarious offers.

One afternoon a group of us visited someone's grandmother, over at a nearby mountain. It was a few hours' trek away and the children were so excited to be going. Grandma was out so we waited for her to return. She was in the forest, gathering food for the arrival of the grandchildren. What delights! Held in thick wedges of bamboo, with grass stuffed in the top, were hundreds of fat, white caterpillars and juicy bugs, while bundles of leaves unfolded to produce a mass of tree insects and beetles, fungi and dark red berries.

The squirming food was piled on a grass mat for the children. Squeals of delight took over from their usual squabbling and banter, and they finished the feast in minutes.

My days passed easily, working in the fields and helping around the village, mostly cutting grass for the hut roofs, digging for peanuts and cabbages, chopping down bamboo to make utensils and reinforcements for huts. The bamboo leftovers would be used as pig food. Would anyone believe me if I told them how I was living? I doubted it.

I thought about home less and less. I could have disappeared and no one would have known.

Once a week I would disappear down the mountain and come back to the village laden with sugar cubes, chickens and coconut pancakes. The villagers accepted me readily; indeed seemed to be amused by my presence.

For some strange reason families began bringing their sick children to me. Despite having very little in my bag in the way of medication, they were impressed when I boiled water and salt to be used as an antiseptic. It had great results on serious skin infections. A few bandages, aspirin, camomile, lavender and Thai brandy made up the rest of my nurse's bag.

There was a baby with an insect in her ear and the pain kept both her and her mother awake for days. A drop of brandy in her ear either killed it from alcohol poisoning or drowned it. The following day the mother of the child was delighted and brought me bags of peanuts and enough bananas to feed a family for a week.

My patient list grew. A young boy who had put a machete through his hand caused the children of the village to shout for me to come and fix him. His thumb, raw and ragged, was hanging off so I cleaned and patched it as best I could and the following day he returned to see me, a baby strapped to his back. As I removed the old bandage he moaned ever so slightly. But he couldn't stop smiling.

Little girls would pierce their ears with thin slices of bamboo and if the bamboo got wet their ears would infect. Some of the swellings were the size of golf balls. One day, while walking through the village I heard what sounded like a pig being slaughtered; the animal seemed to be screaming.

Many of the villagers were gathered outside a hut, the size of a small wardrobe, and when I peered inside a girl, aged around four, was being held down by her grandfather while her father held a rather rusty-looking scalpel. The girl had a swelling bigger than an orange on the side of her head and her father was about to slice it open.

The girl looked at me. Her father sliced the side of her head and green mush and blood oozed from the wound. A large piece of banana leaf was held against her head and the puss flowed onto the leaf. When the leaf was full they threw it to the pigs, idling nearby. The child continued screaming while her grandfather held her and her father sliced again. Some more screams and some more food for the pigs.

When they had finished they wrapped her in a blanket and laid her on a bed inside the hut. Her wound lay open and I was sure she would die, either from shock or infection, and I tried to explain to the father that she needed to see a doctor. Immediately.

The next morning I left the village to buy antibiotics, aspirin and bandages but by the time I got back the child had gone. Fortunately, my protestations had got through to the girl's father, who had taken her to the hospital. A few days later she returned to the village and was soon running around with the other children, wearing a large pad on the side of her head. Doctors had removed a four-inch square area of skin from behind her ear to clear the infected area.

Aha was the main opium smoker in the village and a renowned ladies' man. He sat every day smoking in a hut, doing nothing else. He was great fun and very good with all the children, and had several wives with numerous children. Everyone, including Aha, thought that I would make a good wife for him and it became a persistent joke.

One evening I told everyone Aha was a useless man who never did anything. 'What good is he?' I joked. The following day Aha rose before dawn and went into the forest. He arrived back later laden with goods and that evening prepared a meal for his family; he also made two large bamboo baskets and mended the roof. I showed him a photograph of Holroyde, my friend at home, and that was the end of his courtship.

My life was absolutely wonderful for those five weeks but gradually I grew restless. For some unexplainable reason I imagined that the village was turning against me. Perhaps they had? Maybe they were fed up with their uninvited guest. In a fit of paranoia I began to fear they might even sacrifice me. It was late December and definitely time to leave, so one morning, amid a breeze and a bright blue sky, I slipped away as quietly as I had slipped into their lives.

I arrived in Chiang Mai only to find hordes of drunken tourists hanging off young, pretty Thai girls, celebrating the New Year. It was ugly, urban and fake. The following evening I returned to Bangkok, with its seedy bars, souvenir shops and brothels, and felt the gnawing desire to leave immediately.

Perhaps I would find some more luck in the south. I headed to the islands.

FOUR

In Sickness and Health

Please excuse my terrible handwriting again. My nervous system has taken a bit of a battering over the last six months and I am feeling a little shaky. I shall explain this to you at more length in another letter. Things are now looking up and I have no doubt that I have come out the other end of it all a better, stronger and more experienced person. I'm sorry I cried so much on the phone at Christmas, but it was very emotional for me to hear your voices…

I hope to be home this year, but I don't want to come back an insipid, sick, underweight, broke failure. That's the way I feel at the moment and it may take me some time to sort things out. I love you all and think of you all daily. Everybody kiss each other for me. Big one for the baby.

Letter home, early January 1993

One evening, shortly after the sun had gone down, I was lying on the bed in my bungalow, on the island of Koh Samui, listening to the most wonderful, exotic music drifting from next door. I don't know what it was but after hearing it I realised it was impossible for me to go home.

It was now almost three months since I had left England and the idea of returning filled me with dread. I felt like a child in an Enid Blyton adventure where everything was unknown and irresistible. From coral gardens to freshwater falls and secret lagoons, the allure of the island was more than I could have ever imagined. Slowly, the cracks of my recent paranoia were papered over.

For five weeks I was part of the transient island community life. There was volleyball on the beach at dusk, paragliding, snorkelling, swimming and motorbike day trips or just lounging around the beach. Chaweng and Lamai beaches were the two most popular areas of the island. There was a hint of mischief at night and the clubs, discos and bars heaved with revellers, but they had little appeal for me. I was constantly searching for deep and meaningful conversation, which usually consisted of solving all the world's problems at a stroke. In paradise, it was requisite. If the state of the world didn't improve overnight I would take midnight swims and long walks along the soft, sandy coastline.

My money was running out and I decided to head back to Bangkok to pick up some work that would hopefully provide enough money to fund the rest of my stay, however longer that might be. I packed my bag and set my watch for six the following morning, in order to catch the only boat off the island. Some time later, I told my parents of my plan. As long as I was careful they would be happy. After all, what could go wrong?

The desire in Thailand, like many other developing countries, to acquire foreign language skills, particularly English, had led to a major teaching industry in Bangkok with schools appearing overnight. However, when I arrived back in the city I had very little money and my clothes were unsuitable for teaching. Most days were spent walking the streets, looking for work. I would go into office buildings pretending to look for someone that I knew did not exist, knowing the local custom is always to offer a guest a glass of water. As someone went to enquire about the person I was looking for, I would drink the water and then disappear.

Yet despite the initial difficulties, and having no formal teaching qualifications, I soon got work without any real problem.

From February 1991 until October 1992 I worked in a number of places including a university, various language schools, the United Nations-related international school, and many business establishments. I also taught students privately in their homes several times a week, and I got to see a side of the people and their country that was truly Thai. I loved teaching and I learned far more than I taught my pupils.

Before long I found a nice place to live close to the Chao Prya River, and quickly developed an intriguing circle of friends. The days passed and, almost surreptitiously, Bangkok was better than I had anticipated. The chaos, pollution, traffic jams, noise, heat and constant hustle and bustle were now adorable instead of reprehensible.

Wearing a silk-lined miniskirt, I often found myself riding around the city sitting side-saddle on the back of a motorbike taxi, listening to Sting, Tracy Chapman, Lou Reed and INXS through a Walkman personal stereo strapped to my head. It was way too much fun to be real.

Incredibly, I got parts as a movie extra in Thai films, music videos and later I would take part in the making of several television commercials. This was my life, and it was perfect. I was young and frivolous and curious about things. The streets were alive, the people were alive; the city, with its magical allure, was too.

I felt a new excitement in my life. I sensed a watershed in my relationship with Thailand and, in the weeks that followed, I gradually developed a sense of antipathy for my old life at home.

Around the middle of 1991 I began a relationship with an American guy by the name of Hurley Scroggins, the third. It took him ages to convince me that he was worthy of any attention, but after a few months his Jack Nicholson looks took my fancy. Hurley was fun, well-travelled, rather eccentric and very sociable. For a while he had lived in Spain, and spoke the language fluently; he could also speak Dutch. What impressed me most was that he was extremely knowledgeable and spoke, in such an eloquent fashion, of things I had never heard of. More importantly, he was much wilder at heart than myself. Much to my surprise we fell in love.

Hurley worked as a journalist for an English language magazine, and our life together was exciting and full of surprises. No longer did I consider myself a tourist in Thailand. I was now a bona-fide ex-pat.

The ex-pat community in Bangkok is a small group, an island amid an ocean, where everyone knows each other, but is not always necessarily dependent on, or close to, each other. British, American, Australian and European – the ex-pat community in Bangkok is spread over different geographical areas, simply because it is a huge city. Like anywhere, different people migrate to different sorts of areas.

Sukkumvit tends to be the place loosely regarded as the middle-class area, where the rich foreigners go. Older travellers, many of who have been on the road for years, and old hippies go down to Soi Nam du Plee, where they hang out with the Thai ladies in bars. It can be a rough area, occasionally spilling over into violence. Young travellers on a shoestring budget, backpackers and teenagers migrate to the secure and sheltered area of Banglamphu. Here they will find banana milkshakes and American movies playing 24 hours a day. All tastes are catered for (you can always tell a young traveller from the bright, outrageous clothes they wear that would never see the light of day at home). Banglamphu is the 'old' area of the city where the King's Grand Palace is found, and historic buildings scatter the region. No building can be higher than the height of the palace and so Banglamphu is saved from a surfeit of skyscrapers.

Street markets cover most of this district, selling everything from rice soup at 3 o'clock in the morning to reggae music during the afternoon. Clothes, food, electrical goods, birds and small animals are sold in abundance and masses of people come down from the provinces into Bangkok every year to sell their goods.

Living in Banglamphu I enjoyed the best of two worlds. I was close enough to things familiar, like European sandwich shops, and at the same time was able to indulge in the exotic.

The community I lived around was a small, tightly knit group involved in various activities. One friend ran a second-hand bookshop, some taught English, while others worked for non-governmental organisations. There were poets and writers. There were many who had married Thai women years previously and settled in Bangkok, working in bars and restaurants.

Bangkok is a place where everything goes on, and others got by selling cheap drugs. It was part of the culture, and I found myself smoking cheap marijuana along with many others.

Every three months I would leave Thailand and travel to Penang, in Malaysia – a journey taking around 22 hours – to renew my Thai visa. The Thai Embassy rarely granted visas for foreigners for stays over three months, and for the next few years I made these regular trips. Just seeing a new place added to the excitement of the times and my sojourns were a welcome break from the hectic lifestyle in Bangkok. Yet I was always relieved to get back. Bangkok had quickly, and ever so deftly, become my home. I could feel the past breaking off in chunks.

There are many names and faces from my time in Bangkok that remain a blur but one of those individuals who stay with me is Karolina Johnnson. A Swedish girl who spoke several languages, including Thai, Karolina, like many others around me, had travelled widely. She was very well educated but her greatest difficulty was applying her intelligence to normal life.

Karolina was an awkward girl, with frizzy, fair hair. She drank too much and did not make friends easily. At the many parties she threw at her flat she was the only girl I knew who appeared excluded in her own home. Yet, despite this, Karolina was involved in a side of Bangkok that I had heard of but never experienced.

Karolina lived a life I had only ever seen in films. Many of her acquaintances were involved in the business of buying and selling passports; the exportation of young Thai girls to different parts of the world; gold, silver and gem smuggling and, of course, drugs.

Before long I was introduced to various men from the large West African ex-pat community. For reasons I could never quite fathom, Karolina believed she fitted into this rather dubious community and was wholeheartedly drawn into their world. By pretending to Karolina, or any other vulnerable female, that they were in love with her, these men operated by constantly showering her with attention and, invariably, fought amongst each other over her.

She was flattered and in no time had started working for them. At least once a week she would disappear somewhere, usually a foreign country, doing something illegal for these guys. My friends knew about it as I knew about it, but we rarely spoke about it amongst ourselves or to Karolina.

Dressed as a businesswoman, she was constantly off to exotic locations, usually flying first class. Sometimes she carried bags filled with either drugs or gems and at other times escorted young women to places like Japan, where they would work as prostitutes. They had been sold for the price of a television.

The men she worked for were always on the lookout for new recruits and, on a couple of occasions, Karolina came to me asking if I might be interested in listening to some proposals from her new acquaintances. Whether through curiosity, stupidity or both I decided to meet them. More than anything I was interested in seeing the sort of people she was dealing with, what the offers were and how they carried out their plans. Why was Karolina so interested? What could possibly be the attraction?

I met a German with a large, round face and popping out eyes. As befitting a man in his position he was wearing way too much gold and he was also far too smooth. Smuggling gold to Sri Lanka was his speciality. It turned out that the German was no longer able to use his regular people because they had been through customs too many times and he was now looking for new people. Would I join him? Would I take several kilos of gold to Colombo, in Sri Lanka?

After buying me a beer he outlined his plans further. It would go something like this – he would take me shopping for new clothes; they needed to be baggy, loose-fitting ones. His associates would make a fitted body belt that would hold the gold, which would be worn under the clothes. He went on to explain that I would be introduced to another of his associates and that person would also be on the plane, with the gold, flying to Sri Lanka. At no point should I acknowledge him.

On the plane the second smuggler would take the gold bars to the toilet and leave them in there. In the meantime I would have followed him and been the next person in the queue for the toilet. From there I would fill the body belt with up to seven blocks of gold, go back to my seat and enjoy the flight.

In an attempt at reassurance, the German told me there were no metal detectors at Colombo Airport and, more importantly no female customs officers, so I could not be rubbed down or body-searched. He was willing to pay me or anyone else stupid enough to do it £500.

I sipped my beer. Throughout our conversation I marvelled at how ludicrous his proposal seemed to me. What on earth made him think I would be stupid enough to do something like that? It was preposterous, like something from the film *Midnight Express*, the true story of Billy Hayes, a young American sentenced in Turkey to 30 years for a drug offence. Hayes had strapped drugs to his body and tried to smuggle it through customs. Who would be stupid enough to do such a thing?

'I'll think about,' I said, knowing I had no intention of taking him up on his offer. 'I'll do it if you organise a dry run for me.'

If he would pay for a ticket for me to go to Colombo then I could see, for sure, if he was tricking girls into smuggling for him.

'No,' he said, 'no dry runs.'

'Well, how do I know what to expect? How do I know you're telling the truth and not setting me up?' Did he really think I could be so stupid?

'What happens if something goes wrong over there?' I asked.

'We'll get you out,' he said, looking deeply into my eyes, almost as though he was trying to seduce me.

'Well, then,' I replied, 'I don't think I'll bother. Cheers for the beer.'

Karolina was either a whole lot braver than I imagined, or a great deal more stupid. Either way I was amazed at the type of people she was working for and the things she was doing for them. More offers came my way and, with them, more refusals. Hurley was furious that I had even gone to the meeting.

I shrugged. This was Thailand, and this was how the country seemed to operate. From street to governmental level Thailand, for all its beauty and wonder, exists on various forms of corruption; it is not simply a problem, it is part of the way of life.

Smuggling gold to Sri Lanka was one thing; trafficking people was quite another but Karolina asked if I would go to meet someone she knew and just listen to what he had to say. I agreed to meet her African friend. On the surface the deal was straightforward and slightly more lucrative. I would receive £1,000 for escorting a Thai girl to Japan.

The African arranged for girls to go to Japan, allegedly to work in restaurants or bars, while all her travel arrangements were made in advance. All I would have to do was spend a bit of time getting to know her before rehearsing a concocted story that we were going on holiday, or a shopping trip, or something equally innocent.

'All you're doing is making sure she gets to Japan,' he told me, 'without any problems.'

I didn't go with her to Japan. What he neglected to tell me was that all the girls would end up in prostitution, feeding the insatiable appetite of the multi-billion dollar, commercial sex industry. Typically, the family of the girl involved would be paid the equivalent of two years' wages for a manual Thai worker and told their daughter was going to work in a hotel or perhaps as a factory worker. The money was simply an advance on her wages. The daughter would pay off the loan quickly from her wages and her parents would not have to pay anything back. The girls are ordered like pizzas.

Most of the girls are young and attractive with immature bodies, and desperate to escape the crushing poverty in rural areas of the country. They will take extraordinary risks for promises of a better life as a waitress or a dancer. Yet, when they arrive in the so-called Promised Land, pimps confiscate their passports, usually forgeries. Often, they are raped before being sold and those lucky enough to stay alive often end up in jail. I found it ironic that a black man was involved in the slave trade.

In Tokyo, or whatever her destination, the girl would pay back her own travelling expenses, and pay for all her clothes, make-up, accommodation and food. There would be a levy to pay to the bar she would be working in and also interest on the 'loan' given to her parents, which took her abroad in the first place.

There were so many things in Thailand that were obviously criminal acts, but many Western people living there accepted them as part of the benevolence of a country that grew increasingly more liberal by the day.

The buying and selling of passports, in particular British passports, is big business too and when I was in need of money for a ticket home I was encouraged to sell mine. I refused. I recalled years ago, sitting with my mother in Hollingbourne, when she said to me, 'Be proud to be British, Sandra, it's the best nation in the world. Never give up your British passport.'

I quickly realised that Karolina, absorbed in her secret little life, was bad news. I saw her less and less and became increasingly involved in my teaching work.

Karolina had successfully got away with so much over the months I knew her but her luck had to run out. On 20 August 1994, she was arrested at the Don Muang Airport under her full name of Eva Karolina Johnnson, carrying 7.8 kilograms of pure heroin in her luggage. She had been about to board a flight to Zurich.

It is hard to say exactly when things started to go wrong but in May 1992, I was quite unprepared for what was about to happen. One day Hurley and I were walking through Bangkok and there were soldiers everywhere; tanks rolled through parts of the city and razor wire had been erected around parliament buildings.

'Is this normal?' I asked Hurley with supreme naivety. 'Was it like this last week or have I missed something?'

'No,' he said. 'Haven't you heard? There's been a *coup*.'

A koo, I thought, *what the hell is a koo?* I didn't ask Hurley what this coup thing was because he had said it in such a way that he presumed only an idiot wouldn't know what it was. I couldn't find the word 'koo' in the dictionary. When I eventually found out I was intrigued, fascinated by the notion that the military could just boot out the prime minister. Or so I thought.

In February 1992 the Royal Thai Army, led by General Sunthorn Kongsompong, the supreme military commander, and army chief General Suchinda Kraprayoon overthrew the government of Prime Minister Chatichai Choonhavan, leader of the Thai Nation Party, who had been democratically elected in 1988, in a bloodless military *coup d'état*. General Suchinda was appointed Prime Minister in April 1992 by the ruling coalition of pro-military political parties, who held a slim parliamentary majority. Shortly afterwards public protests at his appointment began and increased over the following weeks. At the time, of course, I knew none of this.

Huge demonstrations were mounted and the military introduced martial law across the whole city, declaring that any gathering of more than nine people at any one time was illegal. They also introduced a 10.00 pm curfew. My reaction was simply 'So what?' What would they do if more than nine people were together after 10 o'clock at night? It seemed ludicrous, but before long gatherings of tens of people multiplied to thousands.

Thai people tend not to be short-tempered, nor quick to react yet, while Thais had been prone to political apathy, it gradually unfolded that there were limits. Essentially, what happened was that among the Bangkok middle class – those with a strong stake in Thailand's economic future – feelings of increasing discontent arose and they voiced these feelings alongside students on the streets. Everyone had grown tired of military rule; they wanted a democratically elected government.

On 17 May the security forces opened fire at head height on thousands of unarmed demonstrators in the streets of Bangkok, reminiscent in all but the scale of the atrocity of events at Beijing's Tiananmen Square three years earlier. Hurley and I stood amongst crowds of around 150,000 people, calling for the resignation of Suchinda.

At three minutes after 10 in the evening, just behind what had developed into the front line between students and military, as we turned to leave the demonstration, the army opened fire. The place exploded. With water cannons and truncheons, machine guns and automatic rifles, the government dealt with the protestors in characteristic style.

Every third bullet had a red tracer on it so we could see where they were firing. I saw young men and women being hit, and they dropped like flies as the streets filled with their moans and ran with their blood. I saw a boy, of perhaps 16, lying on the street with his leg blown off. Everyone seemed to have been shot from behind. We ran, carried along by the crowd, away from advancing, shooting soldiers. Sometime earlier I had read in the *Bangkok Post* about rioting in Brixton, England, but that was nothing like this. This was brutal.

Thousands of demonstrators were wounded, many of whom were left permanently disabled. Many more died. Of those who went missing none of the bodies has ever been found, and rumours swept Bangkok that many of the bodies had been taken to a nearby crocodile farm and fed to the hungry beasts. This, of course, was never confirmed, but most of the workers at the farm were apparently sent away at 1 o'clock in the morning and given no reason as to why they were being asked to leave.

General Suchinda resigned days after the crisis and military commanders implicated in the killings and violence were later moved to inactive posts. After the resignation of Suchinda, the ruling coalition agreed to a package of constitutional reforms. Amongst these was the provision that the prime minister should not come from the ranks of military.

Following the massacres, I regularly burst into tears when I saw a Thai face. The dramatic events came as something of a shock. Having grown accustomed to the beauty of life in Thailand, the deaths at the hands of the military were hard to cope with. The beauty was now complex. This was not what I had expected of the country that I had grown to love so much. I wanted to go home.

There was only one problem. Money. I had discarded my return ticket over a year previously. I resolved to begin saving for the return trip.

It proved virtually impossible. The Thai military bank in Bangkok where I worked terminated my contract, possibly for talking politics. I also lost my job at the university I taught in and all of a sudden I found myself with very little income to pay my rent, food and travel fares.

I still worked at a school on the other side of the city, but it took almost two hours to get there by bus. The canals were often a better option and I rode the long, narrow boats that crossed the city quickly. The canal water, however, is a problem, and the black mass is more like a sewage system, as it pumps raw waste from the

9 million city dwellers. While canal commuters usually cover their mouths with a piece of paper or a handkerchief, one day I forgot to cover my mouth and the black water splashed me.

The following morning I was so ill I believed I was dying. My stomach seized terribly, and I began hallucinating. Nine days later, after my weight dropped rapidly, a visit to a local doctor confirmed I had amoebic dysentery. The amoeba was reproducing inside me. Until then my weight was always 55 or 56 kilos and even with dieting I couldn't get it to drop to 50 but when the amoebic dysentery hit me I soon weighed in at 50 kilos. After that I couldn't seem to keep weight on and I began worrying when it dropped to 47 kilos.

Weeks passed in a flash and everything seemed to be going wrong. On 4 July Hurley and I split up. Things had not been going well with us and we had fallen out of love. I was far from home and alone. Months passed.

What should I have done? Well, like most young people in dire circumstances I should have sought refuge in the financial arms of my family or friends. But how could I? I didn't want them to know that things had gone so badly wrong and that I felt like a failure. I was useless and not good enough. I would get out of this mess myself.

September 1992

Dear Mum and Dad,

What exactly is the situation with the baby? I'm sorry for sounding so demanding but her arrival to the world means a lot to me, for various reasons. I feel so far away, so in the dark over here as to what's going on with her. Please send me a couple of photographs so that I can see her…

Sandra

At home my family were having problems of their own and I resolved not to burden them with my own troubles. My brother and his wife had decided to start a family and everyone was delighted. Both my grandparents and parents longed for a baby in the Gregory family but, knowing that they wouldn't get a child from the wild one, they had always hoped that my brother would do better.

I was thrilled at the idea of a baby and I wanted home even more knowing that we had a little one coming. My mum telephoned to say she was knitting a baby suit; both my parents were so excited at the prospect of becoming grandparents. When the baby arrived in August 1992 she was born with slight physical imperfections that no one had known about before she was born. The family was devastated. Why our baby? It hardly seemed fair.

I felt even further from home. I really wanted to be with them, but my financial crisis prevented this. I certainly wasn't going to ask them for money now. I phoned home.

'Everything's fine, Mum,' I lied, 'nothing to worry about. I'm having a great time.'

Why should they worry about me as well as the baby? The real baby of the family needed attention, not me. My heart was breaking because the last thing I was having was a great time. Almost 20 months had passed since I had arrived in Thailand.

'Bye, Mum. I love you, take care.'

A community ceases to be so once the members become less than resolute in their support of each other. Many of the people I had considered to be friends in Bangkok began avoiding me and I was being dropped like a sack of dirty laundry. To be fair I was no fun to be around any more. I never wanted to go out, and I certainly didn't want to go to the park and play Frisbee, or shop for materials to take to the tailor for the latest fashion. I was miserable to be around. Like most fair-weather friends, they didn't want to know.

Two people I had known for over a year were planning a trip to one of the islands in the gulf and asked me if I wanted to go. I didn't but they said it would be inexpensive.

'You're going nowhere fast in Bangkok,' said one, 'and it would be good for you to relax, get well and be with friends for a while.'

Shortly after arriving on the island my sickness and fever returned. Almost delirious, I couldn't get to a doctor but I managed to visit a chemist who told me I had been stung by a large, black-and-white striped mosquito; quickly I developed dengue fever. I'd never heard of it, but the chemist assured me that it would pass. *'Jai yen yen.'* Take it easy.

Finally it did pass, but I was not having fun nor was I fun to be around. My friends and I fell out and we parted company. I moved into a little bungalow on my own. Not long after I had recovered I picked up a serious reinfection of dengue and my body cramps were so bad I could hardly move. I barely slept.

Something strange was happening to me. I was turning blue. Blood vessels throughout my body had burst and I was petrified. My feet and ankles were flecked with huge pothole sores that wouldn't heal. Yet more medication and then it passed. This was it, the final straw; I was definitely going home. I needed to leave the island.

Days passed and I was still there. It was almost Christmas and I wanted to call home. Unbelievably, I couldn't remember my parents' telephone number. How could that be? The number hadn't changed in years and I had always remembered it before. I had written it down in Bangkok and I needed to get back there. Every day I set my alarm for 5 am to make the 15-hour trip, but I would wake up telling myself that I would 'leave tomorrow'. Physically, I was incapable of making that journey. I can't remember how many days I spent lying by myself in the bungalow, out of sight and out of the light. Any amount of light and my head felt as though it was being split open with an axe. How I wished I could sleep.

By now I was desperate to return home. I wanted grey skies and rain; I wanted custard and the British sense of humour. Above all I wanted my family and friends.

★

There wasn't a sound. So I closed my eyes and remembered the sounds of home, the sounds of streets and schools and girls in high shoes and wind whistling through the Calder Valley. I listened as my memories vibrated like strings.

'Hello,' came a voice from a man who had moved into the bungalow next to mine. 'How are you? My name's Robert.'

He looked as though he had just stepped off a plane from London. He was alone and looked friendly. And pale, as pale as yogurt. I was drawn to him straight away. Robert reminded me of home. He was British. The first time I met him he wore a pair of green cord trousers and a light shirt. There were no beads around his neck or dangling from his wrists, no sun-bleached blond hair, no silver jewellery and no sandals.

All of a sudden my spirits lifted and I smuggled out a smile. We talked about red double-decker buses, terrible food and the foul British weather. Wonderful. He asked about my life and how long I had been away. We didn't get to know each other that well, or even spend a lot of time together, but it was so nice to be able to have a few words with someone who reminded me of everything good about home.

Robert wasn't really a part of the island life. He was just there in the bungalow next to mine and it seemed perfectly enjoyable to exchange a few words in the mornings or afternoons. One evening we went out together for dinner and it was only mildly interesting.

Robert knew I was in a bad way, and knew I wanted to go home. I had told him my story and, in return, he told me he was a jewellery dealer, importing and exporting precious stones from Thailand to various destinations; this was how he funded his trips and long stays in Asia. When my dengue fever eased we said our goodbyes and I retreated once more to Bangkok.

My family were sitting around eating mince pies, drinking sherry and watching the Queen's speech when I called. How I wanted to be there with them. We chatted, again, briefly.

'Happy Christmas, Mum and Dad,' I said. 'Everything is fine. I love you all. 'Bye.'

The writing was on the wall. In Bangkok I went to a hospital and they confirmed that yes, it was dengue but no, they could not really treat it. It would pass. It did and in its place I developed stomach pains. I prayed my life would improve.

In January 1993 it improved slightly and I travelled to Pataya, with a Danish girl, to make a film for a Thai television production company. It was a promotional film about the virtues of Thailand to be shown all over Europe the following autumn. The format was simple: it was made into a sort of game show and we played golf, tennis and on water slides; we donned gloves and pretended to be Thai boxers and raced go-carts. I still don't know whether the film was ever actually screened.

One afternoon around the middle of January, I bumped into Robert. He was still wearing his green cord trousers and had managed to avoid a suntan. Hindsight, of course, is an exact science, but now, looking back, I doubt our meeting was a coincidence. Is it possible to create an apparent coincidence? Yes, I think it is.

'Have you managed to sort everything out yet?' he enquired, with flimsy concern. 'How are you feeling? Have you managed to get a ticket home yet?'

'No, I haven't sorted things out yet.'

Bangkok was pleasant and warm. An ancient old woman passed by, puffing impatiently. Robert adopted a posture of concentration.

'I have an idea how you can raise the money for your ticket home. Would you like to listen to it?'

I never paused. 'Yes,' I said. 'I would.'

FIVE

Nothing Like the Sun

Drug smuggling carries a maximum penalty of death and will almost certainly get you from five to 20 years in a Thai prison. Even more alarming, drug enforcement squads are said to receive 25 per cent of the market value of seized drugs, so are liable to exaggerate the amounts involved.

Thailand, *The Rough Guide*

No one ever knows it at the time but there are always signs or incidents in your life that try to point out the rocky path. Most of the time we fail to heed them. When I was 17 I went to Amsterdam with a friend. On my way home, at the customs checkpoint at the ferry dock, it suddenly dawned on me that I still had a small piece of hash in my pocket that I had been using during my trip. In a panic I began sweating. I could feel my arteries hardening. The customs men would know for sure that I was carrying drugs. Look at my face. The expression would almost certainly give me away.

Tap, tap, and tap. A hand touched me on the shoulder. I ignored it. *Don't turn round*, I said to myself, *he doesn't want you. It's a mistake.* I was terrified. The tap came again. There was nothing for it. I swallowed hard and turned around. A young American guy who I had never seen before was standing beside me

'Whatever you've got on you give it to me,' he said.

I looked at him, spitting defiance, scared out of my mind.

'What?'

He repeated himself. I told him I didn't have anything.

'Listen, I can see you've got something, and if I can see it *they* can see it so give it to me and I'll take it through for you.'

Is this guy for real? Was I that transparent? Was I that obvious? Should I give this stranger the hash? What if he was setting me up? We looked at each other for a minute. Then I took the tiny piece of hash from my pocket and handed it to him. He pocketed it and walked straight through.

'Keep it,' I said, when I passed through the 'Nothing to Declare' section. I should have known then I would never make a drug smuggler, but I just couldn't read the signs.

Robert Lock's mind often wandered. One minute he would be telling me about Japan, where he frequently travelled; the next he would switch to a wholly unrelated subject as if he was talking to someone else. In an instant his eyes could turn chilly, sombre and strange, as if the weight of the conversation itself was impossible to soothe him.

We were having tea outside one of Bangkok's European sandwich shops, where the owner charged the earth for cheeses and German sausages, and Robert was telling me about his planned trip to Japan. Nearby was the P Guesthouse in Pra Athit, where Robert was staying. I had booked into the Peachy Guesthouse 200 yards away. It was a beautiful day and a rumble of feet passed us by every few minutes. Robert asked if I would be prepared to take a package to Tokyo for him, for which he would pay me £1,000.

His left hand had swollen terribly, like a large grapefruit; it looked out of proportion to every other part of his body.

'Robert,' I asked, 'what on earth have you done to your hand? Did you trap it in a door or something?'

It was obviously a stupid question. His face, minutes ago animated, fell harder than a coffin nail. 'No,' he replied, 'don't worry about that. I hit an artery instead of a vein.'

It was drugs he wanted me to smuggle for him. I thought it was precious gems. There were always a lot of rubies, diamonds and emeralds coming in from Cambodia through Bangkok and people would take them out from there. The idea of smuggling gems was wrong but if that's all it was then it was worth thinking about. I had even begun thinking how I would do it. When I looked at his arm it hit me.

God, no, it's not gems. It's heroin.

He looked at me and sort of smiled.

Robert told me he had been injecting heroin for a while although he was trying to get off the needles. The recent accident with his arm had been the result of hitting his artery, which had scared him. What was to be in the package was his personal supply.

'It seems like quite a lot,' I said, 'if you don't mind me saying.'

'That's because I'm not putting it in my arm any longer; I'm putting it up my nose. It's taking four times as much for me to put it there as it does to put it in my arm.'

'Uh-huh.'

That was his explanation and I shrugged. Bangkok was the kind of place where conversations like these were fairly commonplace. The idea of smuggling heroin seemed absurd, but the £1,000 struck a chord. It was far more money than I needed for a ticket home.

'I'll need some time to think about it,' I said to Robert. We finished our lunch and then we separated.

That night in my apartment I couldn't get Robert's proposal out of my head. It seemed like such a simple solution to everything. £1,000. One thousand pounds. I counted them over and over and the more I counted the more it sounded almost like a legitimate way of earning money. Occupation? Drug smuggler. Lovely. How much do you earn? £1,000. Any perks? Oh, yes, a trip to Japan. Wonderful. Sign here...

Robert's problems were really not my problems. He's a big boy and he can take care of himself, so why should I worry about him?

He wasn't going to sell it, he said, he was just taking his personal supply on holiday. All I would be doing was earning some money to get myself home. Robert knew what he was doing and assured me that he wasn't planning to sell it on to anyone else, and I believed him. Beyond this I never really thought about it at all. It sounds crass, and selfish, but all I thought about was that money. It was simple. All I had to do was take a package to Tokyo.

Yes, this was the easiest way. There would be no pressure on my family or friends back at home, and this way I would be there with them very soon. I decided I wanted to take the chance. Part of me was scared that if I passed up the opportunity I might be left here for months, perhaps years. A few days later I called Robert.

'OK,' I said, 'I'll take you up on the offer.'

My relief was overwhelming. This really would be my ticket home and no one would know a thing about this episode in my life. Once I had agreed to do it I really didn't think about it again, somehow imaging that it was much less serious than it actually was. I was going home. What did it matter how I was getting there? And only Robert would know.

When I was younger and my father went away on business he always returned with lots of presents for the family. It was always an occasion in the Gregory household. I sat in my apartment and took a piece of paper and wrote down the names of all my family and my friends and all their children. I would go home with a bagful of presents. 'Look what I got you,' I would say and they would all smile. It's all I thought about. It was all that mattered.

Shortly after I spoke with Robert we arranged to meet. The next few days were filled with apprehension as tickets were hastily arranged and plans were made. Around this time I met Ruth Billingham, Robert's girlfriend, for the first time. I never discussed the details of what Robert had suggested just in case Robert had not told her anything, although I know that Ruth booked the air tickets for me and for her. We would be flying out of Bangkok on 5 February 1993. I didn't see Robert and Ruth again until the day we planned to travel to Tokyo.

Only once before the flight did Robert call me to say that everything would be OK, that there would be nothing to worry about.

'Customs have been sorted out,' he said, 'and everything will be fine.'

I didn't want to hear any of that. 'Of course things will be OK,' I replied. 'Why are you even saying that? Why are you talking like this?' I refused to allow him to go on. I took a deep breath; I had an indescribable feeling of fear.

Dear Mum and Dad

I seem to have been away for so long that I have to think very hard to imagine what it must be like where you are. How I long to be there with you all. I was stung by a small scorpion last week, they hurt! Beans on toast, in front of the fire, while the rain lashes down on the window sounds great. I'll be home soon.

Letter home, November 1992

My apartment at the Peachy Guesthouse was, by local standards, good accommodation but my recent moods relegated it to something miserable and neglected, and I longed for something familiar. It was a bare, squat room, painted a stubborn white. Except for the comfort of a thin mattress and a few bags containing two years' worth of possessions, there was only a table, a wardrobe, some insects and ranks of unfinished letters sitting forlornly like upright cats' tails. Vivid moments. Orphaned, Bangkok memories. It was simply a makeshift shelter.

Chris Rea was singing on my cassette-recorder, from his album *New Light through Old Windows*. How many times had I heard his voice? I sang along with Chris for company. The window shutters, bereft of any real features, were good for keeping out the constant drone from the streets but the lurid sunshine still managed to get through, making me more agitated. I hugged myself briefly, partly amazed at what I was about to do, partly terrified of the consequences.

Midday had just drifted here. The heat was burning my throat, filling the room. I wanted to lie down and sleep, but I couldn't. Whatever was about to happen to me induced a kind of saturated panic, which was bewildering. A consuming dread overcame me. A moral freeze.

Robert duly arrived, smiling thinly, and I let him in. He carried himself the way most people do when they pretend they are taller, or tougher, or more confident than they actually are. Walking with an elusive gait, as if he never quite understood himself, as if he was desperate to *be* someone else.

Robert, with his large nose and a risible English hairstyle, looked almost vulnerable. He was, in fact, capable and audacious. Our conversation was brisk, scrupulous and uncomfortably polite. Then, for what seemed like an age, neither of us could think of much to say.

Robert walked over to the mattress and produced four small packages, each wrapped carefully, but tightly, in heavy, black tape. The packages were identical, possessing the horrible finality of an abattoir. He laid them down casually upon the bed. I tried to smile. I tried not to give in to the paralysis that was slowly gripping me. I tried not to look at him. The packages were filled with heroin.

I assumed I would drink some water, swallow the drugs and they would go down. It would go beyond simple physics. They would disappear, like magic. Abracadabra! They're gone. But not those packages, they're too big.

'You know, Robert,' I said, 'there's no way I'm going to be able to swallow those.'

He turned away, unimpressed. Sophistication was not his strong point. Subtleties escaped him.

The heat rose in my face, and the room spun. *Pass out, Sandra; you're not ready to go along with this stupid plan.* I didn't like what he had brought to my apartment and I didn't like him. But I had invited him here; I had agreed to smuggle his drugs.

Robert moved around the room. 'No,' he said, agitated at my ignorance, 'you're not going to swallow them. You'd die if you did. You would choke on them.'

He produced a tube of lubricant and indicated exactly where I should hide them. *Jesus*, I thought, shaking my head, *what the hell am I doing?*

That afternoon I had eaten very little but my appetite had gone. My stomach was in knots and my hands were sweating. Robert kept talking, a low humming coming from his mouth and I found myself nodding, agreeing, saying 'yes' when it sounded appropriate and 'no' when he frowned. There were no conciliatory gestures. Robert left.

We met at the station, and then headed to the airport.

'Mr Lock,' said one of the customs officials, 'you've come already, please come this way.' None of them looked at all surprised to see Robert. 'Are you with him?' they asked me.

'Yes,' I answered.

When I was a teenager my mum once asked me if I had taken drugs. 'Yes,' I answered her, straight away. It wasn't a boast; I wasn't being confrontational or spoiling for an argument. I was simply telling the truth. She had asked me a question deserving of an honest answer and I had given her one. Then she asked me how much. Again, I explained that I had tried a few different drugs. We talked about it and she shared her concerns while I held fast to my teenage ideas that everything was fine in moderation.

Later, I told some friends and they were stunned at my confession. 'No,' they said, 'that's the last thing you do if your parents ask you about drugs. You never tell them the truth.' I couldn't quite understand this. My parents had brought me up to be honest and I had given my mum an honest answer.

I could easily have said that I wasn't with Robert, but it never dawned on me to lie. I didn't know at that point that there was a problem. I could have walked away when the customs officer asked if I was with Robert. He genuinely had no idea we were together. 'Yes,' I told him, just as I had told my mum all those years ago.

When Robert saw the X-ray his face buckled, and he turned away from me.

'I don't know this woman,' he shouted. 'What's going on? I don't know her. This is disgraceful. Will someone please tell me what's going on?'

Robert's words echoed around the customs room. This wasn't possible. My God, no, it wasn't possible. What did he mean he didn't know me?

It's me, Sandra. The girl you met on the island. We spoke about home. We spoke about England and double-decker buses; we talked about good old English weather. We spoke about your mother, for Christ's sake. What about the packages in my apartment?

'I don't know this woman, this is just disgraceful.' He was furious.

Everything happened very quickly. Threats, screams and accusation filled the room. We were made to sit down on plastic seats with chrome handles. I was staring at Robert. *You bastard,* I thought. *You bastard! What did he mean he didn't know me?*

Ruth appeared to go into shock, putting the palms of her hands across her ears; she was trying to be angry, but ended up looking terrified. 'I don't know what's going on,' she screamed. 'I don't know her.'

Not once did I think anything like this would happen. After Robert had been cuffed, led away and then kicked by the customs men we were all separated. They put a set of handcuffs on me and I shook uncontrollably. *Oh my God, what was I doing? How did this happen?* My eyes burned, and began filling with tears.

One of the customs officials, who spoke good English, walked over to me, his face a mixture of delight and resignation.

'Do you know why we X-rayed you?'

I presumed it was because I was with Robert.

'No,' he said. He told me that while his men were searching Robert and Ruth someone was watching me to see my reactions and my eyes never stayed focused for more than four seconds. Four seconds. He repeated it again. And as he said it, the pitch of his voice leaped higher. I counted them out in my head. *One. Two. Three. Four.* The lines of his clean brown face tightened.

It was true. I couldn't focus. I barely managed to look at anything and I knew that my eyes were giving away all my secrets. The customs official looked at me again. 'We would not have X-rayed you,' he said, somewhat respectfully and rather sadly, 'if your eyes hadn't given you away.' He stood there, in his crisp shirt and neatly pressed trousers, looking taut and unnerving.

The first set of handcuffs they placed on me was for men, almost twice the size and weight of the ones normally used for women. They were massive with an enormous chain and I found them impossible to handle; they frightened me. I began to feel a deep dread and numbness descending; a slow-motion consciousness.

One of the customs officers noticed my shaking and told his deputy to remove the cuffs. Instantly they were replaced with an ankle set, like elephant chains, and I sat with my feet tucked up onto a couch while they attached the other end of the cuff to the chair. I covered my legs and the chains with my coat. *Out of sight, out of mind...*

'We know what has happened, we know you have nothing to tell us.' They wanted to question Robert, they said.

Someone brought me a bottle of whisky and a chipped white mug. I had never liked the taste of whisky but I took it from him anyway. Perhaps he wanted me to get drunk and tell him all about Robert. Maybe it was because I was so obviously upset and this would help to calm me down. Whatever the reason, I sat and drank cupfuls of it. Surprisingly, the shock kept me sober. I was sure I could hear planes taking off. I wanted to cry, but I couldn't.

Some time later – I can't quite recall how long – a representative from the British Embassy drugs squad arrived in the customs room. Accompanying him was a young, female Thai translator. The embassy official was quite young, smartly dressed and seasoned-looking. The Thai woman was very pretty, with long dark hair. She looked like everything that I wasn't – cosmopolitan, confident, successful and mature.

'Has anyone searched your bags yet?' asked the British official, his voice sour and unfriendly.

'No,' I answered, 'they haven't, but you might as well.'

The translator said there was no need.

'Go ahead, search them,' I said, and I sat there, shrugging, like a scolded child.

Unzipping my bags, she carefully took the contents out, piling them up one by one on the floor. I had some family photographs and she delicately placed them to one side. There were some musical tapes and slowly she brought them out. Tracy Chapman. Chris Rea. Then Sting and his album *Nothing Like the Sun*.

The girl looked at me and then, from nowhere, quietly started crying. It took me completely by surprise. What was wrong with her? She wiped her eyes and leaned in. She listened to the Sting album at home, she told me.

How do I say this without sounding melodramatic? Right there, at that exact moment, I understood what a terrible situation I was in and I could see that she understood too, probably far more clearly than I did. There we were, two young women, one in leg chains, and the other in a beautifully tailored suit. One was going home to listen to Sting; the other might never hear him again.

The man from the embassy wasn't exactly offhand but neither was he sympathetic. Why should he be? He had probably seen countless idiots like me. I got the impression he was annoyed that I had been the one carrying the drugs and not Robert. I discovered much later that the British embassy had received a 'tip off' about Robert and they had told the Thai anti-drug authorities about him. That was the reason the customs men had been waiting for him at the airport.

I could tell what he was thinking. *Stupid little cow.* He talked for 10 or 15 minutes. 'We don't really want you,' he said, 'but there's nothing we can do about that now. We want Robert Lock. We definitely don't want Ruth Billingham.'

I shuffled in my seat. My shoulders sloped.

'If you tell me that she had nothing to do with this I will let her go,' he continued. 'I won't charge her. Now, was she involved in this? Did she know anything about it?'

Whether he was in a position to charge Ruth with anything I had no idea but there would be little point in blaming Ruth for anything even if she had known about it.

'No,' I replied. 'The first time I met her was this evening on the train. She doesn't know anything about this.'

'We know whom the drugs belong to. They're Robert Lock's drugs.'

I nodded. 'Yes, they are.'

Robert had already lied and pretended not to know me. So why should I protect him? It sounds vaguely ridiculous, but his denials were almost immoral. How dare he deny all knowledge of what had happened? I wasn't denying anything, so why should he?

A short time later Ruth appeared, while Robert was still being questioned, and came straight over. 'Don't worry about it, Sandra,' she said. 'It'll be all right.' I think I managed a smile.

The Thais needed some convincing before Ruth was released without charge and allowed to leave the customs room. I never saw her again.

Robert was brought back into the room. They wanted to photograph us. Robert sat down. Next to me was a small Thai official who moved a table out of the way of Robert; another guard ran across the room and kicked Robert in the throat.

'Did you see that?' Robert screeched. 'I'm going to sue. I'm going to press charges.' He was holding his throat.

'I don't really know what I saw there, Robert.'

I was told to get up for the photograph, but first they had to retrieve the packages of heroin. My heart sank. *Oh God, not here.* I could feel myself blushing. I was taken behind a screen where a woman stood clutching a Polaroid camera.

'Remove them,' she barked. She stood in front of me, staring. It was humiliating. I had to retrieve the packages that were lodged inside my body and she took pictures of me as I took each package of heroin from inside myself. The woman stood there, unblinking, a curious kind of midwife, attending to me with her camera.

'Please don't take pictures of my face,' I pleaded, twisting my head to one side. Click. The Polaroid developed. I took the first package out and handed it to her.

'We want the other three,' she said, aggressively. 'We know there are four.'

Click. Another picture. Click. I could hardly believe this was happening to me. Smiling like a shark, the woman waved the photographs dry. I stood gawping at a far wall. This was not what Robert had promised.

Back in the main room there was a very low table and I was placed in front of it. On the table was a very large set of old-fashioned scales, similar to those used by butchers. My four little packages barely registered, and almost disappeared on the table. A long, thin blackboard was produced. The scales were moved a little and replaced by the blackboard which had been scribbled with our names, dates of birth and day of arrest.

'Look straight ahead,' a voice boomed.

I've always hated having my picture taken. Now, in the customs room, in front of that heroin, my vanity had been replaced by shame.

'Look at the camera.'

I couldn't bear to and I twisted my face away. Eventually they got their picture.

The official handling the heroin pulled on a pair of thin, surgical gloves. With a scalpel, he slit open one of the packages, took a small amount of the powder out and placed it in a small vial. Inside the vial was some kind of chemical. He shook it gently and the liquid inside turned purple.

'Do you know what this indicates?'

'No,' I lied, 'I don't.'

'It's showing that this is heroin. Did you know that you were carrying heroin?'

I lowered my head. I was gasping for air. Once again we were separated and Robert was taken away for questioning. The following few hours passed in a fog of apprehension. Now I was beginning to feel tired. I think I nodded off.

Robert appeared again. My leg cuffs were replaced with handcuffs and we were walked through the airport, towards the car park outside. We were going to the police station.

My memory jumps from being scared to fits of panic, to calm, to absolute fear. I thought about home in Yorkshire and the brightness of my family. I thought about my brother and the baby and also my pets. Thailand disappeared from my thoughts and I replaced them with the cold and grey of West Yorkshire. My history and my future appeared all at once, completely muddled. Was I actually alive? Shortly before midnight I fell asleep.

I woke abruptly when the van stopped at the police station.

'That was a dream, wasn't it, Robert,' I said. 'Tell me that was a dream.'

'It happened,' he snapped. 'Now get out of the van.'

It was still pitch black. The police station was somewhere in the heart of Bangkok although where exactly I'm not sure. Up a set of rickety steps we climbed into a dark room, where I could hear something moving in a corner. My mind was racing overtime and I was sure I could see the faces of screaming prisoners. A hundred different thoughts competed for space in my head.

Someone switched on a light. The office was very large and on one side there was a small, folding bed, on which a policeman was lying. He rose slowly and the customs officials signed us over to the police. Words were exchanged.

Our bags were searched and our pockets were emptied. Robert had a good camera, an electronic chess game and a Walkman amongst other things and the policeman took them. They took most of my money from me and I signed for it. It would be stolen, they said, if I took it downstairs. I was allowed to keep my book of family photographs. The customs officers left and we heard their laughter as it echoed down the walls of the corridor.

We were led through one gate, then a second and finally into an area with fluorescent tube lights. On the right-hand side was a very large room with bars all the way down the front. On the left side was a much smaller room with bars down the front and side. Robert was placed in the larger of the two rooms with some older men, probably prisoners. I was put in the smaller room. For some reason they never locked the door.

Two sides of the room consisted of bars; it had a floor and a partitioned section at the end which, I discovered, was the toilet area – a concrete spot with a hole in the floor and a cement trough full of slimy water. It smelled putrid. The floor was crusty from years of dirt. The smell from the water I was supposed to wash from was so foul that my head spun whenever I went near it.

Mum and Dad, I whispered to myself, *I'm so sorry. I didn't mean this to happen.* I started to cry.

The guards left me with a few items of clothing and I rolled up my coat and placed it on the floor against a wall at the back of the cage. I lay down and began drifting to sleep. A policeman appeared.

'No,' he said, pointing in the opposite direction from where I was lying, 'you must not sleep here, you must sleep there.' I moved hastily, and then slept.

The next morning I realised there was a thin window in the brick wall, towards the back of the cell and through this I could see the steps that went upstairs in the police station. The policemen could stand on a certain stair and see into the cell where I was sleeping. This must have been a regular practice with female prisoners. They seemed to want to point me out to their friends.

What would I do now? A metal plate, covered in sloppy rice with a little bit of overcooked cabbage, had been placed in front of me on the floor. Breakfast. There was something in the corner. Two large eyes stared at me. I rolled over on the floor and saw the largest hairy rat imaginable and it was eating my food. He was two feet away from me. I was glad that I wasn't hungry.

Years before, in America, I recalled my mum thinking that I was crazy because there were always half-eaten cherries on the kitchen table. 'Sandra,' she said, 'this is no way to dispose of fruit. If you're going to half-eat it throw the rest out as well.'

But it wasn't me. It turned out that we had field mice in the house, coming in through the back of the cooker. 'The trouble with mice,' she laughed, 'is that if you've seen one you've probably got a hundred. You never see them together.'

As I stood there staring at the rat in my cell, I thought of that conversation with my mum and I began shaking. Shit, there must be hundreds of rats there, underneath me, crawling around and over each other's wet bodies. Suddenly, more than anything, I was embarrassed to be there, and having to take food from my gaolers with rats scuttling inside the cell. The rat could have it. I stuffed my coat down the hole where the rat had appeared. I would figure out a pillow for that night later.

There was nothing to do, for the moment at least, but get on with things. The grime and dirt had built up over the years like paint and I decided to get comfortable. I got some water from the toilet, ripped up a shirt for a cloth and then scrubbed the floorboards and the bars.

No matter how ridiculous this situation appeared to me I would get out soon, I was convinced of it. I was a British citizen. They wouldn't keep me here for long. Not in this filth.

SIX

Suicide is Painless

Dear Mum and Dad

My head is spinning with shock, sorrow, shame and remorse over this disgusting situation I have created. I feel dirty all the time, I don't know if I will ever be able to get used to this place. I went out to court yesterday and one of the guards let a Thai prisoner up to the court to act as translator; he only had one leg and spoke no English at all really…

Letter to Mum and Dad, May 1993

I walked the narrow corridor between the two cages daily. For six days I could speak with Robert and we would stand at the bars chatting, swapping unlimited angst, which was such a ludicrous scenario that I still wonder why we spoke, given what had just happened. Why was I doing this? It was simple. I desperately wanted conversation with someone familiar, even if it was from the guy who had landed me in this mess in the first place. And I presumed Robert knew the ropes.

Robert constantly asked me to protect him, to say that he knew nothing about the drugs and to ensure that he went free. Over and over he told me that he would be more help to me on the outside than he ever would be from the inside. I was terribly confused. The whole episode had sent me into shock and I could hardly collect my own thoughts, let alone make a rational decision about what to say about Robert and his role in smuggling the heroin. But why should I take the blame?

One thing was clear; he never had the belly for the trouble we were in. A worried woman knows a worried man when she sees one.

'We'll escape,' he said, pointing out rusty bars high above the cell I was being held in. 'Pull them to see if they'll move and feel along the walls for a way out,' he continued. 'It'll be easier to get out of here than it will to get out of a prison.'

I thought he was mad. Surely we wouldn't have to escape from the police station, never mind prison. We wouldn't be there that long. If he wants to escape then fine, he can go ahead. I was too scared to try to do anything that might upset the police.

Although Robert still wanted me to say he had had nothing to do with the heroin, the least I expected him to say was that he was sorry. Nothing.

Jean Sharpe, a representative from the British Embassy, came to see me on my second day. She was wearing a pretty floral dress. Her attitude was stiff and brisk. 'Your parents are going to be told what has happened to you,' she stated, baldly.

I passed her the letter I had scribbled to my family telling them to forget all about me.

'No,' I said, 'no, please don't tell them. Don't tell anybody where I am or what is happening to me. Just go away and don't come back.'

She glanced at the letter. 'The media might be interested in this case, so it would be better if your parents hear from the Foreign Office than from a journalist or from reading about it in a newspaper.'

'The media? Don't be ridiculous. The media won't be interested in this. I'm sure there are far more interesting things for them to report on than me.' Her eyes widened.

I wondered what kind of sentence I might receive; at worst weeks, perhaps even a month. 'Jean,' I asked, 'what am I likely to get for this?'

'The minimum sentence is 25 years, Sandra,' she said, 'but they could uphold the maximum, which I think you know is death.'

What? What? What the hell are you talking about? Minimum? Maximum? 25 years? Death?

'No, Jean,' I blurted out. 'That's not possible. No way! I can't do that!'

She barely moved. 'Oh, yes, you can,' she said, 'yes, you can. You'll find the strength.'

The air was dry and I sucked on it for moisture. I looked up at the cell ceiling, imagining I might never see natural light again. I almost threw up at the thought of the rats. Jean's conversation echoed, sounding almost berserk. Was she insane? 'Find the strength'? She had to be joking.

'No, I won't,' I repeated. 'I'm not that sort of person.'

Jean looked away again, handed me a small booklet containing a list of lawyers, saying she would see me at Lard Yao, and promptly left.

What a horrible woman, I thought. Yet over the coming years I grew to rely on Jean so much and thought so highly of her that when the Foreign Office transferred her out of Bangkok I must have cried for a month. She turned out to be one of the loveliest women, who fought my corner more times than I can remember.

There were quite a few Thai men in the cells of the Crime Suppression Division and, after the rat ate my rice the first morning, I gave the sloppy rations to those in the cage opposite me. They devoured it. The food was pale and disgusting. The cells for both the men and women faced directly opposite each other, so there was no such thing as privacy. I watched them as much as they watched me because there was nothing much else to look at.

Two teenage brothers in the men's cell were thin, poor and dirty. Every night they slept entwined around each other. They had been offered £100 to drive a pick-up truck down to Bangkok. They were stopped and the police found several hundred kilos of marijuana, all professionally pressed and baled. I looked at them as they hugged each other. Fear sat in their gut like broken glass.

There was no natural light in the cells, although it was never dark because the fluorescent strip lights were kept on all the time. After I had scrubbed the cell a few days earlier, I had stuck large pieces of old newspaper over the bars to stop the lights keeping me awake at night. My sickness wouldn't go away, and the light burned my eyes, giving me splitting headaches. A light in another room silhouetted a policeman.

Every day I was taken upstairs for questioning and on the third day, the policeman in charge of the case, who seemed fairly decent, handed me several sheets of typed A4 paper and told me to sign at the bottom. Up until that point I had been as cooperative as could be expected but when I saw an official document typed in Thai, without translation, I panicked. My father's voice came back to me.

'Never sign anything, Sandra,' he had always warned me, 'until you have read and understood all the small print. If you don't like it, don't sign it.' Even 7,000 miles from home he made perfect sense.

'No,' I said, 'I won't sign it. What does it say?'

'Nothing,' said the policeman. 'Just what you have told me.'

There was a silence between us. It was obvious he was lying about what was in the document. His brown eyes hardened. I could be signing my death warrant.

'No,' I repeated, 'I'm not signing.'

'You sign,' he shouted, with increasing purpose to his voice. 'If you no sign the court give you the big sentence. You sign.' It was obvious he was talking about the death penalty but it was another chance I would have to take. Still he persisted. 'If my king gives an amnesty to prisoners, you will not get the amnesty if you no sign. You die in Thai prison. If you apply for Royal Pardon, you no get it if you no sign.'

He repeated his signing mantra over and over, telling me that I would spend the rest of my life in prison. I was scared but I would not sign. The following day he came downstairs for me at around 4 o'clock in the morning.

'Get up, get up, you sign.' I refused and the tension between us increased. Later, he returned, offering to go out and get me anything I wanted to eat. He knew I hadn't eaten in days. 'You sign?' he pleaded, pretending that there was some intimacy between us, as if he understood my predicament.

'No,' I said, again. 'I won't sign it.'

We continued this for a few more days. His frustration finally got the better of him and he took me upstairs again to his interrogation office. He shut the door and whispered. 'I cannot stop my men coming in to see you in the night if you no sign. They like you, but I tell them "no".' It was obvious what he meant but I didn't care if they raped me. If it happened I would deal with it but I still wasn't going to sign their stupid paper.

'Do what you like, I'm not signing anything.'

Robert bought a bottle of Thai whisky from one of the policemen and that night we split it. I had eaten nothing and fear orbited my body like a satellite. With a bottle of paracetamol and a packet of antidepressants I drank the whisky. I'd had enough of this shit. It seemed like the easiest way out of everything. I wanted to make it easier for everyone concerned: my family, friends and even the Thai officials.

'I'm going to sleep Robert,' I said to him, at around seven in the evening. 'Don't bother waking me up.'

In the early hours of the morning I woke up, the usual fluorescent light buzzing overhead, hoping that I was dead. Although I knew I was alive I pretended that this was what death felt like – not too sore, just a little hazy, a little grey. *Stupid cow.* My pathetic attempt at suicide had failed miserably. I stumbled into the slimy toilet area, slipping and cracking my head on the concrete tank.

Lying on the wet floor, I realised that I was not in heaven but still very much in Thai hell. The ruinous stench of the police station lingered on.

Christ, Sandra, you are an idiot. You can't even kill yourself without messing up.

The next morning Robert told me that he had suspected I wanted to kill myself. I think he had wanted me to die.

Two women walked into the main office of the police station while I was being interviewed. 'Ugh, the press,' said one policeman.

The women both looked British and roughly the same age as me, and were blonde and pretty. I don't know why, but I was so happy to see them that I jumped up from my interrogation seat and ran to greet them both.

They're here to see me, how wonderful. They'll probably get me out.

'A friend of ours told us you were here.'

Panting like a Labrador I was so relieved to see someone who wasn't Thai that I began rambling on hysterically. 'They want me to sign papers that are written in Thai. What do you think, should I sign? Will I sign? What do you think? How long will I be here? What...'

Both of them said that in the same situation they probably wouldn't, but asked me what my lawyer had suggested.

'Lawyer? What do you mean?'

I didn't have a lawyer. I hadn't even thought about a lawyer. Had I phoned home or anything? No, I hadn't. I hadn't thought about that either.

The officer-in-charge told one of his deputies to take me downstairs and the two women followed. We were allowed to stand and talk. I stood on one side of a set of bars and they stood on the other. Their names were Victoria and Olivia. One worked for Radio Four and the other said she worked for the *Guardian*.

Before long I had told them everything about myself, where I was from and how I had loved horses and how silly I sometimes was and how I came to be in Thailand and how the hell I had ended up here. I showed them all my family photographs, told them about the baby that had just been born into our family and how I couldn't ask my family for money because things were difficult at home too.

I thought they had just popped in to visit me. It never dawned on me that they were there for a story. When Victoria asked if I would mind if she took a couple of pictures, I felt embarrassed, but they had been so nice that I said, 'Why not?'

She paid the policeman some money and opened up her bag containing lenses, different flashes and several cameras. I stood there, hands behind my back, then hands out front and hands holding onto the bars, hands clutching my face. Whatever she suggested, really.

Victoria snapped and flashed while I prayed no one would ever see those pictures of me behind bars. I have not seen Victoria since 1993 but I have seen those photographs repeated scores of times in newspapers over the years.

The following day both Olivia and Victoria came to the police station and brought huge bottles of strawberry milk, a large bag of cookies and a small bag of oranges. The penitents' gifts. I drank some of the milk, leaving the cookies and fruit until I got to court. Food for photographs, it was a fair swap.

'Do you remember those two girls from Birmingham that were arrested years ago?' I said to Robert. 'I'm sure it was in Thailand and they got a lot of press coverage. Jean Sharpe said the press might be interested in this case. What do you think? Do you think the press might be at court tomorrow?'

Karyn Smith and Patricia Cahill, two young girls from Birmingham, had been given 18- and 25-year sentences respectively, after they were found guilty of attempting to smuggle over 60lb of heroin, worth £4 million, out of Thailand in 1990.

Fortunately, they avoided the death penalty despite the high quantity of heroin they were carrying.

I remembered seeing them on television when I was in England, but had left the country three months before they were sentenced and never found out what sentence they had received. Before I left for Thailand an old man from a local pub warned me about going. 'You don't want to go over there, mate,' he sniffed. 'You're going to end up in that prison with those two Brummie girls.' Just over two years later, when I was taken to Lard Yao prison, one of the first faces I saw the following morning was Karyn Smith's.

'Seriously though, Robert,' I continued, 'you don't suppose there's going to be any press when we go to court, considering the amount of coverage those two got?'

'Don't be so bloody stupid, Sandra.'

He made a bet with me that there would be little or no media interest in this case. A bottle of champagne, he wagered, if there are any reporters there. I wanted to believe Robert but felt sure his champagne would be going on ice.

On the Thursday following our arrest we were taken to court. The night before court I was told to have all my stuff together and that I would not be returning to the police station. *Thank God*, I thought, *nowhere could be as awful as this place*. Once again the cell door was unlocked so I strolled outside into the corridor and hung my Thai dressing gown on the bars outside the cage.

In the morning I went to get it down before having a wash. Shit, I couldn't believe it. Through the gate at the end of the corridor were a large group of men with television cameras while others buzzed around with notebooks and pens, looking, poking and prying. The press had arrived.

For a minute I stared blankly, before racing back to the cage. Hurriedly, I began hanging clothes on the bars where the police had been looking in some days earlier. The press would be up there, I was sure, trying to take pictures of me in this stew of a cell.

No, no, no. My family and friends would see me like this, scampering about like an animal. I didn't want anyone seeing me there at all. *Please, just leave me alone.*

At around half past eight, one of the policemen came to the cell, smoothing his hair down, then combing it. 'Come on, we go.' Grabbing all my clothes from the bars, he shouted at me again. Everything that was still on the floor he was shoving into my bag. I was prodded out, with Robert not far behind, and we found ourselves in the middle of a horrendous media scrum.

I had not slept and, apart from the milk, had still not eaten. Earlier I had washed my hair with water from the septic tank, hoping that I would not look as bad as I felt in front of the judge. A pair of blue polka-dot culottes, a white shirt and a pair of green court shoes might also make an impression, or at least help me appear respectable.

The police returned my bag and, to my surprise, the officer who lived up the stairs gave me back, in a brown envelope, the rest of the money he had taken from me earlier. Although not very much, it later proved very useful. Some friends of Robert's were at the station and he signed over his Walkman, camera and electronic chess game to them. Ignoring me, they talked in whispers.

Some days earlier, when I had written the letter to my parents, it had been a strange kind of relief to do so. From that point on I had told myself I was no longer the person that I had been and I no longer had a family. It would be so much easier this way, to do this on my own. Somehow I had convinced myself it was possible to survive this ordeal, but the only way to do it was to do it alone. The only way to do this would be to lose my past; if I could cut myself off from my past then whatever happened in the coming weeks, months or, God forbid, years, wouldn't really matter.

All this changed when I saw the press. I remembered everyone at home. Now they were going to know about me and I didn't want anyone knowing who I was, or anything about my family. I didn't want anyone laying any blame at the door of my family.

One of the cameras had ITN written in large letters down the side and all I could think of when I saw that camera was my grandfather. He had always watched ITN news and I knew he would see me being bundled to court by Thai police. The shock of it all would give him a heart attack and probably kill him. *Get that fucking camera out of my face!* I screamed to myself. I was pushed forward, while trying to hide my face. *Don't worry, Pa-Pa,* I said to myself, *I'm fine.*

Much later, people would tell me that as they watched me they could see how emotional and shaken I was. But I wasn't crying for myself, instead it was for my grandfather. The last time I had seen him he was already frail, already an old man.

'I am so sorry,' I shouted above the crowd. 'Please, wait for me, Pa-Pa! Please don't die.'

'How do you feel?' 'What's the charge?' 'What's it like in the cells?' 'Why did you do it?' 'Whose idea was it?' The reporters shocked me. They had not come to the police station to see me, but to look at me. Pushing and shoving for positions, they continued to fire stupid questions at me. How did they think I felt?

The cameras rolled and flashed. I was an animal in a zoo. I was somewhere between dead and alive. Did my parents know? What did I think of the death penalty for drug smugglers? *Jesus, what's wrong with these people?*

'Mum, I love you,' I sobbed at no one in particular. 'Dad, I love you.' I felt obliterated. I missed them so much. I just wanted to be at home with them and say sorry for all the stupid things I had done over the years. *Dad, you were right about me, I did always have to have the last word.* Now look where I had landed myself. *Mum, I'm sorry for being so selfish.* Now look where I was. I hated myself.

Robert was sitting in the back of an open truck, his head in his handcuffs, but he said nothing except, 'No comment.' I had heard people say that in films, but I never imagined I would hear it for real. Trying to separate himself from what had happened, his words sounded vaguely guilty and confused, as if they had succumbed to the pressure of some kind of truth much too great for him to comprehend.

'Granny, and Pa-Pa, I'm so sorry. Wait for me, wait for me.' My words sounded terribly hollow and so weak.

We were put in a rusting pick-up truck. I sat in the front, without handcuffs, while Robert was placed in the back, alongside two policemen. He was handcuffed. We were driven through Bangkok and it took roughly an hour and a half to get to the court. Although I didn't look like a prisoner, I certainly felt like one.

We drove past the Palace of Thailand's King Bhumibol Adulyadej, and it was very surreal. So many times I had strolled past it over the previous two years and now I was being driven past it in a prison van. There is an area of farmland to the rear of the palace, with iron railings and gardens around it. The king gives over most of his grounds for agricultural purposes and fat cows graze lazily in the sun. Much of the land is peppered with greenhouses.

The truck rolled on. I watched children going to school, people going to work on buses and bicycles, people selling things on the street. Some people were shouting, others wagging their fingers. Hard- and soft-faced men strolled by. All of a sudden I loved the country all over again.

What have you done, Sandra? What have you done? I couldn't stop the tears welling in my eyes. I couldn't help thinking that if we had not been stopped at the airport I would probably have been flying back to the UK that day. It was such a strange feeling knowing I could so easily have got away with it. But I felt different now. In a way I almost felt happy; I wouldn't be returning home with a secret. I doubt my conscience would have kept it safe for very long.

The truck came to a stop at a set of traffic lights. Nearby someone was selling Buddhist prayer beads that are made from little flowers; they usually hang on a string from car mirrors and around the small spirit houses that are set up to guard people from evil spirits. I bought two sets and later carried them into the court, hoping the flowers would grant me some kind of special dispensation from my crime. I needed something to say I was sorry. I needed to pray. I also needed all the help I could get.

We were taken through a back entrance at the court, passing a massive cage full of men, who were shouting and screaming. 'Look at the Westerner,' shouted one. Beyond the cages were the prisoner's families and the noise was unbelievable as everyone was desperately trying to communicate. There seemed to be cages and bars everywhere. The whole place was a teeming mass of bodies; it looked like a swirling Goya or Bosch creation. The noise was deafening. Everything was so dark and venomous. All the prisoners wore muddy-brown coloured shorts and T-shirts. The prisoners looked like beasts. The brutalities in here were not done in secret.

This isn't happening. It just wasn't possible that I was involved in all this. It must be happening to someone else. *It must be a mistake. Yes, that's it; it's all a big mistake. They can't possibly put me in there; we must be just passing through.*

We continued walking past the front of this horrendous cage, between the visitors and the prisoners, into a brightly lit, air-conditioned room. At one end there was a glass partition with counters and wooden benches placed in a row. Robert and I were told to sit down together, more or less at the back. I sat down, placed my bags on the floor, and then proceeded to peel an orange, which I had with me. A group of Thai faces turned around towards me and gave me a horrified look.

'What are you doing?' they seemed to say. 'It's not a picnic.'

I kept peeling, though a little nervously. I just didn't know what to do, or how to act. I was unable to make sense of anything. I looked at the orange and felt like a fool. I ate it and felt the juices choking my throat.

The guards, in their dark beige uniforms, were dotted around the room. Then another two of them walked in. In between them, flanked by their sides, was a loose-looking figure, wearing a sickly brown, heavy T-shirt and the same coloured shorts. He was burned dark from the sun. The poor soul looked hellish. He had a face like cancer under a microscope.

Most Thai people, unless they work in the streets or on building sites, are light-skinned; they do everything possible to keep out of the sun in order to keep their skin as light as possible. His hair was shorn off and he was shackled with a pair of elephant chains around his ankles.

The chains have large iron rings that double over on themselves, and the rings are roughly three-quarters of an inch in diameter. In between the rings is a length of chain, roughly three feet long and an inch thick. In the middle of this chain the prisoner ties a heavy string so that he can hold the chain up and walk without tripping over it. It makes a heavy clanking sound as it is pulled along. The prisoner cannot walk properly while wearing it and is forced to shuffle, dragging one foot at a time.

As this man was brought into court Robert and I looked at each other and just stared, in total shock and disbelief and disgust. We were absolutely horrified. *What the hell has he done?* I wondered. Whatever it was it must have been something really dreadful to end up looking like that. Perhaps he was a serial killer, or a rapist? The chained man sat at the back of what I now realised was the courtroom. Embarrassed, I stopped eating my orange. I had thought we were in a waiting room.

There were lots of officials sitting around at the front of the room, all wearing the typical military-style clothes of office. Eventually one official took a piece of paper and handed it to one of the seated individuals. From nowhere I heard my name, then Robert's. A policeman whom I recognised from the station strode to the counter and was handed two pieces of paper, which he brought over to Robert and myself. He handed me one of the sheets and told me to sign it.

I had no choice. Nervously, I signed and was given a copy. Several weeks later I discovered that what I had signed was simply the paper to remand me in custody. We were bound over for 11 days while the police drew up formal charges. Prosecutors would have 84 days to bring the case to court and in the meantime we would have to wait for their decision, going to court every nine to 11 days for further remanding.

Following the proceedings, we were taken back the way we had come in, past the screaming hordes. Now it was official; we were prisoners. Robert was taken to a cage on our left as we walked. Later he would go to Klong Prem Men's Prison. We said, 'Goodbye and good luck' to each other and strangely enough I think we both meant it. We would need it. Despite what had happened he was still my reminder of home. And anyway fear had got the better of us, so saying goodbye was just a way to ease our insecurities about the future.

I was on my own now. Step, step, step, down a little corridor I was escorted by the guards, past lots of officials doing paperwork. We came to yet another set of bars that ran from the floor to the ceiling. There was a gate in the bars and an office stationed there, partitioned off by even more bars. There were bars everywhere I looked. Two female officers stood idly by, wearing military uniforms and rubber flip-flops on their feet. They came out, signed some papers and took me into their custody.

Without a word they tipped the contents of my bag out onto the floor. One of them grabbed hold of all my underwear, stuffing it into a plastic carrier bag. With a broad smile they put my carton of cigarettes to one side and took the rest of my clothes, putting them aside also. A few items of toiletries and some make-up were stuffed into the carrier bag, along with my album of family photographs.

Everything else was placed back inside my travel bag and taken to their office area. 'No can, no can,' they shouted, together. The strings of prayer beads were also taken off me. Was I really so undeserving of such a holy object?

My small shoulder bag was searched but they missed a packet of cigarettes I had placed in the inside pocket. They left me with oranges and a bag of biscuits inside my shoulder bag. A rub-down body search followed; then I was told to remove my shoes. They opened the gates, shoved me through the bars of the cell and the gate clanked shut.

The room held around 30 people and I immediately thought they all looked subhuman. Everyone wore dark brown dresses, like sacks. Each creature was barefoot and dirty and they scuttled around on the floor. Two girls sat over by a wall and one appeared to be grooming her friend's hair for head lice. My shoes had been confiscated. I was in the same situation as the others. A tentative expectancy hung in the air.

Olivia and Victoria were standing on the other side of two sets of bars. Noticing them, the guards looked at them and said to me, 'You have two friends, we give them your bag?' Before I had a chance to reply my bag was passed through to them. It was my only connection with my old life and although there was nothing of any importance in that bag, watching it being passed to two virtual strangers, my heart sank. My life was disappearing with it.

When the gate shut I went over to where Olivia and Victoria stood. The gap between us was about 12 feet wide and the light was not good, but it was good to have them near.

'Can you contact my grandfather for me?' I asked. I worried about what he would see on television. If he knew beforehand it wouldn't come as such a shock. I gave Olivia my brother's address and telephone number.

'Tell him to call my grandfather, please.'

She did call my brother and he duly warned my grandparents.

I wondered how Robert was getting on, whether things were the same for him as they were for me. The pain in my stomach had intensified during my time at the police station, and at the court I was barely able to walk upright. It was the same in this holding cell. My stomach was in knots.

The holding cell had no natural light, and the air was oppressive and musty. It was such a dirty area, smelling like every bad toilet I had ever been in. To one side were two, small sectioned-off areas housing Thai-style toilets – basically, a hole in the floor with large tanks of water beside them.

I could feel the thick air in my eyes, on my skin and up my nose. While all the Thais were completely disinterested by their surroundings I sat alone and looked around in stunned amazement. A woman came over to me and began to speak in English. Her name was Anna and she was Nigerian. Anna had heard me talking to Olivia and Victoria and she told me that I could order food from them.

'Whatever you want to eat you can have,' she said.

'I'm not hungry.'

She looked at me peculiarly. Food was the last thing on my mind but Anna was desperate for me to order something. The prison provides no food or water for people going to court and because Anna had no friends, family or contacts on the outside, she'd had nothing to eat or drink that day.

Anna was going to court because her husband had told her to go to Bangkok and bring back a bag that a friend of his would give her. Whether she knew what was going to be in that bag or not, I don't know, but a year after I met her she received a life sentence – 99 years – for attempting to smuggle a kilo of heroin out of the country.

I still had the bag of cookies and oranges but it never crossed my mind to give them to Anna; I assumed that everyone's appetite would have waned like mine. Little did I realise that most of them had been in prison for months, some of them years, and they were as hungry as dogs.

'You will be going to Lard Yao tonight,' said Anna. 'Tomorrow you will see the two other British girls who are there for smuggling heroin.'

Lard Yao was the women's division of Klong Prem Prison. The notorious Bangkok Hilton. She was talking about Patricia Cahill and Karyn Smith.

Anna lost interest in me shortly after and I felt terribly deflated, alone and by myself. One of the officials, who was fat, abrupt and quite aggressive, came over to the bars and shouted out a few names. Those girls who were called scrambled over to the bars and promptly dropped to their knees, then sat with their legs to one side on the floor. Obedient and prostrate, they looked like zoo animals before the trainers. It was awful.

The officer handed out pieces of paper from the court and some of the girls appeared quite happy at the contents placed before them; others looked miserable. The smiling prisoners had just been informed they had been offered bail and they were going home that evening. Bail had been denied to the rest and they had just received another 11-day remand hearing. A few others were given the official document to confirm the sentence that had just been handed down to them by the courts.

Relatives passed rice, fruit, cola-in-a-bag and other Thai delights to the guards who proceeded to check them, before they were passed into the cage of women. The frenzy around the opening of each bag was pitiful, but even then I guessed that it was not only food and drinks being passed through in plastic bags. Lighters, cigarettes, money, snuff, pills and powders were all smuggled beneath egg fried rice and vegetables.

Those who weren't smuggling ran to the back of the room, promptly sat on the floor in a circle and ripped open their gifts, shovelling food into their mouths. Throughout this rather surreal feeding frenzy I remained silent. Hours had gone by since my last cigarette and I was beginning to feel twitchy. Then I remembered the ones the guards had overlooked. Some of the prisoners were already ahead of me, smoking in the toilet area. They must have smuggled in their own. I took out my cigarettes and, for the first time since my arrival, the girls took an interest in me. I offered the pack to one girl, hoping she might take one and talk to me. No such luck. She grabbed the packet and, in Thai, called the rest of the women over.

They scuttled to the toilets while I waited a few seconds before plucking up the courage to follow behind them. I asked for one of my own cigarettes. I squatted down alongside them. It was the most wonderful, delicious cigarette. We hunched down lower before crawling out of the toilet. I offered the girls the bag of cookies and oranges and within a few minutes the whole lot were gone. We sat there smiling. I had broken my first prison rules.

At 5.30 pm all the girls gathered their shoes and lined up at the gate. We were leaving.

SEVEN

Prisoner 228/36

Dear Mum and Dad

... I have spent the whole afternoon on the verge of tears, again... I'm doomed. A life sentence here is 100 years and most people seem to be getting life from the courts. Most pardon applications are being refused... and 'the death sentence' means death here... one of the teachers from the university came by to see me yesterday, he brought soap and shampoo with him and I found the whole thing totally embarrassing. I can cope with this weird world of walls but when the real world shows itself to me I crumble...

Love you both

Sandra

Letter home, June 1993

A gloomy, pearl-coloured light descended as we were driven through the city in a lorry with a cage on its back. The people in the streets watched us, pointing us out to their children. We were public property to be ridiculed and held up as degenerates.

Two handsome young men sat at the back of the lorry, both holding rifles, as it rumbled through the streets. *Perhaps I should make a run for it, in the hope that the guards will shoot me dead.* In a consoling almost paternal voice, one of them told me that they only ever shoot fleeing inmates in the back of the knees to stop them. They would rather they served their sentence to the full than kill them.

An hour or so later the lorry pulled up reluctantly in front of Lard Yao; as if it felt the unwillingness of the women it carried. There were so many women on the lorry that I had trouble seeing the large, very stiff pair of pale green gates, past bodies and bars. The gates opened and the van pulled through.

This is it, I thought, *this is real prison.* There were more bricks and bars and fluorescent lights than I had ever imagined, followed by that unmistakable rasp of rattling metal keys that would stay with me throughout the following years. We were shoved off the back of the lorry, counted by two officers, and passed and piled into a narrow, damp and dark, concrete cage. Tiny frogs, less than a centimetre long, jumped around on the ground. Nothing much else stirred.

The curious thing was that the prison already felt familiar, as if the memory of the other women who had passed through still lingered. All around me women, young and old, started ripping off their clothes and shoving each other to get to the front of the queue that had formed. I kept my clothes on and remained at the back.

A heavy, steel door opened. Five women passed. I could see through the door. There was grass and a tree. There were pretty grass lawns and flowerbeds. *Oh, how wonderful!* I thought. *This isn't going to be so bad. And at least I will be able to see the sky.*

Another five women passed. Five more, then another five, until there was just a couple of others and myself left. My turn. I was scared but I was also eager to get into prison to see how bad or good, it really was. If there are trees...

The door opened and I spotted a blonde head on top of a blue uniform. She was an Australian girl named Nola Blake. What a relief to see her little blonde head amongst all the dark-haired Thai girls. Too much eye make-up, skinny as a rake, wrinkled and kind of hard-looking, Nola knew her way around the prison. She was one of the prison trustees and had been asked to meet the *farang* – the foreigner – to act as translator. Nola was wearing a blue uniform because she was a sentenced prisoner. She spoke fluent Thai.

'Welcome to the Bangkok Hilton.'

The prison was calm but to me it appeared totally chaotic. The rest of the 1,700 prisoners were all locked in for the night, but everywhere there was the sweet-foul smell of hot bodies. Everyone was given a very intimate and thorough strip-search by another prisoner. I was handed a thick, brown denim sarong, the colour of a remand prisoner, and a shirt. This was my uniform. Most of the few personal belongings I had left were taken away by Man Kwillean, a Hong Kong Chinese woman I later nicknamed Rifkin, the name of the prison grass in the film *Midnight Express*.

Rifkin emptied my carrier bag and leather bag out on the floor, took my watch and the few pieces of jewellery I had, but allowed me to keep the book of family photographs, filled with pictures of my family and the new baby at home. My shoes and clothes were stuffed into a leather bag and that was the last I saw of them. I felt like I was free-falling.

I was given a small, stained sandbag for a pillow. Nola walked me over to a slimy, green concrete area for a wash. Directly in front of us was a massive, blue-tiled water-tank on the ground but there was no water inside apart from a little pool at the bottom. I had a toothbrush and soap but I couldn't figure out how I was meant to wash from the tank with the dribble of water.

There was a cadre of bored-looking women milling around, all of them topless. They wore short sarongs around their waists, but looked like boys.

'That's the tomboys,' said Nola, when she saw me gawping. I had never seen anything like it; they had coarse, home-made tattoos, covering their bodies in a swathe of blue and green lines. Some had rough love hearts and symbols, while others had gouged words like Smak, instead of Smack (heroin), on their arms, legs and torsos.

The presence of the tomboys freaked me out. Their eyes were

bloodshot and wild. Nola kept laughing and joking with them in Thai but I had no idea what they were talking about. Besides, I was too busy trying to figure out how to wash.

'Have you got a bowl?' Nola asked.

'No.'

Off she went and brought back her bowl while I stood around staring at everyone, stunned.

The plastic bowl Nola brought me was about six inches in diameter. It was used to scoop the water from the tank and throw it over you, the typical Thai way of washing. This is how I would shower. But how would I get the puddle of water out of the tank? One of the tomboys placed a bucket under the tap, and it quickly filled up. She was dunking the bowl into the bucket.

In Lard Yao Prison a bucket is like gold; they are expensive to buy and getting one is an indicator of your privileged status. When you get one you do almost anything to keep it.

Nola told me the 'boys' showering at the tank liked the look of me so I should just go ahead and share their bucket of water. Prudishly, I didn't want to take off my clothes, and the heavy sarong made washing properly rather tricky. After a long day in the courtroom holding cell, I was hot, dirty and tired. I scrubbed my teeth with the plain brush. Nola went off to get me a pair of thin, cotton shorts and a T-shirt; my new pyjamas.

'Have these,' she said. 'They're better than the things you're wearing, they're awful for sleeping in.'

'Thanks.'

'Are you hungry?'

'No.'

'OK.'

I felt like a child. On Thursdays, she said, the Christian missionaries come to visit and are allowed to bring in food with them. Nola had a burger in her bag, and would I like half? A burger! In here? Fantastic. My hunger pangs returned. On the floor of a deserted building, as the lights flickered and a guard strolled by, I ate my first proper food in over a week.

'How long have you been here?' I asked.

'Seven and a half years.'

'What?

'Seven and a half years.'

No way, I thought, *no way. That's not possible.* No wonder she looked so exhausted. What had I been doing for the last seven and a half years while she'd been in this place? I was horrified. It wouldn't be possible for me to be in here for that length of time.

In the darkness I stared unbelieving at Nola. I had been in Bangkok for two years and I had never known that she, and women like her, had been here all that time. *Shit, Sandra, I thought, that's terrible.*

Nola had been arrested in Bangkok after heroin had been discovered underneath her baby in a pram. She had been caught along with her husband and a Thai local who were all heroin addicts. Over the next few years she proved to be quite a distant friend to me but that night, sharing a hamburger, we felt like bosom buddies.

'Seven and a half years,' she said again.

A loud siren sound pierced the air and Nola said it was time to go upstairs. She took me to a room where an officer was standing, waiting for us. The officer opened the gate. Like a losing prize-fighter, I rocked slightly before turning around to look for Nola but she was gone. Slowly, tediously I walked a little further. The room was packed tightly with bodies. Despite the numbers I felt so alone.

Lit with three long fluorescent strip lights, the room was incredibly bright. No one paid me much attention. There were over 70 women in the room and most of them were kneeling over their pillows, hands clasped together, chanting in rhythm to the sing-song voice coming over a loud speaker somewhere.

'You,' someone snapped. 'Sit. No walking. Thai people praying.'

The voice, unravelling with anger, repeated herself again in broken English. I sat and looked around, amazed at where I was. I was in the remand room. This was where I would attempt to sleep for the following three and a half years.

Each night between 70 and 120 women slept in that room, an enclosed block on concrete stilts, which was roughly 26 feet square – I paced it out over the years – with bars down two walls opening out onto the prison courtyard. We would lie side by side, and head to head with legs overlapping up to our knees, squashed together in rows. Women sometimes had to sleep sitting upright, others slept in toilets, while many barely slept at all. They stayed up all night crying because there was nowhere for them to sleep. After a while I would get used to waking up entwined in the arms and legs of the woman next to me. Conditions were cramped and primitive.

The only way adequately to explain what it's like sharing a room with 70 to 120 women is to say 'Close your eyes and imagine everyone in a crowded train lying side by side for four years in a space not much bigger than two carriages.' None of it was ever pleasant.

Twenty minutes later and the praying ended. A Thai woman, the 'mother of the room' – a prisoner who took charge of sleeping arrangements, money and cleaning of the room – walked to the far side next to the toilets and made a row of women shuffle up. She pointed to a 15-inch space and told me that was where I was to sleep. Two linoleum squares on a concrete floor was my bed.

I sat down and the people in the row rolled their eyes at me; they had lost 15 inches of space because of me and none of them looked happy about it. The rest of the women in the room, those situated away from me, breathed a collective sigh of relief. I hadn't been put in their row.

What the hell would I do now? Despite my nerves I smiled awkwardly, shrugging my shoulders as if to say, 'Well, here we are, it's not very nice is it?'

Everyone looked awful. Ragged, pitiful and diseased. One woman, roughly in her early fifties, had two-tone long hair. Half of it was jet black and the half nearest her scalp remained deep grey, five inches of grey. How long had she been in here? She had obviously run out of hair dye a long time ago. Her eyes drooped into huge bags of dark flesh under her forehead. She waved a hand to no one in particular. There was an obvious craziness about her that was unsettling. I felt as though I'd been given a starring role in *One Flew Over the Cuckoo's Nest*.

It was virtually impossible for me to sleep. I was poked every hour or so by the person next to me who shouted, 'You stay in two squares.' OK, OK, OK. From now on I was going to do as they said and teach myself to sleep like a sardine in my two squares. I was sure I could hear rats scrabbling around me somewhere. This was madness and it would probably kill me for sure.

The only thing worse than the lack of sleep was the pain in my stomach that refused to go away. A toilet roll belonging to one of my neighbours was the perfect solution and I rammed it under my ribcage, to force the pressure. It was made-to-measure. The only thing worse than my stomach was the heat. It was unbearable.

I woke the next morning in a daze. Here I was, prisoner 228/36 – the 228th person arriving in Lard Yao in the year of Lord Buddha 2536 (1993), and the noise of the prison startled me. I did not want to have to confront whatever it was. Water was being splashed around in the toilet area as people moved in preparation for the day ahead. It was around five in the morning. Already colonies of strange-looking insects had incubated around the toilet area – and anywhere else wet for that matter – adding to the unsavoury atmosphere.

A large group of women stood over and all around me, but none of them were looking at me; instead they were all queuing to use the toilet. There were two holes for over 70 women. Some of them stood chatting to a friend using the loo, but most just stood blankly. To get to and from the toilet each morning usually took an average of 20 to 30 minutes.

While this was being done the rest of the room were putting their beds away. Large towels and tiny pillows all had to be folded in a certain way and stacked in exactly the right place in the centre of the room. Once all the beds were away the women sat around until the gate opened, waiting to be let out.

As the sun came up I heard the heavy iron gate clanking and the sound of garbled voices. Lard Yao was now officially open for business. Prisoners swarmed everywhere like locusts.

'Go shower,' ordered the mother of the room. I followed some women who carried buckets, home-made bags, cats, shower bowls, large plastic cups of water and sheets of plastic. *My God!* I thought, *how could there be so many women?* I went down the steps to where Nola and I had eaten the burger.

Everyone imagines that they know how it is in prison, how prisoners act and react to such an environment, but they don't. I thought it would be quite easy to adapt and get used to it all. I had thought that I would know what it would be like and I was so wrong. What I sensed immediately is that prison is not like the movies, or television dramas. It's far more insane, terrible, emotional and disgusting than any of those.

The empty space from the previous night was now full of people and they sat around on plastic sheets wearing sarongs, or stood in corners undressing. Many prisoners were almost naked. One woman combed her pubic hair while another scraped at her tongue with something blunt. Some sat, others dashed around. Over by the tall prison wall, hundreds of women showered under the sky and I could see they were already ankle-deep in dirty water. I saw a face I vaguely recognised.

My God, it's her! I recognised that face, pale skin and blazing red hair. It was Karyn Smith, the Brummie girl I had seen on the television over two years earlier.

Karyn was wearing the regulation shorts and shirt that every other prisoner wore. She stood there in front of me beaming a huge smile that I can still see to this day.

'You're English?' Karyn asked.

'Yeah, I'm afraid so,' I replied.

'Never mind this lot, I'm not going to work this morning, come with me.'

Karyn had heard I had arrived the night before and had made the effort to find me. *It was kind of her to search me out*, I thought, although I later realised that most new arrivals in prison relieve the monotony of prison life. It was only those inmates who had been inside for years who usually avoided new arrivals because they were such hard work; they need looking after and tended to be a terrible emotional strain.

Karyn was in prison with me for six months and we became good friends. During those first few arduous weeks she helped me settle much better than I could ever have managed on my own. Gradually, though, I noticed how hard and abrupt she was.

'Have you always been the way you are now?' I asked her.

'No,' she said, sighing. 'But the trick is not to let these fuckers take the piss.'

'I don't want to end up as hard as you.' But I did.

Karyn and her co-defendant Patricia Cahill had been in Lard Yao for two years. She was still fairly new to prison protocol. I asked about Patricia and Karyn told me they were not on great terms. Karyn nicknamed her 'Plastic'. I reserved judgement until later.

Karyn ran ahead of me around the edge of the prison and I struggled to keep up, hardly able to muster a walk with the pain in my side.

'Need the toilet?' she asked.

'Desperately.'

She passed me a plastic bottle that had been cut down and directed me to the toilets. There was no door, no privacy and no choice either.

'Watch the sewer.'

We jumped over a deep drain. The water running through it was as black and awful-smelling as the canals running through Bangkok. It was a haven for disease; the smell of prison never leaves until you do.

Up ahead a group of miserable-looking girls were dragging wooden poles with batons attached to the ends along the sewers. Every morning they did this in order that the sewer would not overflow; they dragged the putrid contents to one corner of the prison.

A large tank sunk deep into the ground was the area where the sewage gathered. There was a general air of suffering and resignation in the area. A woman stood in all this shit up to her waist, swishing the black water out through a large pipe in the wall.

'God!' I said to Karyn, 'I hope she gets paid well for standing waist-deep in that crap.'

She didn't, of course. Like most women in the prison – because they never produced anything considered a commodity, anything that the prison could sell – her wage was less than £6 a year.

'That's nothing,' said Karyn. 'Wait until you see what they do under the toilets twice a year.' She laughed like a drain. A few months later I saw what she was talking about. A group of young girls, usually the girls from the *soi* – the punishment block – had been selected to dig out the tank of solid material that fills up under the toilets. The tank was over 10 feet deep and to dig it all out they had to get inside it. They worked there for several days, digging out six months of shit and carrying it away in small, rusting buckets.

If the punishment of having to do that wasn't bad enough, the shame of being seen doing it certainly was. It was an ugly, awful process. The smell was unbelievable. On a positive side, those girls usually found themselves with larger sleeping spaces in the room.

*

Karyn showed me the prison. We walked around the inside edge of the walls and I was amazed how small the place was. Through a tall chain-link fence, we could look at what was on offer for breakfast that morning. This was the *gonglean* – a large, enclosed area housing three rows of wooden tables and benches. Women lined up and down either side of the room, holding metal plates, and they each collected a mound of brown rice from a server at the doorway. Waiting their turn they filled the benches. It was like something from *Oliver Twist*. A Buddha statue and religious trinkets were kept here on a stage. The *gonglean* was also where announcements were made. A monk would come in there every week too, to pray. Mainly it was the place for eating.

The women who worked there dragged massive metal pots along the ground, doling out boiled cucumbers onto each plate. After a five-minute prayer, where each woman held her hands together and chanted, they started their meal. Everyone wore brown clothes, they all ate with short metal, Chinese spoons; the women looked as sick as hospital patients.

'Are you hungry?' Karyn asked.

I wasn't.

We continued walking.

'You're not well, are you?'

I didn't answer. Karyn headed off towards a group of people milling around outside the prison shop. Minutes later she emerged brandishing a piece of bread and a fried egg in a plastic bag. I really wasn't hungry, so Karyn said she would save it for later. I don't think she really knew what to do with me that morning, and I had no idea myself. This was all so strange. When would the embassy sort out this mess?

I kept asking questions. 'Who's that?' 'What's that?' 'What's she in for?' 'Where does she come from?' 'How does this work?' 'Why do people act like that?' Anything. Everything.

There were women everywhere: old women, young women, fat women and thin women, women from all nationalities. There were so many women that it didn't seem possible that they had all committed a crime. Some sat on plastic mats, eating or looking at themselves in tiny little mirrors. Others walked about, while some hung around in the toilets. Many more were scrubbing clothes on the ground. We fell silent for a while and I watched the activity around me. The sun scorched the ground. I had no idea what time it was.

And cats. There were almost as many cats as women. The prisoners carried them around on their shoulders and in their pockets. One old woman with scraggly grey hair and no teeth had a mat full of cats. They sat with her, eating rice from plastic bags as she coo-cooed them all. Why was she here? She barely looked sinister enough to sneeze.

Every now and again the guards would come in at night and bag up as many cats as they could manage into rice sacks and take them out of the prison. Many found their way back in, but women went through agonies worrying over the fate of their own little beast. There were cats that had never seen a dog or a man. It didn't take very long for me to get a cat too. First it was Jow-Son in the bakery and later my lovely Upstairs.

During the daytime, prisoners kept all their possessions with them, which were never very much: a few prison clothes, toiletries, a hairbrush, the ice buckets we used to make and some food. All kept in plastic bags from the factories, or bought from the black market.

When prison officers carried out raids – usually done with regular monotony – they would take away any possessions that were not well enough hidden. Often they would sell whatever had been confiscated back to the offending prisoner.

If you had a book in the room, or had one too many pairs of pyjamas, it would cost a box of washing powder to get it back. The bags and ice buckets we made out of old plastic rice sacks and tubs. These would always be taken; if you wanted the contents of the bag returned you had to pay for that also. The guards usually kept the bags. The factory girls – prisoners who worked in one of the five factories within the prison – always looked forward to the searches. A search meant that they would do a bit of business afterwards and earn some money making replacement bags. The guards in charge of the factories, who got the work contracts, were usually given some kind of payment from their girls. It was a free market, but nothing was ever free.

We passed a very dark woman who was green and black with bruises, chained by her arms and legs to a pillar. Shrieking like a drowning child, tears running down her face, she lurched at us as we passed.

'What the hell is wrong with her?' I asked Karyn.

'Oh, she's just come from the police station. She's one of the nutters.'

Perhaps I had been treated a lot better by the police than I had imagined...

Further on in our stroll we passed a floor full of babies, scrabbling around in the dirt. A women's prison was the last place I had expected to see them but I counted roughly 20 young babies lying on their backs. Where were their mothers? I asked Karyn. She told me they were getting ready for work.

It was impossible to walk past a floor full of unattended infants so we sat down next to them. Most of them were naked except for the occasional torn garment. None wore nappies. One little mite screamed until his mother arrived back from washing; she dumped a load of washing down and tried to feed the baby a bowl of very wet, mashed white rice. He refused and continued to scream.

'The poor baby wants milk, not rice,' I told Karyn, who translated to the mother. She smiled a toothless grin at me and tried to breastfeed her baby. She was thinner than straw and I doubt she had any milk to give to the baby. There was nothing we could do, so we left.

Another time, sitting alone early one morning, a little black child ran past behind me. *Surely not*, I thought, *not a child in here.* Then another girl roughly three years old, with braided hair and bare feet, stole through the crowd. They were two little African children, Mama and Toyin, who lived in Lard Yao with their mothers. They had been born in the prison and all they had ever known were walls.

New prisoners arrived daily and I could barely distinguish one person from the next. However, a young girl who arrived on a pickpocketing charge sticks out in my memory. She was thrown into the room housing all the heroin addicts. Around 4 o'clock in the morning everyone woke up to constant, hysterical, high-pitched screams that sounded as if someone was being murdered.

A guard in her pyjamas came by, took one look through the bars and left. She returned with Boosecan, a prisoner working as a nurse in the hospital. The guard opened the door to the girl and pushed Boosecan, who had a syringeful of sedative with her, inside. Things went quiet.

By all accounts the guard who had come by had been so scared that she hardly dared open the door to take the girl out; the other prisoners in the room were petrified the girl was going to kill them all. It sounded very odd so the following morning I went to find the girl and see what all the fuss was about.

Four heavy-looking tomboys were escorting her towards the hospital. She looked roughly 18 years old and weighed around eight stone. Judging by the effort it took to take her I guessed she was much stronger than she looked.

Another injection of Valium followed and she was walked back to the building where women sat making umbrellas. Curious, I followed behind. Suddenly the girl flew into another furious rage; considering that she had just been pumped full of sedative I was astounded.

The four tomboys called for help and several more ran to hold the girl down. Her eyes darkened, while her head rocked furiously from side to side, so fast it appeared to rotate. She was foaming and spitting and growling deep groans. I had never seen anything like it. It was as if the devil himself was screaming. She sounded possessed.

Eight prisoners held her down until Boosecan was summoned. She thought the girl was putting on an act and wouldn't inject her. The girl started howling. Over and over Boosecan stabbed the needle deep into the muscle of the girl's leg and when she didn't react she thrust it into her arm. The girl collapsed unconscious.

Karyn and I decided to visit her. She had been taken to Mare Mooway, an officer who claimed she could exorcise spirits. Karyn and I stood watching over the girl as Mare Mooway sat cross-legged beside her, holding her right hand up over the girl's body and mumbling something incomprehensible.

'Don't stand there,' someone shouted. 'When the spirit comes out it will go straight into you. Stand at the side and the spirit will flow away.'

For 10 minutes Mare Mooway sat mumbling. Then, all of a sudden, something seemed to move from inside the girl. Her eyes closed, her head relaxed and her body lay still.

'Stay lying down!' Mare Mooway shouted.

'I'm thirsty,' said the girl.

Whether the girl was possessed or not and whether or not it was a spirit I saw leave her body I will never know for sure. In Lard Yao you never knew anything for sure.

There were more nutcases in Lard Yao than cats. Many of them had a condition the Thais called 'jump' that caused them to say or do anything when they were poked. Some women spent hours torturing these souls, making them jump up and down, or making them do the most ridiculous things.

One woman spent her days hugging a coconut tree, singing at the top of her voice, or calling out to anyone who passed. In the mornings she shouted at her tree because it had not grown very much, telling it what a useless tree it was. Then she started her hugging once more.

Another was a completely mad kleptomaniac. Jee-up's nerves twitched constantly and she stole whatever she could whenever possible, even when someone was watching her. She received constant beatings but she never stopped stealing. Another sat around most of the day, her sarong around her waist, masturbating.

Karyn told me to get a shower and Patricia would come to find me. Why? What was happening? Karyn went to work.

I dried myself and changed into a second set of the heavy, brown clothes I had been issued with the day before. Patricia Cahill arrived later in the morning, fully made-up and wearing a blue sarong and shirt. She looked almost dazzling against the wrinkled old ladies I had passed earlier, and totally out of place. For some reason she didn't appear too happy to see me.

'Your parents are here,' she said, almost coldly, 'they're waiting for you.'

My parents? No, that wasn't possible, someone was mistaken.

EIGHT

The Bodysnatchers

Dearest Mum and Dad,

It seems years ago, but you left only eight days ago. As I said when I saw you both it really did mean the absolute world to me that you came and although we parted in such strained, negative circumstances, you gave me strength. That is probably the only thing that will see me through the next X number of years... If I get life though you really will have to forget me. I can't do a life sentence in here. I love you both.

Sandra

Letter home, February 1993

I could feel Patricia's breath on my ear. I looked at her as if she had just told me that my parents had died and not that they were here, visiting me. Their death would have made more sense; but visiting me here? That seemed impossible. The morning sun multiplied as Patricia talked.

Did they not receive my letter? Had they not listened to me? I told them explicitly to forget all about me, forget they had a daughter. *Patricia, you must be mistaken*, I thought to myself. It was impossible to speak so I just stood there, open-mouthed. My mum and dad wouldn't be here, how could they be? Unless that bloody woman from the embassy hadn't posted my letter. That was it; the selfish cow had binned it. I was sure at the time that she hadn't bothered to post my letter.

Patricia took me to an office, saying very little. Thump, thump, thump, my heart was pounding again. Patricia spoke in Thai to an officer, then told me to go stand at the main gate.

'What will I do if it is my parents?' I asked her.

'It's them all right,' she said. 'I saw the passports. Run in, grab your mother and quickly give her a hug, then they will put you behind the bars.'

'Behind bars? No, no! I can't see my mum and dad from behind a set of bars!'

'Well, it's either that or nothing. You decide.'

The embassy had arranged a visit in the embassy room, instead of the public visiting room. A visit in the latter usually lasted for 15 to 20 minutes in a dark crowded room, explained Patricia, and people shouted across a four-foot gap to each other. No contact, no hugs, and no time for real conversation.

How do I look? Is my hair OK? Oh, God, they shouldn't have to see me like this! Every step I took was heavy and painful. I fingered the hem of my brown sarong.

There they were. It *was* my parents, but they did not look like my parents. I thought my grandparents had come. Both seemed to have lost weight, as if their bodies had regressed somehow, as if the strain of my actions had caused their movements to become frail, even childlike. Their temples were lower than I had remembered, and they walked slower. They looked as if they might break.

They stood there, tears streaming down their faces. The news had aged my mum by 20 years. I could see them wondering, as I was, where had it had all gone wrong? How did their beautiful, blonde baby daughter, who rode on ponies and took French lessons, end up here?

They sat on a black, PVC-covered couch. Before I could run and hug them, I was put in a small cage in the corner of the room. We were separated by a heavy set of bars; strung over the bars was mesh chicken wire. My mum put her brittle fingers through the wire and our fingers touched. The feeling of relief that surged through me was insane. She stroked my hand and then tried to kiss me. My father put his large, warm hand up to the bars and we touched fingers through them. I think we were all crying. I had not seen my parents for more than two years.

I do not remember what we said to each other that day but the feeling of closeness remains with me as if it happened yesterday. I can feel it. I can almost touch it. For a short while, our touching lit up the room like fireworks on a dark sky. Most of the dialogue is gone but the scene remains.

'You must go!' shouted an officer. 'Go!'

'What?'

'You go. Now!'

'But they've just got here… '

The officer hurried over to a window and pulled on a shuttered blind. Jean Sharpe from the embassy had arrived, informing us that the press were outside taking pictures.

'The prison is sensitive towards media coverage and they want the cause of all this attention to leave.' She meant my parents. Two more minutes together and they were taken away.

'Please, Jean,' I begged her, 'please keep them out of the papers.'

Her look left me in no doubt whose fault it was that the media were interested in them. She left to deal with the reporters.

Later that day I was called to the office. Inmates are allowed food to be sent in from a relative, and it is collected at the end of the day after a guard has checked it through. My mum had brought boxes of protein supplements and her home-made fruit-cake to Thailand for me. I looked at the parcel and felt as though my dear mother had entered the prison with the bag of food. I could see the shops where she would have bought those things, saw where she would have kept them at home before leaving for the airport. She had bought things that she had given to me years before when I was a child and here she was again, nursing me with a bag full of groceries. My eyes filled with tears.

That afternoon a guard watched me struggling with the pain in my stomach and sent for the prisoner from the hospital that had carried out the intimate checks on the new prisoners. 'You no well, you stay hospital.'

With the embassy staff having visited me that day, the prison officials tended to worry about all the paperwork they would have to fill in if anything serious happened to a foreigner so they put me in the hospital wing that night. In the hospital block the horror of everyday prison life paled into insignificance. The place was tiny, with only five small rooms each holding about ten women. For many of the prisoners, the hospital offered little hope of recovery or treatment. In its wards, women of all ages – in prison for a multitude of crimes and serving sentences from a few years to life – wasted away and often died gruesome deaths.

One room was for heavily pregnant women and those who had recently had a baby. Another was for women over the age of 60 and a third appeared to be for those who had access to large amounts of money; it was slightly more comfortable and the women who spent time there tended to be treated with a great deal more care. I was in the room for 'others', people who fell into none of those categories.

In this room there was one young girl aged around 20. She had a brown tube protruding through the middle of her stomach, attached to a bottle underneath the bed. Naked as the day she was born, something was being drained out of her. She smelled and looked dreadful. Another had what looked like a football exploding from her throat. I wanted to leave immediately.

At the end of the corridor there was one further room, where the Aids and the TB patients were placed. Putting them in together usually finished them off in weeks and most of these critically ill women were not even given a paracetamol to relieve their pain.

My mum and dad had promised to return but there were no visits at the weekends. Lying in my hospital bed I was determined to get better. I also wanted to look OK for them when they came again to see me. I decided a suntan would do the trick. For hours I sat on a step directly in the sun. People are amazed when I tell them we were not locked up all day in cells. There was no real need for this: a high wall with barbed wire and a guard brandishing a machine gun was sufficient enough to keep prisoners under control. I baked.

I was fascinated by the idea of escape. Sitting in the sun, hoping to get well, I thought I heard helicopters. Then one flew directly overhead and I knew I wasn't dreaming. It returned and hovered over the prison for what seemed like an age. Then it went away again. Then it returned. Disappeared, then returned. That was my dad, it just had to be. Of course, it was. He's coming to get me. And he's coming in a helicopter!

This was wonderful. The sun was beating down and, for the first time in ages, I was happy. My dad was going to free me. I felt like a little girl all over again, only this time he wasn't leaving me in the way I had presumed he was, all those years ago, when I had fallen in the water. Now he was coming to save me. He was coming to get me out.

There was a large sandy area in the centre of the prison and I hadn't yet figured out what it was or what it could be used for. It was either a massive cat-litter tray for all the prison cats or a helicopter-landing pad. That was it. That was where he would land. That was the only explanation as to why he was flying overhead. He was trying to set down in the landing area. But why was he coming today? We hadn't discussed anything. OK. He would tell me his plans on Monday. He would tell me what time I should expect him. And I could tell him about the perfect landing pad. I couldn't wait.

When Monday arrived my face was burned brown from the sun. I didn't hear my name being called for my visit until late in the morning. I thought they had forgotten to come.

'Your parents are in the embassy room waiting for you,' said a guard.

They had been in there for hours but the guards had only called me, in Thai, for a visit once and had not bothered again. I could hardly wait for my dad to tell me about his helicopter plan. It would be great. Imagine, flying out of Lard Yao with my dad, waving at the rest of the prisoners and the guards, with their shiny boots and gold-rimmed glasses. They would hate me and I would just shrug and say something like, 'You see, I wasn't really supposed to be here, anyway.'

OK, Dad, tell me about your helicopter plan. I didn't actually ask him, I wanted him to surprise me with it. *OK, Dad, I'm ready*. Did my mum know? Probably not. It was a secret, just in case, in her excitement, she let it slip and the plan would be foiled. *OK, Dad, I'm ready*.

We had only half an hour to speak but that was plenty of time. If we had paid the guard we could have had all day, but none of us knew at that time.

OK, so he hasn't mentioned the helicopter. He still doesn't want to involve my mum, but he'll be back tomorrow. He'll tell her to go to the toilet or something and then talk me through it. The following day it was the same; there was no mention of him coming to get me in a helicopter.

The fourth day I saw them was Wednesday, but this time everything had changed. They were both cold towards me and looked traumatised.

'What's wrong?'

'We are leaving today, Sandra.'

'Why?'

'Our local newspaper said that we are visiting you in Thailand, published where we live and printed a picture of the house along with a massive valuation. Someone's broken in and we've been burgled. We are going home to deal with this mess that we wouldn't have had if it hadn't been for you.

'So you deal with your problems and we'll deal with ours.'

They left. My parents had always loved their home. When I was growing up, I often asked them why they didn't go out at night like other parents. I couldn't understand why they were always at home. They laughed and told me they loved their home as much as they loved each other. They had things at home that they had collected and treasured for years.

I felt sick when I heard they had been burgled. Later, in letters my mum told me that 'nothing special, just some booze, a television and a bag of jewellery' had been taken. It was only part of the truth. Eight years later when I asked my mum why she never wore her engagement ring, she told me it had been one of the things stolen. It was a beautiful white gold ring that my dad had saved hard for over 40 years earlier, and it was gone.

After their visit I didn't see my dad again for nearly five years. There had been no helicopter plan at all.

Over the next few months I would return to the hospital, mainly with the same complaint. Most of the time the pain was emotional rather than physical and being there helped me overcome any feelings of self-pity. Talking to a young woman who had just had a baby in the prison, or to a teenage prostitute dying of Aids, put my own situation in perspective. At least I had some kind of hope.

Lard Yao ran on money and not rehabilitation. The notion of rehabilitation was an anathema. It was a miniature city and a world unto itself where money talked and the prison officials listened. Prisoners, of course, were not allowed real money; instead coupons were handed out every day and used as an acceptable currency. They were only valid for the morning on which they were issued. At 1.00 pm the coupons became void.

Hardly anything in Lard Yao was free. Everyone had to pay for everything they used except the sandbag pillows, a large towel that was used as a blanket, tap water and the plates of gritty brown rice with something sloppy and boiled placed on the top of it. Toiletries, sanitary items, thin uniforms, washing powder, coffee or any food items from the prison shop, stamps and stationery all had to be paid for. The black market was rife. It was possible to buy just about everything from hot water for tea and blocks of grey ice, twice a day, to illegal substances and items such as small knives, radios, snuff, cigarettes, pills and powders.

Those who ran the black market would lend large amounts of money at an interest rate of 50 per cent. Prisoners washed clothes for 30 baht a week and other traders had portable 'shops' in carrier bags, where you could get something to eat in the middle of the day. These items were also charged at a mark-up price of 50 per cent and you had to pay up the following Tuesday.

You could get most things done and could buy almost everything from the black market girls, at a price. Failure to pay a debt on the agreed day increased the debt by 50 per cent per day and, if it was still not paid, violence regularly followed. Normally, the black market girls would simply find the debtor, surround her and take whatever money she had until it was paid off, or they would take everything the girl owned and sell it. Or they would beat her.

On one occasion a Nigerian woman had her bottom lip bitten off and fed to a cat, for not keeping up the repayments. In another incident a Thai woman was battered senseless, with prison-made truncheons, for not forking out what she owed. Even the guards took their share of any black market profit.

The lights were never switched off at night in the Lard Yao dormitories to ensure that everyone could be seen at all times of the night. Couples slept together in full view of anyone remotely interested in watching their lesbian relationships: prisoner/prisoner, guard/prisoner, guard/guard. A myriad of combinations. Girls eager to embark upon relationships often approached me but I refused. Not because I wasn't interested – I just smiled and told people I was a 'try-sexual', I would try anything once – it's just that I never fancied anyone.

Most nights I just put a small towel over my face to help me sleep. I was like an ostrich, burying my head away from what was going on around me.

In those first few months I slept alongside some of the strangest women I could ever have possibly imagined. One of my neighbours had killed her husband because he had been showing his second wife more attention than her; she chopped him up into eight pieces, took the meat off his upper legs, put the pieces in large biscuit tins and poured his remains into the river as fish food.

With images like this in my mind, it was no wonder I baulked at the food placed before us every day: gritty, dirty rice, full of maggots and bugs, whole fish soup, boiled cucumbers with egg or hairy pork. The kitchen girls simply sliced through the dead pig, bones and all. They would slice off most of the meat and sell it on the black market, so what was left was a chunk of fat, topped with thick skin, sprouting coarse hair.

I was in desperate need of some peace and quiet. So I was sitting with Karyn, in what we called the Boathouse – a little wooden building standing on stilts over a green, slimy pond full of enormous fish. We used to go there whenever we could, enjoying the relative peace and quiet, sitting chatting.

Suddenly the most awful stench wafted over from the hospital building nearby, and Thai prisoners were running around with their heads down, shouting and screaming. They wore scarves, fashioned from shirts, over their faces, to block out the putrid smell. I thought a sewerage pipe had burst in one of the upstairs rooms.

Some kind of gooey, brown liquid was pouring through the ceiling and a large puddle had formed on the tiled floor below. The liquid fell in a constant flow; the smell was overwhelming. It turned sickly and we could barely catch our breath.

Three days earlier a woman had died of Aids and tuberculosis, and the undertakers had not been round to pick up the remains of her body. Left untreated, in temperatures over 100 degrees for three days, her body had swelled and eventually burst in the heat. The woman exploded.

Not surprisingly, the prison officers stayed well away from the burst body, while two prisoners placed a bucket under the dripping mass in an effort to catch what was flowing from the dead woman's insides. Most of the mess missed the buckets and was swept aside from the floor onto the grass, by the edge of the building.

Buddhist Thais don't like touching dead bodies themselves, believing that everyone has a spirit inside them that does not die when the person themself dies. Apparently this spirit can, very easily, jump into another body if interfered with. So the bodysnatchers were summoned. Usually of another faith, the bodysnatchers took most of the people who died in Lard Yao away to be dissected by medical researchers. They made quite a decent living from the prison, given the number of dead bodies that were carted out of there.

By the time the bodysnatchers arrived to pick up the body of the woman, she had stopped pouring through the ceiling. Upstairs, they could barely stand what was lying in front of them and almost as soon as they entered the room they ran back out again. Dressed in what looked like astronaut suits, and carrying a heavy-duty body bag, they eventually carried the body down the stairs. The body was dropped on the floor and her photograph was taken. One of the men snapped her fingers broken, to make it easier for him to take her fingerprints, before she was removed from the prison grounds.

Lying there, drained of life, and most of her fluids, the stiff body of the woman resembled a grotesque piece of modern art. Most of the prisoners who witnessed this scene simply turned away, knowing that they might well end up in the same condition. It was a horrible, ugly death, and no one seemed to care about her; just the smell she had created. This was just another day in Lard Yao.

As the truck left the prison grounds, the woman's name was called out, over and over and her spirit was asked to leave the grounds with her.

'Please,' a voice shouted, 'go now. It is time for your release, please leave the prison.'

I felt nausea. I wasn't just shocked but also terribly frightened. There are places where perhaps death is expected, but here, in prison, it was even more disturbing. It was a beautiful morning, the sun was splitting the sky and the contents of this woman were pouring through a ceiling. The hospital was simply a public memorial to the dead.

I've always wondered how I would react if I ever witnessed something truly tragic. Now I know. Like the rest of the women I breathed a sigh of relief that it wasn't me. No one cried. We just looked on in astonishment. There was no noise, just the silence of a woman who was dead. I wish I could, but I still cannot recall her name.

At some time while in prison everyone dreamed of having their name called out, just to leave that squalid place, but no one wanted their spirit called. It was like being trapped in a horror movie.

From 6.00 am to 6.00 pm we were all out in the courtyard, a space roughly the size of a football pitch into which 1,700 women were crammed, later increasing to roughly 3,000. Communication was initially difficult and my lack of Thai proved a hindrance. Learning the language, and something of the national way of life, was the only way to become accepted into the prison culture and to understand what the guards were saying. Otherwise I would have remained an outsider and would have known little of what was going on. Shortly after being arrested I had begun working in the officers' laundry, and communicating how I felt or what I wanted was tricky without Thai.

The Thai social structure is made up of definite hierarchies, and Thais constantly reinforce their own social positions as well as those of others with respect to themselves. It's a big deal for a Thai to tell a European what to do, especially in prison where the pecking order is constantly being reinforced, so they would tell me to do things that weren't necessary, and boss me around, just because they could. They would go through my things when I wasn't there, and help themselves to what they wanted. From the start, I had to stick up for myself.

'How do you tell these people to fuck off?' I asked Karyn.

'Just say it in English,' she told me.

When the need presented itself I did. 'Fuck off. Just fuck off!'

They laughed at me. From then on I knew I needed their language. Slowly I mastered it and I now speak it fairly well. With the language I also developed a temper and at times regretted the fact that I was now proficient. Every day I seemed to be arguing with someone in my new language. None of it was ever pretty.

The first time we got a letter handout from the censor, I was handed a large stack of mail. I couldn't believe how many people had written. People from all walks of life – some known to me, others complete strangers – had made the effort. They wrote to condemn me and they wrote to console me.

In between receiving letters though the days passed slowly and, most of the time, I wondered what was really happening back home. My parents' arrival had been one of the most wonderful experiences, yet it was tinged with such sadness that it was now almost unbearable to think about. As good as it had been to see them, I wished that they had stayed at home. I was going to have to do my time without them.

The only time the daily prison routine changed was on 5 December, which was the king's birthday. That day the whole prison rose at four in the morning, washed quickly and attended prayers for an hour and a half. The same day Buddhist monks came into the prison and collected bags of dried food and toiletries that some of the women donated for the poor people of the city.

Initially, the routine was unbearably dull although, as the years passed, I would find more and more to occupy my time. Mostly, we behaved like zombies. Yet it was the inmates who generally ran the prison, although they were never in control of it. When the officers gave out the orders certain prisoners began the process of unlocking or, at least, the unbolting of their fellow convicts. Prisoners calculated the prison and factory accounts, constructed and repaired buildings, fixed faulty wiring, ran the hospital, cooked the food and, basically, did whatever else needed doing.

The Thai national anthem rang out at eight in the morning, followed by 10 minutes of prayer chant, in which many if not most of the prisoners participated. The Thai flag would be hoisted up a pole and the whole prison had to stand to attention, in rows of blue, brown or brown-and-cream uniforms. The category of the girls wearing brown and cream was 'appeal'.

We had to be at work between 8.15 am and midday. Between 12 o'clock and 1 was lunchtime, then back to work until 4.30 pm. From then until 5.30 or 6.00 pm we ate, and washed ourselves and our clothes. Between 6.00 pm and 6.00 am, we were locked in the rooms for the night. If we were lucky we found some time during the day to relax. After work everyone sat outside on mats. It was like a time-share arrangement. You could claim a space as yours as long as you used it, but only between the times not allocated for work.

Everything needed to be washed as soon as it was taken off so there were two washes per day. Women who did not have a washing line had to get their clothes washed and dried before the 8 o'clock bell. In the rainy season, drying clothes proved to be extremely difficult and most of us went around wet. During this time most clothes and personal belongings turned mouldy and rotted.

Constantly, the rats would come out from the overflowing sewers to invade our spaces and any food left around would be chewed or eaten whole. The prison shop opened between seven and eight in the morning and we had to buy our food for the day during that time. It also opened between midday and 1 pm but that was lunchtime, and if you didn't prepare your food, eat, wash bowls and cutlery and collect your washing at that time then you never managed it at all. Lunchtime was no time to stand in massive queues.

When a prisoner wanted to speak to a guard (they were all female) we had to get down on our knees, clasp our hands in front of us in the attitude of prayer, and bow. Provided we showed respect for our superiors – and everyone was our superior here – we could usually get by without too much trouble.

Newspapers or news cuttings were not allowed, although some magazines were permitted. Radios and televisions were prohibited and no access to a telephone was ever granted, not even upon arrest.

Letters got through to us, although the censor handed them out sporadically, and on no given day of the week. If we were lucky we would receive mail roughly three times per month, although weeks might go by when there was no mail handed out at all. By the time mail came through it would often be at least four weeks old; it was never usually received in the order that someone had written it. A letter written in July might be received after one written in August or September.

Three one-page letters were permitted as outgoing mail each week, and every word that we wrote or received was diligently censored. Often the censor would tire of reading our mail herself and would get one of the other foreigners to read through it for her; gossip usually ran rampant through Lard Yao as a result. If deemed unfit the whole letter would go straight into what was known as File 13, without a trace or a word.

Whenever I went to court, for another attempt at a trial, I would smuggle out a roll of written aerogrammes and a book full of unwritten ones too. It was a tricky business getting them out, especially so because Rifkin always stood over us as we changed into our court clothes. Rifkin had no reservations about grassing on her fellow inmates. The guards who searched us going out were never the same as the ones searching us coming back in so there was little chance of anyone noticing that I took out blank aerogrammes, spent the time in the holding cell writing as many letters as I could, passed them to a friendly court official for posting, and came back with none. As well as the court post I would pay a guard 50 baht a letter and she would post it for me, although I couldn't afford to send many of those.

Writing home was a task because I always tried to sound upbeat and positive, although I was nothing of the sort. Yet letters were one of the things that kept me alive: from my mother, father, brother, friends, strangers. It was wonderful to receive their correspondence, even if it was just a short note or a scribble. Suddenly I was transported home to them. I could smell my home in those letters; especially letters from my family. I would pull the pages and the folds of the paper close to me and breathe them deeply. Sometimes I would not open them immediately; instead I would take them into my cell at night and just sit and imagine them writing. Maybe they would be at home, or in a coffee shop, or at work. It was wonderful.

Better still, if there was a photograph inside I would grab it from the envelope and hold it to me, looking around to see who had seen me with it. I would fly into a rage if other prisoners tried to look at it, which they often did. It was bad enough that I was there but to have my family in that prison with me while others poked their noses at them was too much.

I was never completely truthful in letters to my parents. It was just impossible to tell them how things really were. How could I tell them, for example, that a teenager had been electrocuted in the room I slept in?

She had arrived in Lard Yao the previous week with a girlfriend, looking like a couple. Both of them were young university students. The father of one of the girls had been a policeman and he had suspected them of stealing money from his house. He had pressed charges against them, in order to show them what life is like in prison.

Even the hard-faced 'mother of the room' had a soft spot for those two and she allowed them to sleep next to each other. Each night one of the girls would go to the toilet area and take a rag hanging on one of the many pipes before proceeding to wipe the floor where they were to sleep. A lot of the prisoners did this because the floor was always so dirty.

This particular evening the young girl took the cloth and wet it. Then she scrubbed the floor. A few minutes later she took the cloth back to the pipe. As she hung the cloth up, the pipe broke. Inside the pipe was a live 220-volt wire. The girl's right hand went through the pipe and she grabbed hold of the wire. There was a soft buzzing noise, then a sizzle of light. She was standing in half an inch of water and her left hip bounced off an old, metal, disused water cooler.

For a few minutes the sparks flew until her girlfriend, in a panic, grabbed a towel, twisted it into a makeshift rope and threw it around her friend's neck, pulling her off the wire. She made a short sound with her throat and a low cry as she fell onto the floor. Her young body had fried and she lay on the ground, in a puddle, with smoke coming from somewhere inside her. It was one of the most horrendous and saddest things I had ever witnessed. All of a sudden she was dead. It was as if she had just slipped out of her own skin and disappeared.

The young girl's father dropped the charges. He had taught her a lesson the hard way. The prisoner who was in charge of overseeing the electrics received her punishment. Following a cover-up, nothing happened to any officials at the prison.

Eventually I mastered the art of sleeping. I have no idea when this was because I had no real concept of time in prison. Days and months all looked the same. Sleep was the only possible escape.

At some point everyone gets used to sleeping in such conditions, but no one ever really sleeps straight through a night. With so many people it was just not possible. Often I would wake up to find the whole roomful of women had put away their pillows and towels and they were sitting around the door waiting to be let out. Curled up, in the middle of the linoleum floor, I would be lying there, completely alone. Why were they in such a panic? Why were they hurrying?

Every morning I would get up, go out and sit down on my blue mat. My priority for all those years was hot water in the morning so I could have a coffee. It was my own way of beginning the day in a fairly civilised fashion. The toilet could wait, the water tank could wait and the prison could wait.

Underneath a large, square area of parallel washing lines I would sit, next to the sewer, drinking my coffee. On good days I could stretch this out for half an hour, while on bad days I barely sat down and it would be time to get on with the day. If I was lucky a magazine or comic from home might have been passed by the censor and I would be dazzled by the current affairs of the day, or the latest mad-cap antics in *Viz*. *The Spectator*, *Time* and *Private Eye* magazines all helped keep me sane and oblivious to my surroundings.

But repetition soon becomes a prisoner's enemy; at first it allowed me to grind out each day with at least a basic sense of purpose. Before long everything and every day became a carbon copy of the last, and nothing could relieve the resulting tension.

Whenever an officer was walking towards a prisoner, we would have to stop, turn sideways on the path, face inwards towards the officer with our heads down and wait for them to pass. Passing them without following this slightly ludicrous ritual was deemed to be insulting and disrespectful. As much as I hated having to do this, I was in Thailand and this was the way the prison ran. It was degrading, but it was also the rule. Yet I was still a fairly belligerent and bellicose individual who found it hard to prostrate myself before the authorities. Usually I just went through the motions.

If an officer was sitting, in order to speak to one of them, we had to kneel on the floor; we had to be lower than them. We had to show every one of them that we were a lower form of life than they were. But it was painful to bend. I had developed terrible skin infections on my feet that made it difficult. There were so many boils that I took a perverse delight in counting them almost daily to see if the numbers were going up or down.

Over time I kept a diary, of sorts. Not every day, but just enough for me to remind myself of certain events. It became a way to help me understand what I was going through, what my family were going through and what the rest of the thousands of women in here were going through. Although I was never completely certain of dates and time I tried, as best I could, to be accurate.

Diary extract
14 May 1993
Three people came to see me, three old friends, from Bangkok. It's embarrassing for people to see what I've been reduced to. Hearing about my childish existence and how I have to wash clothes on the concrete and sit around watching the frogs and birds slip about on the wet concrete floors. They ask me if I need anything. I hate being so useless, so dependent… The restrictions here are endless, just like being at primary school. I hated Susan seeing me in this awful situation, but it was so good to see her… life before the arrest is still a terrible blur. I don't know if it's the shock, but I'm finding it difficult to remember people and names…

Being in Lard Yao was like being shipwrecked on an island. It was our island and the metaphor suggested we were all in this together. Most prisoners wanted to make this temporary community work but, because of all the pressures brought to bear upon us by the prison system, it proved impossible. In many ways, as I have said, we prisoners ran the whole place, but the feeling of unity was not very strong. We always tried to keep some sort of harmony, though, in the hope that we might one day be rescued.

Some months after I was brought to the prison, I had a split with most of the other foreigners; basically, we never got on as well as I – and no doubt they – had hoped. I enjoyed mixing with the Thais and was happy enough with my superficial friendship with them; I could relate to them more than I could with the others. There were a few Americans in prison at the same time as me but few of them had ever travelled before and I found them overly contemptuous of Thailand and Thai people. I didn't hate Thai people, but defending them all the time earned me a bad reputation.

One evening, when we had all been locked in, a fight broke out between some Americans and all the Thais. It was vicious and bloody. One Thai woman grabbed me and threw me in the toilet.

'We don't want you,' she said, spitting, 'we want them.'

The following day I was labelled a traitor by the Americans and, after this incident, I spoke to very few of them ever again. I accepted this without much difficulty; I had come into prison alone, and was going to leave it alone, so I figured I'd do my time alone too. I didn't need anyone.

When you fight a Thai you don't just take on an individual, you take them all on. It's not possible to fight just one of them, because they stick together, hunt in packs and make sure their friends are looked after. Perhaps my split with the Americans wasn't such a bad outcome really.

Karyn Smith and I did remain good friends, but we lived different lives. She worked in the *gonglean* and I worked on the other side of the prison in the laundry. The age difference between us – she was still a teenager and I was approaching 30 – meant that we had different interests. To be honest, I didn't want to become dependent on Karyn nor did I want her to become dependent on me. For a while, at least, I was always sure I would be released. It would be terrible for her if we had become too close and I had to leave her there…

Sunday afternoons were the only time not allocated to working and this was the time that the black market would set up 'short-time hotels'. All over the factories, under washing lines and tables and in toilets they would build what looked like a child's den. Here a couple could pay for an hour in the den together, while the black market woman stood watch, alerting them if an officer came by.

Sunday afternoons were also when the guards got massages from the inmates, had their nails done or their grey hairs plucked. An all-round Lard Yao pampering. Effectively, what this meant was that they had no time to be busting the short-time hotels. It was shocking at first to see women publicly engaged in sexual relationships, but over time it became acceptable and, in many cases, completely understandable.

Diary extract,
17 May 1993
My Thai is improving but I still don't really know what they are talking about. I somehow prefer to remain alone. I don't want to be drawn into the silly, giggly conversation and idle gossip…

I don't know whether people come in here with limited intelligence or whether the routine and mundane existence causes them to be petty. I still pray that I can think individually if I ever get out of here. I'm worried about the court trial. What should I say? I do wish that I was sentenced and all this was over…

I had no idea when my trial was going to take place. Trying to get information from anyone remotely official was virtually impossible and I was growing increasingly frustrated at the lack of activity surrounding my trial.

Every day I could hear trains passing the prison, and when I did my heart would beat faster. Every time I saw a plane flying overhead I cried. My head exploded at the thought of other people – holidaymakers and tourists – ordering their first drinks as they disappeared into the clouds above me, leaving me in this dungeon. All I seemed to think about was returning home. When would it be my turn to step onto a plane and see my family?

Lard Yao became a horrendous slow-motion dream where there were people everywhere and, in that dream, I could always see where I wanted to go – it was always through the heavy prison gates. It took forever to get there because of all the people around me pulling me back. Every night for six months I dreamed that I was running away; I was on buses, planes, trains, bicycles, bobsleighs and boats. I ran, walked, ducked and dived through forests and towns but always, always got caught.

After a while I began dreaming about the prison I was in, as though my mind had accepted where I was and had got used to it all. These dreams were the scariest.

At the end of May 1993, around the time of my first birthday in prison, I was sitting in the *gonglean* waiting for Karyn to finish cleaning up after lunch. It was a Saturday. One of the guards, bored by the lack of activity, had found a tape of music and was playing it over the tannoy system.

Slowly, the tunes filtered into my head. It was beautiful music and, gradually, I realised what it was. It was the Beatles, 'The White Album'. How amazing! The voices of Lennon and McCartney lifted the whole place and I could see the faces of so many prisoners – Thai and foreign alike – lifting, as they started to hum or sing the songs.

For the last few months I had lived in a strange state of denial, convinced that I would be leaving Lard Yao. Sitting there in that filthy hall I suddenly realised *this is not a dream, Sandra. This is real. You are here, you are a prisoner and you will probably be here for years and years to come. So you had better get used to it.* This time I couldn't suppress the tears. Karyn looked at me, saw the horror in my face and knew immediately what I was feeling.

'You'll be OK,' she said as she walked away, leaving me alone with my sorrow.

I would be staying in Lard Yao for a long time; there would be no bail; the judge would not throw the case out of court; the police would definitely charge me and I would not be escaping. Lennon kept singing. I began sweating, and my ears pounded and throbbed. I had heard 'The White Album' first as a child, before listening to it properly as a teenager. I had it on vinyl at home in West Yorkshire.

How could I have been so arrogant as to think that I would be different from all the other women? I was no different. We were all the same. I was a prisoner, a convict and a criminal. They knew it. Now I knew it too.

Karyn saw how upset I had become, but didn't need to ask what was wrong. Like everyone else in here, she had been there too. Quietly, slowly, she left me.

By June of my first year I was at the stage where I no longer looked forward to anything. Half the time I didn't even know if I was alive, nor did I care. Sometimes I would wake up, look around at the half-naked torsos lying around me thinking that I was dead. Not just dreaming I was dead, but actually thinking it. *You are dead, Sandra, for sure, because no one alive could possibly live like this.* It was subhuman.

Occasionally, I would look at myself in a mirror or in the reflection of a window. I was gaunt, thin, wasted, weak, tired, a wreck of my former self. My back was painful, my kidneys were sore, my eyesight occasionally stalled. I no longer felt like Sandra Gregory. I was simply using her name.

I had never been in prison before and I had no previous convictions. The amount I had been carrying actually became a standing joke among the other prisoners. Why had I gambled with my life attempting to smuggle so little?

*

I know when I was born, and when I had my first fall-out with my dad, and the moment I first kissed a boy, and the instant I said goodbye to my parents. I also know when I was so sad that it almost finished me. On 21 July 1993 I was sitting on a mass of concrete, scrubbing the officers' dirty clothes when, at around eight in the morning, Karyn came bounding over to me.

'You know Dana's got an illegal radio and listens to the news every day? Well, she said she just heard that two British girls in Thailand on drug charges are going to be released today on a pardon.'

My heart stopped. 'What?'

She repeated herself.

'No, Karyn,' I said, 'don't be so stupid. She must be mistaken. The media wouldn't know you are going home before you knew yourself. Go to work and just forget about it. It can't be true. Dana's winding you up, you'd know if you were going home.' I could barely stand the thought of my only friend in that place leaving.

Karyn went to work and I tried to carry on scrubbing clothes but my mind was elsewhere. I was imagining Karyn leaving me in this hellhole, never turning round, and just walking through the gates to go home. *Don't leave me.*

A loud yell erupted from the middle of the prison shortly after Karyn headed to work. It must be true. The place had erupted and I then knew it was true. Karyn and Patricia were going home.

Suddenly, I was so happy for them. I jumped out to look for Karyn, trying my best to pretend that I wasn't that concerned with my own fate. But part of me was weeping inside.

Everything happened so fast that we barely had time to speak. That evening Karyn undressed, threw her uniform to the floor and put on casual clothes that marked her down as someone from the outside. She was no longer a prisoner and neither was Patricia. Although Patricia was never a favourite of mine, I wished her well.

They walked out through the green gate; the gate shut and she was gone. It was as simple as that. Tomorrow she would be a memory. I knew I would never see her again.

That evening I thought my heart would break in two at the pain of seeing them leave without me. My only friend in that place had gone and now I was alone. From that moment I never watched another woman walk out of those gates; it was simply too painful.

I have never felt as lonely in my life as I did in the month that followed Karyn's departure, and I cried constantly. Every time I saw anything that reminded me of my friend or any time anybody looked at me and asked, 'Ah, are you missing Karyn?' I crumbled under the weight of my loneliness. Yet Karyn had taught me well and I would survive, I decided, without her. She deserved to be home and I deserved to be here.

Karyn wrote to me many times when she was back in the UK but after a while I decided not to write back. Not because I didn't want to or had nothing to say but because she was a young women who needed to get on with her life. The last letter I received from her was, as usual, warm and understanding, chirpy and fun. I read it, and then tucked it away. And Karyn Smith was out of my life.

Shortly after Karyn and Patricia left, a woman died of an asthma attack in the room I was sleeping in, and I was amazed by how unaffected I was by that young girl's death. She had forgotten her asthma pump before being locked in the cell. When the attack happened and someone had called out to the guards, two officers came strolling by in their pyjamas and stood at the bars of the room, asking the poor girl why she had forgotten her pump.

'What do you want us to do about it?' was all they said to her. They thought she was pretending and that she was wasting their precious sleeping time. They stood there talking about what kind of punishment they would hand out to her the following day.

Within ten minutes the girl had fallen to the floor from the kneeling position she had been in, holding her throat. Right there in front of us all, in a matter of minutes, she died. The body count was rising. After this incident I no longer cared for the fate of others.

I grew weary of *everything*. The noise, pollution, filth and the constant heat became unbearable. But there was nowhere to go, nowhere to hide, and nowhere to cry or shout or lash out in private. The sewers overflowed in the rainy season and it was putrid. The smell became unbearable as the rats, cockroaches and centipedes came out from their hiding places to invade our space, like aliens planning on taking over the world.

Lawyers showed up at the prison constantly. Thai prisoners would tell their lawyers that there was a foreigner in Lard Yao and if the lawyer got their case the prisoner would get 10 per cent of the lawyer's fees. They all seemed to think that being European I was some sort of money tree and I lost count of how many lawyers came to the prison to see me. They all said the same, of course, that they could get me out, but after the third or fourth offer of release I figured that if it was so easy then nobody would be there.

The advice they all seemed to give was to say that Robert was innocent, that he knew nothing about the drugs. 'Plead guilty to possession,' everyone said. 'It's a lesser charge than trafficking and you'll have a quick trial and get the minimum sentence.'

I had no idea what to do or what to say at my court hearing, whenever that would take place. Everyone, including most of the prisoners, told me to tell the court that Robert knew nothing about the drugs. But why should I? It wasn't true. He knew everything about the drugs. *They were his drugs.*

It might be better to lie, though, I thought, because being a grass, an informer, in prison is not the best way to do a sentence, and pleading guilty to possession could mean a lower sentence. I told myself I would think about it.

In August 1993, a breezeless day, I was herded onto a bus with some others and taken to court. I was served with the official charge sheets. Remand was over; the trial had begun. However, the trial would last a further two and a half years and once a month I had to go out to court for a day. I met up again with Robert. He looked rough and had lost weight.

'Look, Robert,' I said to him, 'I'll go halfway with you. We can both plead guilty to possession and we'll get this trial over with quickly.'

'Go fuck yourself.'

'What?'

'Go fuck yourself.'

If that's the way he wanted it to be, there was no way I was going to lie to protect him. From that conversation on I decided that I would tell the absolute truth about Robert and I would testify against him. That was the last time we ever spoke together.

The next time we were taken to court was the first day of our trial. An old, brittle-looking judge sat high on a bench flanked by two people who looked just like students, and a hush descended on the room. The prosecutor and lawyers were in attendance and my poor mother had made another trip to see me. Although I wasn't really mentally prepared to see her, her appearance was wonderful to see and my spirits were lifted immediately. Unfortunately, she had arrived at court thinking that the trial would take a few days or maybe weeks. She intended to stay every day until it was over, which proved impossible considering it was to be such a long time before its conclusion.

Seeing my mum in court, my head went blank. I found myself just staring at her. It was such a horrendous, emotional time. The court was a sea of strangers apart from my mum, and both of us, red-eyed and bleary, just looked at each other thinking, *How? How did this happen?* The hardest part was when she walked away and I had no idea when, or if, I might see her again. My heart ripped at the corners.

One of the customs officers, speaking only a little English, sat down next to me and said simply 'If you lie to protect him,' pointing at Robert, 'and the court find you to be lying to protect him, they will uphold the maximum penalty. You know that, don't you?' His advice trailed away to a murmur.

We were sitting on old wooden benches and when I turned to look at my mother she had paled and I thought she was going to fall off the bench.

'For God's sake, Sandra,' she pleaded, 'you're already in enough trouble. Tell the truth, please. For God's sake, whatever it is, just tell the truth.'

I told the truth, about how Robert had asked me to smuggle his drugs and how I had agreed and how we had been caught and how I had regretted every minute of what I had done.

Back in the prison, after the court appearance, I got hell from the other prisoners for saying this. Everyone had heard all about the trial because the British press were reporting on it at length. For telling the truth about Robert I developed a reputation as a prison grass.

Months later, a group of Robert's friends showed up in court and told me that there were people who knew where my parents lived and, if I didn't keep my mouth shut, they would nail-bomb my parents' house. The protocol of prison life is so different from anywhere else. In most places outside prison there are rules, but when the rules are broken, the consequences are usually minimal. In prison you are constantly vigilant about transgressing rules, codes and beliefs. How does it work? What should you do? How do you behave? There were countless questions that could only be answered by experience.

One day I was called for a visit and was greeted by a recognisable face although I couldn't quite place her. The woman had an Australian accent and she smiled as she spoke. Did I know her from the UK or Bangkok? She told me her name was Natalie and she chatted away for ages as I tried to figure out our relationship.

She was in great form and I couldn't tell her I found it hard to place her so I carried on the charade for the duration of the visit, which lasted 15 minutes. Some weeks later she returned and by then, thankfully, I had remembered I had known her reasonably well in Bangkok. It had got to the stage where I could barely recall people's faces, never mind their names and, in truth, part of me just wanted them to leave me alone. Initially, visits were welcome, but as the months wore on, they reminded me that people had lives outside my own, where they could walk, talk, eat, sleep and drink freely. I was just a memory.

Nothing in Lard Yao made sense, and nothing seemed real. No games of any description were allowed: no ball games, no cards, dice or board games. Yet the large sandy area I had thought was either a giant cat-litter tray or helicopter-landing pad was in fact a pitch area for French boules or volleyball for the officers.

We could watch but we were not allowed to play. Every evening for a month the officers would practise volleyball, and the closest an inmate would get to playing was to fetch a stray ball for the guards. Every volleyball practice was yet another quantification of the passage of time. Anyone caught with a home-made game, or found kicking a ball of rolled-up paper, risked confinement in the *soi*, or the dark room, for minor misdemeanours. They would be kept there for several weeks.

If you had money, you could get your hair cut and fingernails polished by the inmates who worked in the 'beauty salon'. If you had no money to pay for the service you would ask one of the girls in one of the factories to cut your hair. If a prisoner was caught cutting hair, or even if someone was recognised as having just had a haircut that wasn't from the salon, the guards would enforce a punishment. Most of the time my hair was cut illegally.

The laundry I worked in was only for the guards. Every day they would bring in their dirty clothing and every day we would wash, dry and iron it for them to collect that evening. If anyone working in the guards' laundry was caught washing a prisoner's clothing, those clothes would be confiscated and a punishment or fine would be enforced. I never understood, and I still can't, the idea of physical punishment as rehabilitation. However, the punishments handed out to prisoners, that had so horrified me initially, gradually become almost unnoticeable.

The guards would make women bang their knuckles on the concrete anything up to 100 or 200 times, but the guard had to be able to hear the sound of her knuckles knocking on the ground five paces away. If the girl missed one knock she had to do the whole lot over again. By the time the punishment was over, the offender's fingers were usually bare of skin to the bone.

Another version of this saw women crawling on all fours, up and down the length of the prison over the cement path, for hour after hour in the blazing sun.

Then there was the punishment where groups of officers gathered around and called out that there was to be a beating. Once a crowd had gathered, the victim had to sit and receive a thrashing with a rattan cane or a solid truncheon. When it was over, the wrongdoer had to raise her hands in thanks and say out loud, 'Thank you for rectifying my bad ways.' Punishment and this curious need to cleanse offenders usually began with orders from above, and the malignity of it increased.

Other officers preferred humiliation as their form of chastisement. They would hang a large sign around a girl's neck advertising her crime, and she would have to walk around the prison for the rest of the day. The sign might say 'I am a thief', or 'I have the mouth of a dog'.

Couples caught by guards in intimate liaisons were usually tied up together with ropes and made to sit in the middle of the grass, under the blazing heat of the sun all day. The heat was bad enough but the grass presented an altogether different problem.

First, despite appearing lovely and lush, the grass was full of vicious ants that not only bit, but also managed to hang on to human skin until they were individually plucked off. Second, the grass was watered daily with sewerage water.

Every morning a woman lowered a basket into the sewer. A pump had been placed inside the basket and a pipe was attached to the pump. The basket filtered out the shit from the sewer and ensured the hosepipe didn't get blocked. While the sewerage certainly kept the grass a fertile green, exposed wounds on the wet grass infected terribly. Most of the women had plenty of open sores.

Those girls forced to sit on the grass, tied up as punishment, ended up with terrible infections, and that was also the idea of the punishment. What I couldn't understand, though, was why women were being punished for having sex when the officers used to do the same, many of them with the prisoners. An inmate gets to know herself well in prison and through punishment the knowing is much more profound. Prisoners construct their memories from brutality.

By December of my first year the prison was getting the better of me; my feet were covered in huge sores and I was depressed. I cried at the slightest thing and felt hopeless. I barely knew what was happening with my family, nor how they felt about me and, half the time, I didn't really care. My case? God only knew.

On some mornings as I hung out my washing, a wood pigeon would call out and I would close my eyes and stand listening to him cooing. I had heard them years earlier as a young child in Kent and, just for a few seconds, I would close my eyes and travel back to those happy times. Then the bird would fly off as I opened my eyes again to face the piles of dirty clothes and squabbling Thai women working beside me. Did I dream those wood pigeons? I have no idea. But for those few seconds it was bliss.

Increasingly, the nights were the hardest to endure. From lockdown in late afternoon to release early the next morning meant hours and hours of close confinement. It was an awfully long time to be left alone with your thoughts. Nothing made sense apart from pain, both physical and emotional, which existed on the

My christening in September 1965 with Dad, brother and Mum.

Top: My brother and I in Hollingbourne, 1970.
Above: Me on my beloved pony Goldie, 1977.

Right: Outside my house with Kara a few months before I left for Thailand. Kara survived my years away but had to be put down six months after I was released from Cookham.

Below: Fetching firewood up in the mountains, hill tribe style. I was amazed how much weight I could carry in those baskets.

Right: The little girl who had a swelling on her neck slashed open with a rusty scalpel. The wound was left open and I was convinced she was going to die. Eventually her father took her to hospital, and she made a full recovery.
Below: 28 February 1996. Leaving court and going back to Lard Yao after receiving a 25-year sentence.
(*Photo: Reuters/Popperfoto*)

Above: Visitors outside Lard Yao. The embassy room is on the ground floor, behind the walking man. There was no glass in the windows, so it was easy for the press to take photos from the driveway. *Left:* My first New Year in Lard Yao. The girls all worked in the bakery and this was the only time they were allowed out of uniform. They were in fancy dress because they were putting on a show to entertain the prison commander.

About a month before I left Lard Yao I had to stand in front of the office to have this photograph taken. There is a Thai saying, 'Sprinkle the surface with coriander'; not everywhere in Lard Yao looked as pretty as this, but it was the only place they allowed photographs to be taken.

Above: Demanding Princess Anne's attention in the gym in Holloway. She is president of Save The Children and had come in that day to see the work we did with handicapped children.
Below: With my grandfather, just after I was released in July 2000.

Free at last. Mum, me and Dad, July 2000.
(*Photo: Derek Ironside/Newsline Scotland*)

same level. The pain of the cell wasn't actually physical, but sometimes, most times, I wished it were.

Previous to Lard Yao I had always thought of myself as a survivor, but prison life tested me to the limit. Day after day, month after month, I grew so tired of it. It was impossible. The bald, disease-ridden rats that grew to the size of cats and two-inch flying cockroaches never ceased to horrify me. I could stand my own ground with the other prisoners but could never cope with the disturbed chatter of rats or flying cockroaches.

There were times when the gap between what prison and rehabilitation claimed for itself and the reality of the daily performance was so huge it was hard to know which was worse – the reeling motion of your mind or the crawling on your stomach like a snake.

What do you do? Nothing really, except think about why you are here, how you got here and how you have almost crucified your family by your stupidity. All the while the single fan above us chopped away at the relentless heat.

If it hadn't been for my family back home then I am sure I would have killed myself, and taken the easy way out. But I owed them more than this; they were the ones who had got me through to this point, they were the ones who kept telling me that I should hang in there. The first faces I would see when I woke up every morning and the last ones I would see before bedding down for the night were my family and friends. In my cell of women, they visited me every night, just to say 'Goodnight, Sandra', just to remind me they were there. Their faces swam before me. It was a kind of schizophrenia. I wanted them near me, but I didn't want them in there. I was scared for my family, much more than I was for myself.

Towards the end of that first year my feet were still erupting in massive holes. The pain seemed to come from inside the bone and an infection had developed from the inside before exploding. No one cared, though. Why should they? There were some days when

I was so low that I couldn't imagine spending more than another hour in that place. Lard Yao was a madhouse, a rest home for the about-to-be-criminally-insane. I prayed for miracles. I prayed for a sign. I prayed that all this praying might be worthwhile.

Happy Christmas! But 25 December was just another day for most of the other women and me. Part of me still wanted to celebrate something, especially all the letters and little kindnesses from family and strangers, at home, and from around the world. On Christmas Day I wrapped up all the toiletries and new knickers I had been sent and gave them away to some Thai women I worked with. I don't think many of the women knew what to make of a sock full of gifts, but it gave me a little pleasure giving my stuff away.

New Year passed and there was nothing to celebrate. I replaced celebration with surviving and existing and that way I could deal with the enormous weight of the unbearable. I realised that prison confirmed nothing and proved nothing. It was just there.

NINE

Domestic Violence

Dear Sandra

You have no idea how often I have tried to write to you and the number of pages that have gone on the fire and I still can't write what I want to say to you. We love you so much (you stupid cow). Please, please come back...

Letter from my brother, June 1993

Many people passing through Bangkok, often total strangers, would come by to see me, as if I was an object of curiosity in an exhibition tank. In the visiting room I would ask them why they had come, hoping they might have brought a message from someone I knew at home, or a snippet of news, from beyond the prison walls.

'I've just come to see you,' they would say, startled by my bemused and disappointed expression. I couldn't help it.

Having to shout across a four-foot gap only increased my sense of frustration and alienation. 'It borders on the surreal,' said a reporter who came to visit one day. My life belonged to Lard Yao.

One year had passed since I first entered Lard Yao and I was still no nearer to being sentenced. I was a curious sight, embarrassed by living in these squalid conditions and angry with people outside prison knowing how I was forced to live. The impulse for sympathy is ancient and I hated their sympathy even more.

The paradox of Lard Yao was glaring; everyone wants prisoners to be punished and they expect rehabilitation. Fine. But the vulnerability of prisoners, and the lack of self-esteem reduce all the good intentions to less than zero. I wanted to open my own mail or make a cup of tea when I fancied one. I wanted to eat when I was hungry, not when I was told. Even showing emotions was restricted. Everyone felt this, but no one said it. You couldn't, it was impossible. Displaying emotion was a sign of weakness and in prison weakness was often preyed on. I was weak and I grew tired of having to put on a face and pretend I was hard and tough.

There were, of course, days when I realised how lucky I was and how much worse my situation could have been. By turns I grew resilient and found the occasional pleasure in small things.

Court mornings, of all occasions, were often a quiet, peaceful time. Rising early, before anyone else was up, and being let out in the dark was a precious change to the regular routine. It was one of my only chances to be more or less alone.

I would sit outside on my plastic mat for a few minutes with my cat, watching the fat bullfrogs jumping around the courtyard. I would watch them jealously, as they plopped and hopped around on the ground; they were as free as anything could possibly be in the prison. They were freer than the guards who worked there, ate there and, in some cases, lived there. I desperately wanted to be a frog or even one of the pigeons that flew in and out of prison all day.

One morning, on my way out to court, I looked around at the other people going that day and noticed a young girl. She looked too young, like an infant almost, and didn't look at all well. In the damp holding corridor, the rest of us stood up and were counted, but the girl couldn't lift herself from the floor. There were no signs of life in her eyes, and her body looked too thin to be alive.

'Frogs. Frogs.' The jumping of the tiny frogs had caught her attention.

Hers was a typical story. Her parents had been given a 'loan' for their daughter and told she would be given a job in a factory in Bangkok. Instead she was put to work in a brothel. At the time she was 12 years old. Not long after she began selling her body she contracted HIV and, at 15, she developed a heroin habit. Shortly after that the HIV developed into full-blown Aids and, at 17, the police arrested her for possession of heroin. She was going to court from Lard Yao, charged with possession of less than a fifth of a gram of heroin.

Two weeks after her court appearance her skeletal body staggered along the tiled floor of the hospital building. I watched as she dropped to her knees, her hands clasped together, asking the nurse for a paracetamol.

'Go!' The guard flicked the girl away with her hand.

A few days later I saw her again. The bodysnatchers were taking her out of the prison in a body bag. By all accounts the youngster spent the last few nights of her life screaming in pain, but no one had bothered to give her any medication. The Thais would say it was her karma to die. How do you tell such a terrible story? It's easy. You just remind yourself that it's not you in that body bag.

Working in the laundry, scrubbing the clothes of the officers and their families had left my feet in a terrible condition. The officers brought their washing every morning and we had to wash it, dry it and have it ironed and bagged up by 4.00 pm that same day. I developed huge boils and infections across my feet and legs that looked like moon craters and the constant exposure to dirty water was having a terrible effect on the healing process. I left when I could no longer take the pain and began working in the bakery. At least it was dry.

No one working in the laundry was allowed to keep a cat because we worked with the officers' clothes and to send out a bag of clothes with cat hair on it would have been to invite a punishment. No sooner had I started in the bakery than I adopted a young tomcat by the name of Jow-Son. Before long my cat became the most important thing in my prison world.

Family and friends in Britain would write asking if there was anything I would like sending from home. It was never as simple as that. Anything I might have liked would never have been allowed into Lard Yao, and anything that was allowed I didn't really want anyway. While I thanked people for their kind offers, I told them I needed nothing. That changed when I realised that feeding Jow-Son was going to be a problem. (The rats in Lard-Yao were far too big for the cats to catch.)

While other prisoners received bottles of perfume, make-up and underwear – most of it to give to the guards as bribes or for dealing with the black market – I requested boxes of cat food from home.

One morning, out of nowhere, a beautiful, reddish-brown cat appeared and was immediately adopted by the Thai sweet factory girls. This cat was the biggest domestic feline I have ever seen. *He must have escaped from Bangkok Zoo*, I thought, because he just didn't look normal. I nicknamed him Brutus.

After a few weeks Brutus started terrorising all the other tomcats, and often we would come out in the morning to find a fearful tom clinging to the top of a fence with smelly, brown liquid pouring down the wall beneath it. The bakery cats developed infections all over their hind legs from where Brutus had brutally and systematically attacked them all night.

Soon Jow-Son was howling when I picked him up, his infections bursting out over my shirt, leaving me covered in green slime from his wounded legs. Over and over Brutus attacked the male cats. It seemed almost unnatural. Brutus refused to allow the other toms peace. Even the kittens born following his arrival all bore an uncanny resemblance to Brutus. Working late one night in the bakery, I saw him strutting inside. 'That's it,' I thought, 'I've had it.' I could no longer sit back and watch this creature terrorise all our babies.

I picked him up and shoved him in a rice sack. To be honest I didn't know what I was going to do with him but I was raging. I was also trembling. I walked away from the bakery carrying the sack over my shoulder and looked at the wall. I could hear Brutus clawing his way out of his little cloth prison.

If I throw him over, I thought to myself, *he'll get hurt and might lie injured for days*. My palms began to sweat. All I could hear was my heartbeat and the sound of a low humming coming from the bakery. Everything swirled. Looking across the yard I saw the pond where Karyn and I had sat together in the boathouse. I walked over and threw Brutus and the sack straight into the water. A few bubbles rose to the surface of the water. Brutus was gone.

My God, what have I just done? I was trembling terribly as I returned to the bakery, and when the girls asked me where Brutus was I could hardly speak.

'Gone where?' they wanted to know.

'Over the wall.'

It was the first time I had ever killed anything. A few days later the bag with the dead cat floated to the surface of the pond. Surrounded by furious women from the sweet factory, I denied their accusations telling them I had no idea where their precious cat was.

Jow-Son disappeared very soon after that but despite losing him I still didn't regret what I had done. It was a long, long time before I was allowed to forget my murderous incident and a long time before anybody would speak to me. I never went near the Thai sweet factory again.

It's a curious story to tell, and I am always struck by people's reaction. Animal stories. It makes them sad. All the craziness and all the suffering and the moral chaos and the young women dying and all the terrible things that went on in Lard Yao and people say, 'You killed a cat?' I'll never figure that one out.

*

One of the hardest things to adjust to was the way time passed, or didn't, as the case might be. Days sometimes felt like hours, hours sometimes felt like weeks, and weeks often felt like years. Yet it always seemed to be Sunday again. I had received a little pocket calendar shortly after I had arrived in Lard Yao and tried to keep track of time. The months passed rapidly but the calendar was a hindrance. How many more calendars would I receive?

Each year I would be sent a pile of calendars from different people, each sender presuming that it would prove useful. I hated the sight of them; I hated the sight of any calendar, but didn't tell anyone how I felt. I didn't want to sound ungrateful.

People also wrote to me about the seasons at home and year after year I would hear about the spring daffodils and the autumn leaves turning brown. So many times I prayed that I wouldn't miss another British springtime. I wrote and received letters from a man in Scotland and one spring he came over to Bangkok to see me. He brought a small bunch of daffodils with him. They were one of the most beautiful sights I had ever seen as I looked at them through two sets of bars and across the visiting room. The guards, of course, wouldn't allow me to have them but I shall never forget how their graceful yellow faces bobbed in that dark, grey corridor.

There are very few markers of time in prison. One day is pretty much like the last. It goes by slowly and then, suddenly, a year or two has passed and you wonder what's happening to your life and where it is going. It's almost seductive, the way time disappears.

My first anniversary passed and I had barely noticed it. The real way to measure time was by the events going on beyond the prison walls. Life was going on outside without me, without any of us. There were the occasional blips of good fortune – like the daffodils – but mostly we held onto things in our minds as they had been outside before our imprisonment.

I would go over the events of the last few years, wondering who fitted in and who were against me. Did they mean anything or were they simply part of my slow breakdown? For a while I struggled with the absurdity of my prison identity.

Meanwhile, Shanty, my friend from West Yorkshire, had her third child and he was growing up quickly with his two elder brothers. Holroyde had lost his boyish looks and the sagas of his life unfolded in his letters. My dog, Kara, was getting old and regularly attended the vet. My two cats had 'gone'. While my grandparents grew precariously older, my parents tried to live a normal life, but they struggled with the shame of everyone knowing where their daughter was and what she had done to get there.

One afternoon, Jackie, a woman from West Yorkshire, was in Bangkok and she visited me in prison, promising to come regularly until she had to go back to the UK. She lived roughly a mile from my house and her visits brought me so close to home I could almost touch it. For the 20-minute duration of her visit I could almost smell Yorkshire; I could feel the bumps in the pavement as she described the walk between our two houses and I could taste the tea we spoke about drinking from china cups.

Six months later and she had to return to England. I was devastated. It felt like she had just started visiting; it felt like she had been coming forever. When she was gone I felt completely lost. I resolved to forget about her visits and concentrate on doing my time. All that mattered was getting sentenced and surviving whatever sentence they handed out to me.

The questions that mattered now were these: How many years have you done? How many do you have to go? Will there be an amnesty this year? Would you go home if there were one?

My brother sent me a bundle of unfinished letters and also one that he had managed to complete. When I read them through I suddenly realised just how much I had upset my whole family. So many times he had started writing but was too upset to finish them. Hearing from him was marvellous, but terribly emotional.

Dear Sandra

I have tried to write to you so often over the past months but always only get so far and have to give up. What should I say to you? It all seems like a dream to me. I can't bear to think about it... my God, may we never ever have to go through such a period as this again... my God have we cried... please come back when you can.

I still can't believe it has happened to you (I love you) please come back... I can't bear to think about the situation you are in. When I think about it I get too upset. You really are a stupid, idiotic girl, but we want you back... one day we will see each other again.

I have changed a great deal as I am sure you have... this is all rubbish, why am I writing this? I have been trying to write so often and this is going to be sent to you no matter what, even if it is a load of old rubbish...

Sometime during my second year – I can't recall exactly when – my brother came to see me. It had been several years since we had set eyes on each other and he had changed greatly. Gone was the long hair and smelly Afghan coat and in its place were a sensible haircut, a smart suit and a pair of leather brogues. He had turned into our father. Having a family of his own had obviously changed him greatly and I was slightly unsettled by his appearance. Yet in some ways I was glad. He was getting on with his life while my life stood still.

For a few seconds we said nothing; then we talked. It upset both of us that we couldn't touch or be closer to each other. His vitality had never waned but he was more reserved, probably from seeing his sister in such a state, and his face retained a peculiar expression of sadness.

What did we talk about? Everything, I suppose, and all the things that reminded me how much I had let everyone down. Like my brother, I should have grown up by now, I should have had a decent job and started a family, but instead I was sitting here, insane with misery, praying not to be given the death penalty.

It was so difficult saying goodbye and when he left my heart split once again. How I wished I could have gone home with him. My head was bursting into a thousand pieces.

People around me often received news that a member of their family or a close friend had died and I lived in constant fear that someday I would receive a similar letter. Girls would break down, inconsolable, as the news filtered through. Perhaps they hadn't seen their family member for a year, maybe three, sometimes five or it might even be 10 years. The guilt they felt was unimaginable.

Some of them cried publicly, others screeched. Many more just walked to a corner of the cell and stared blankly at the wall. I resigned myself to the possibility that my grandfather would not last my sentence. I tried not to think that it could be someone else.

Letters telling me of bad news were always written in the past tense. Situations that had already happened and were now resolved were OK to pass on, as long as there had been some kind of positive result at the end. 'Your dad was ill and had to be taken into hospital, but he is fine now.' Or, 'Pa-Pa was terribly sick over Christmas and we didn't think he would pull through, but he's back at home now and eating like a horse.' I wondered about the things they were keeping from me.

I dreamed of home so often that sometimes I couldn't distinguish between the dream and the reality. Was I dreaming I was a prisoner? Or, was I dreaming that I was at home? It was maddening trying to figure out what dream exactly was true. Everything became a blur and, at times, I really did question my sanity.

The dreams grew more absurd. I imagined the judge would throw the case out of court simply because I asked him to, or that the police wouldn't bother to charge us or that somehow I would be granted bail and be able to find the money to pay for it.

There was just a wall between freedom and myself. Surely it wouldn't be so difficult for it to disappear? I woke every morning, exhausted from being a fugitive during the night. Even in the daytime I obsessed over it. One woman, who I had got to know fairly well, told me that she would do everything to help me if I found a way. But she would not come with me. Why? I asked her. She would be leaving through the gate the legal way very soon, she replied. She was serving a 50-year sentence and had just completed five.

As hard as it was being in Lard Yao, I remember sitting in the room one night looking at all the Asian faces and realising that, since my arrest, no other British woman had been as stupid as I had been in Bangkok.

Every time I went to court there was a pack of journalists and reporters following my every move and I knew that my case was being covered by most of the national newspapers and television stations in the UK. I sat there wondering whether my case had prevented any other potential smugglers from taking the chances that I had taken. All of a sudden the fog lifted and I didn't mind being there quite so much.

In April of 1994 the fog descended again. Patricia Hussain was arrested at Bangkok airport in possession of 7 kilos of heroin that she was trying to take out of Thailand. Any day now she would be arriving in Lard Yao.

'Fucking hell,' she said, when I met her the morning after she arrived. 'It's you. I saw you on the telly before I left to do this trip and I said to my mate, "Shit, Dolly, if I do this trip I could end up in the same place as that girl on the telly." Dolly told me not to do it, but I reckoned I'd be OK. Guess I reckoned wrong, eh?'

Patricia was from Manchester, a former prostitute and mother of two. She was short, dumpy and wild-looking, with a lop-sided face from having been bashed around with several baseball bats. She giggled a hysterical laugh. We became friends and, for a few months, she was a breath of fresh British air with stories of life at home. Her tales though were so different from my own memories of England and her life in Manchester made me quite glad to be in Thailand. She settled down to prison life and adapted to suit herself; we came from different worlds and had little in common with each other so it was inevitable that we wouldn't remain friends for long.

Some time later Patricia received a death sentence that was converted immediately to life imprisonment. I asked one of my Thai friends in the prison to write her a letter of appeal, and a year after getting the first sentence the court reduced it to 35 years and then to 25 years in a general amnesty. In July 1996, Patricia was flown to the United States to testify in a trial involving the smuggling of cocaine from Latin America, and she left Bangkok accompanied by US marshals. She would later go to Britain to testify in a drugs trial. Her appeal to the king for clemency was heard even though she was arrested more than a year after me, and it resulted in her sentence being reduced to 10 years.

In many ways, the prison was a showpiece. Everything that could be reasonably said to be in good condition was simply for the benefit of both the easy working of the prison machine and the guards who worked there. Nothing was meant to make life easier for the women. There is a Thai expression – 'Sprinkle the surface with coriander' – that basically means 'Create an impression that the whole is as pretty as the surface.' Thai food is usually presented with a sprinkling of coriander and even the blandest food can look appealing after the finishing touches are added.

Pretty fences hide slums in the city, while bushes and hedges were planted in Lard Yao to hide the conditions in which prisoners lived. The surface of Lard Yao was constantly sprinkled, metaphorically, with coriander. It was a reminder of the paradise that lay outside. Anyone seeing Lard Yao for the first time would think it was perfectly fine.

Some factory worker prisoners worked six days a week making plastic flowers, umbrellas or baskets from telephone directories, while others sat all day at sewing machines making army and school uniforms. Most of the women who made the school uniforms had been in prison for so long that they had forgotten what a child dressed for school actually looks like. These women each received around £9 every six months for their work. They sat in neat rows that created an impression of order. If the prison had a contract with a company, the workers would often work their usual eight-hour day and then all night – packing or sewing – to ensure the contract was completed on time. Threats would follow anyone not volunteering to work overtime.

Much of the work was carried out for huge multinational companies, including a famous children's film company, a well-known photographic company and a firm, in London, which sold very expensive bags. Women made ski-suits and baby clothes for the European market, packed playing cards and glued together children's toys with flammable solvents.

Other women worked in one of the five kitchens, or the laundry, or organised the general running of the prison. One woman was the electrician and, for a price, fixed broken fans in the rooms. Groups of girls worked on the gardens, cleaned out the water tanks and dredged the sewers every day.

The bakery ovens were turned on at 3 o'clock in the morning, with the early shift girls, and were never switched off before 10 o'clock at night. Work began at 4.00 am and went on until 8.00 pm, making pastries and bread that were sold in a shop outside the prison gate. The officers could order things for themselves and at New Year the bakery girls worked 24 hours a day getting all the orders together and making sure the shop outside didn't run out of anything.

Those who worked there did so every day for 52 weeks per year. Like the women in the sewing factory, we were paid roughly £9 every six months although one year we received nothing because the officer who ran the bakery told us that 'All the profits have gone into your stomachs, so you'll get nothing'.

Although very little of the baking was for the inmates, there were ways of getting hold of some of it. The 'extras' – what we could steal – always came in useful. A fresh loaf of white bread, straight out of the oven, could ensure a lasting friendship in Lard Yao, especially if you could steal a little butter to go with it. The taste of European-style food was a wonderful way to get away from the endless diet of rice and boiled fish. But after a while even the food in the bakery became boring and dull.

The prison bakery was always being shown off to anyone visiting the prison in an official capacity: guards from other prisons, Department of Corrections officers and the occasional foreign embassy staff. Most of the women would be hurried out the back of the bakery and warned to hide behind the fence until the visit passed. Those who stayed behind were ordered not to say anything that would undermine either the prison, the prison staff or the fate of the prisoners themselves.

The bakery, with its pungent aroma, its smiling officer and its superficial surroundings, made Lard Yao appear almost perfect. It was supposed to be a reflection of how the rest of the prison functioned, a kind of cook-it-yourself metaphor of rehabilitation. If the prisoners had a bakery, then surely life in the prisons could not have been that bad? Sprinkle the surface with...

The rodent population of the kitchens and the bakery ensured that Lard Yao was altogether less than perfect. Every night they would appear and eat whatever had not been locked away. The tell-tale signs could be seen every morning in all the mixing machines and across all the counters. They would chew through bags of sugar and vegetables and trap themselves in pipes.

I began living in the bakery; we all did. And we stored our meagre possessions – some prison clothing, a few toiletries, a little food, some letters – amongst the shelves and bags of flour, or between utensils and under or in anything. We kept our stuff well hidden from the officer in the bakery, one of the most foul-mouthed, bad-tempered and miserable women in Lard Yao. We christened her 'Old Mother Penis'.

She was properly known as Mare – the polite name for an older woman – Dtick. Mother Dick. If ever Old Mother Penis saw so much as a dirty rim of a washbowl or a bar of soap lying idle, she screamed obscenities at the top of her voice, ripping the kitchen to pieces, pulling out all our stuff and throwing it outside.

'Prostitutes!' she screamed. 'Buffaloes!' 'Wankers!' And 'Slags!' She repeated this, over and over, until she was red-faced and exhausted.

Old Mother Penis was not a woman to be messed with. Once, she stood Pee Pom out in the sun for a whole day for warming a bowl of vegetables in the oven for a friend. Another day she beat poor Deng because she had forgotten to put self-raising flour in the bread mix so it all had to be thrown away. Deng had worked in the bakery for nearly 10 years but Old Mother Penis sacked her for not making the bread properly that day, which meant that Deng went almost a year without receiving any money from the prison.

We washed at the back of the bakery, always being careful not to get caught by any of the guards or prison trustees. The general shower area where everyone was supposed to wash was mayhem and being able to wash anywhere but there, even crouched down behind the tank, was a blessing.

One morning, however, while in the main shower, after most other people had finished, one of the Nigerians hovered in front of me, grunting that I should get out and let her into my shower. I pointed to the empty one next to mine but she knocked me over just to get into the shower I was in.

'Do you want to fight about this?'

'Yeah,' she replied.

I was furious. What the hell did she think she was doing? I flew into a rage and began pounding against her face. Bang, bang, thud. *Fuck you!*

She began hitting me back. She was huge and I honestly

thought she would slaughter me, but after a few punches she lowered her head and her punches landed in mid air. I was still pumped with fury and possessed of an unfamiliar strength. Even with her head down, I managed to find her nose with my punches. I wanted to see blood, *her* blood.

I never realised that I was able to fight or even that I would want to, but that morning I fought her as though I had been born to box. God, I wanted to kill her. I punched her again. And then it was over.

After this incident I developed a reputation as a fighter, which had the curious habit of keeping me out of trouble. Only on three other occasions did I have to use my fists in Lard Yao. Sometimes there is just no other way to solve a dispute in prison.

For most of us who worked in the bakery there was never any compelling reason to go anywhere else. It was like a club without secrets. We became part of the bakery and, with the flour and the fumes, the bakery became part of us. The time and the inclination to change our routine were rarely available and, if they were, we were far too busy with officers' orders and keeping the shop stocked to do anything else.

The bakery had a black market of its own and girls would keep food for their friends in the fridge, warm food in the ovens and supplement diets with sugar, butter, breads and pastries. The black market also did a roaring trade in 'hooch' and one of the things that visitors were never allowed to bring into Lard Yao was pineapple. Mashed up, loaded with sugar and left out in the sun, pineapple turns into pure alcohol within 12 hours. Prisoners would brew 'hooch' with other fruits but pineapple was the best thing to use if you really wanted a decent drink.

In the bakery we would stand for hours peeling fresh pineapples, then smash them with lumps of wood, before squeezing out the juice. We mixed the flesh with sugar and cooked the mix for hours to make a sweet, thick filling for pastries. The bakery received deliveries of up to 150 kilos at a time. We were supposed to throw all the leftover juice into the sewer although we could drink as much as we wanted before getting rid of it. We were not supposed to give any of the juice or pineapples to our friends.

One week I made some kind of wine with the juice and quickly realised why pineapples were banned. By the time I had finished a mug full of pineapple wine I could hardly walk. Before I was locked in for the night the effect of it made me cry. I didn't like being drunk in there so I never made any again. But I did manage to give gallons of the juice away to whoever came by. There were a few drunken prisoners that week.

Noontime signalled the dreadful mountains of grey, gritty rice with something threatening to be a vegetable perched on top. Often it was boiled cucumber or a tiny boiled fish, which had not been cleaned, and chillies. These delicacies were dished up three times a day. Somehow, the Thais managed to get fatter and fatter from the food, while I constantly lost weight. Every day, while massive ovens churned out stuffed breads, pineapple pastries and decorated cakes, one of us would head over to the area where the food was prepared for the rest of the prisoners, and bring back lunch or dinner.

The Thais I worked with were usually too busy or felt they were above the task of bringing the food to others, so the duty fell to me. I would take a four-gallon jam pan to collect whatever vile-smelling 'delight' happened to be on that day's menu. It was always a relief to get a break from the cramped confines of the bakery, even if it was to smell dead fish or to be hounded by thousands of flies heading for the piles of carcasses waiting to be hacked into the pot.

The kitchen would hardly be recognisable, to most Westerners, as a kitchen at all. It was simply an area for chopping and boiling food. The girls there would sit on the concrete with meat cleavers, hacking toenails off chicken legs and chopping the mounds of dead pigs into pieces for boiling, surrounded by swarms of blue-bottles and scuttling cockroaches. Hygiene was more of a greeting than a noun.

Over a relatively short period of time, I became quite friendly with Noi, a middle-aged Thai woman who controlled the jail kitchen and was in charge of all the cooking. A stolen bag of biscuits from the bakery would help me get enough vegetables to eat for a week. Noi had a desire for all things European, including soap, chewing gum and chocolate, many of the things I could get sent to me from home – and I would swap these for delicacies such as stuffed chillies and chicken fried rice, when I had the chance to trade something.

Noi had served over 15 years and had a hardened expression on her face that I feared I was developing for myself. She was stockier than most Thais, with a sharp nose, and deep brown eyes. She had clout in the kitchen and was a good person to have as a friend. Gradually I sensed that the other women were somewhat suspicious of my relationship with her and they disapproved of me speaking to her.

One afternoon Pee Pom took me to one side and asked me if I knew about Noi. 'No,' I replied.

Did I know why no one spent much time in her company? I didn't, nor would I care.

'Noi is a cannibal,' said Pee Pom.

'What?!'

'She's a cannibal.'

Pee Pom proceeded to tell me Noi's story. She had set fire to a wooden house where a family slept, and when the fire had burned out she had gone in and taken out the hearts and livers of all five occupants. She ate them over the following days.

This was Lard Yao and nothing surprised me. I did think it was slightly ironic that a cannibal was head cook in the prisoners' kitchen. Someone in the prison administration obviously had a sense of humour. Noi was released under the general amnesty of June 1996.

*

The prison grapevine was buzzing. One of our guards had been arrested on a murder charge and was expected to come into Lard Yao as a prisoner within a few days. The guard resembled a bent-up little crow and was as spiteful as a cobra. We were all very excited at the prospect of Crow coming in to join us. The story circulated that Crow's husband had taken a second wife, as many Thai men do, and they had been found together by Crow in her bed at home.

She left the house and got a handgun, returned home and shot them both through the head as they rolled around in her bed together. Whether the story was accurate or not, I'm not sure, but a few days after hearing it Crow was bailed out of the police cells by the Lard Yao commander under the condition that she be held at the prison. Any guard coming in as a prisoner would have been a delight but the fact that it was to be Crow herself was marvellous.

We knew she would receive immediate protection and special treatment, but hoped she would be forced to share at least some of our space and have to shower out in the open with us. We delighted in the idea of Crow standing knee-deep in foul water, with the rest of the prison population, as soldiers in helicopters hovered overhead, watching everyone bathe.

Crow spent the following weeks, though, living upstairs in he air-conditioned area of the prison, where the guards slept during night duty. Food was taken to the office three times a day by one of the guards. After a few days even the other guards couldn't avoid gossiping and the murder story was confirmed. Some weeks after being arrested Crow disappeared and little was ever heard about her, except that she had changed her name and was working somewhere outside Bangkok.

Increasingly, the guards always took gratuitous and sadistic pleasure in dishing out punishments and tortures, even taking time to prepare their preferred methods. The longer I was in prison the greater the variety of punishments I witnessed. Prisoners who violated jail regulations, even in relatively minor cases such as quarrels, were subject to punishment. Officers would dish out public beatings with either a rattan cane or short truncheon. I saw women beaten, battered, handcuffed, scorched, starved and brutalised, mostly by other women who could at best be described as perverts.

A girl had been caught stealing from the nursery early one morning while the mums were washing their clothes, and when the nursery guard came on duty at 9 o'clock the thief sat on the ground waiting for the guard to deal with her. A large crowd lurked to see what fate awaited the girl. The waiting process was simply another part of the punishment.

The guard ordered the girl to put one hand face down on the table. She lifted her truncheon way up behind her head, then brought it crashing down across the girl's fingers, with a crack that broke them all.

'Other hand on the table,' the guard ordered.

Again, you could hear the sound of the break. Kneeling on the ground, the girl raised her two broken hands up to her nose and thanked the guard for rectifying her bad ways. Slowly she got up and left. 'Seeing is believing', according to the aphorism.

Three guards in particular had the reputation for being the hardest of them all, and to receive a punishment from any of them was something to avoid. For a while many of us sensed that those three guards felt they had lost their reputations for brutality and the women got nervous.

One weekend they strutted around looking for someone to bolster their flagging reputations. One of them was very cute, the size of a small doll, and marched around like a robotic soldier. Her head constantly scoured the area in front of her for victims. I can't remember why she chose the particular girl, but she was made to stand waist-deep in shit, digging out the bunker under the toilet all day. When it was time for 'lock-in' the girl, almost on the verge of collapse, was put in a small empty room without having been allowed a shower, and was left there for the night and most of the next day. The guard just smiled. Lard Yao had fallen deeper into a dubious moral limbo.

Most of the prisoners dreaded the *soi*, the punishment room, where as many as 30 girls would be placed for a variety of crimes, including fighting, stealing, disrespect towards an officer and being caught having sex. Offenders would be placed there for anything up to three months.

There was no bedding, no fan or mosquito nets over the bars, no change of clothes, no books or paper to write a letter on. Everyone was fed on slops twice a day. A bucket, sitting in the corner, in full view of everyone, was used as a toilet; they were allowed to wash once every three days. 'Officer, officer, the bucket's full,' was the regular lamentation from inside the *soi*. A few weeks of this punishment and the girls would come out thin and pale, covered in bites with raging skin disorders.

Often the guards would ask the girls whether they wanted time in the *soi* or a beating and, more often than not, they took the beating.

'It gets it over and done with,' I was told by a girl named Nai.

One morning Nai had been caught fighting and was offered seven days in the *soi*, or seven hits with the truncheon. She took the hits, leaving her covered in purple and green bruises. But she would get over them quickly.

I could barely understand this exterminatory impulse of the guards. The guards sought perfection, a world without enemies; at least none who could strike back. I tried my best to avoid punishment while the guards tried their best to avoid punishing me. The embassies, particularly the British, American, European and Australian, frowned upon physical brutality and beatings. It was impossible, though, to be in Lard Yao and not know who was in control.

★

Angela was a very large American woman who was arrested and then charged with attempting to smuggle a kilo of heroin out of Thailand. Her family provided her with one of the most expensive lawyers in Bangkok, but six months after her arrest she arrived back from court with a life sentence. Her family paid the lawyer thousands more dollars, but a year after her initial sentencing the appeal court upheld the original sentence.

Angela cried about how unfair she thought it was, because other people had been caught with far more heroin than she had yet they had been given sentences far shorter than hers. Again her family paid out several thousand dollars to the lawyer and she hoped for a reduction of sentence at the Supreme Court, but they too upheld the life sentence.

When she returned from court the Thais whispered stories to me about Angela. A visitor had told one of the prisoners about a story in the newspaper that day. It reported that a woman had been caught trying to smuggle a kilo of heroin out of Thailand in the body of a dead baby. Thais generally do not export drugs. They usually get a foreigner to do that for them so the Thai women in the prison suspected that the story was about Angela.

Smuggling drugs was bad enough but to smuggle them in the body of a dead baby was unthinkable, and when other prisoners asked me about her case I told them what the Thais were saying. It sounded logical and explained why the court had not reduced her sentence, although I didn't actually believe the dead baby story and said so when I spoke about it. The story quickly spread around the prison. The following day Angela heard about it but with the added titbit that 'Sandra told me you killed a Thai baby to smuggle your drugs in.'

Understandably Angela went a bit crazy but, knowing that a six-foot-two woman weighing roughly 22 stone was after me, I was in no great hurry to put her straight. I hoped someone else might. Angela, sweating with fury, charged around the prison and for days I hung out in the shadows. I couldn't fight Angela, and wasn't angry enough even if I'd wanted to; I was so exhausted from work I could barely fight sleep. When she finally cornered me I was in the bakery where only those who work there are allowed. As she entered all the Thais immediately left us alone and only the metal workbench came between us.

She was furious. *Here it comes,* I thought, *the fat lump is going to kill me. If I hit her, punches will just bounce off all that lard and she's too tall to punch in the face.* I was tempted to grab one of the 10-inch knives on a nearby counter but I really didn't want things to get out of hand.

She ranted and raved for a bit, letting more and more anger out while I agreed with her that it was a horrible story. I told Angela she'd be justified in beating me because I had been wrong to repeat the tale. The situation was defused. Even though we had never spoken much before, we chatted for a while and soon after became quite good friends. When I finally left Lard Yao she was the only person I kept in contact with.

In late August 1994, a British man and a Swedish woman were arrested on drug-trafficking charges in separate incidents. The Swedish woman was arrested at Bangkok Airport after she was found with 7.8 kg of heroin in her luggage. The woman was Karolina Johnnson. I couldn't believe it when a reporter who visited me told me about the case. It had to be the same Karolina I had known.

One Friday evening a girl with a frizzy head staggered through the gate. Her stuttering walk gave her away. Karolina had arrived, the same Karolina who had tried to get me into smuggling gold and girls; the same Karolina I had thought about when Robert had made me his offer. *If she could smuggle successfully surely I would be OK just this once,* I had thought.

Had she ever thought about me when she heard I'd been arrested at the airport? Had she ever wondered whether her activities had influenced my decision? The following morning some girls told me that the new woman wanted to see me. 'She says she knows you,' they said.

'Yeah,' I replied, 'she does.'

She had known I'd been in Lard Yao all that time but not once had considered visiting me. I went to find her.

'So you've finally arrived,' I said, standing over her. 'I wondered how long it would take you.' She ignored my caustic remarks.

'How do you live with so many women? I can't survive without men.'

I left Karolina on her own to find out that having no men was the very least of her problems. She received a 35-year sentence.

Court appearances took place each month and I prayed that the trial would be over soon. Amnesty was part of the everyday conversation, like food or who was sleeping with whom, or who was being punished for what. Everybody talked about possible pardon. It was something of a preoccupation and then, ultimately, an obsession. How would it affect our sentence, we wondered? What would the amnesty grant you? How much longer will you have to serve? We ate the same food. We asked the same questions. We tried our best to pretend our lives were going to get better. But I knew that if I did not receive my sentence soon then I would be excluded from any amnesty.

If an amnesty were given there were four levels of reduction of sentence. All prisoners had to be sentenced. After that, most of them would be eligible for an amnesty if one were granted. The King of Thailand together with the Department of Corrections decides which cases will be granted amnesty and whether drug cases will be included.

To gain a reduction in sentence, all prisoners had to pass a series of tests, in Thai, in order to gain a 'class'. Six months after sentencing all prisoners took amnesty classes, which increased the level of reduction that could be granted. For example, three classes could give anything from a half to a one-fifth reduction of sentence; two classes and they might receive one-third or one-sixth off their sentence; while one class equalled a one-seventh reduction. If a prisoner failed to attend a class she received one-eighth of a reduction. Nothing was ever certain with amnesties though and if one were given there was never any guarantee that all cases would be included. We lived on amnesty possibilities and speculation.

If you were friendly with an officer, bribes often helped. Prisoners had to learn the Thai National Anthem and rehearse several sets of rules:

FIVE TEACHINGS OF BUDDHA

Do not kill animals.
Do not commit adultery.
Do not steal.
Do not lie.
Do not drink alcohol.

FIVE DUTIES TO BE OBSERVED

Be kind to everything alive.
Help yourself and be law abiding.
Do not be obscene.
Be honest.
Do the right thing and think of good things.

TEN PRISON RULES

No opium, marijuana or any drugs.
No intoxicants.
No escape equipment.
No gambling or games.
No weapons or sharp objects.
No rotten food.
Nothing valuable.
No pets.

No explosives.
No newspapers or diaries.

FOUR THINGS TO DO
Eat to sustain life.
Have good karma.
Respect the laws.
Respect every officer.

SIX DUTIES OF A GOOD CITIZEN
Obey the laws.
Pay taxes.
Protect the country.
Education is compulsory.
Protect public property.
Observe the traditions and customs.

SIX VICES TO AVOID
Don't drink alcohol.
Don't go out late at night.
Don't indulge in pleasurable activities.
Don't gamble.
Don't have bad friends.
Don't be lazy.

1994 had passed into 1995, which had passed into 1996, and there was nothing anyone could do about it. I put my hands around my head and screamed inside at another year of my life posted missing. I couldn't put my loneliness to one side; it was there all the time, growing like a tumour.

All I wanted was to be sentenced, regardless of the severity, then I would find the time to take at least one of the classes needed to grant a reduction in sentence. If I received a life sentence – or worse, the death penalty – I would have to appeal, and that would mean I wouldn't be finished with court and I wouldn't get the amnesty. It was a medieval way of treating people. I had been in this hole for years and still had no idea when I would learn my fate. What a circus.

Deep down I always had hope that I would be treated leniently. But I also learned that false hope is much worse than no hope. When you are a prisoner, everything you experience takes on a completely different meaning to similar experiences on the outside. I listened, and constantly looked for information on who might be getting out, who might be getting pardoned or even who knew how to work the prison system expertly.

I saw myself reflected in all these instances, hoping especially in the case of a pardon that I might be next. I prayed not to be given the death penalty and prayed hard that the trial would be over soon. I wished Robert would just plead guilty so that we could get on with our sentences.

It would have been easy to lose my mind in there; many women did. And the only things keeping me alive were the letters I received from outside and my family photographs. Sometimes, before lock-down, I would run my fingers across the surface of each picture or letter. The contours of each face came alive and the words came to life through the ink. I put them down. Lard Yao was nothing but darkness and shadows.

TEN

Art of Survival

Dear Mum and Dad

The Thais told me 29 February was a very good day to be sentenced on. Leap Day is considered very auspicious here and I was hopeful of a positive outcome. Bangkok was shut down for the Euro/Asia Summit meeting and the day was declared a national holiday. John Major got the lucky day for himself. My sentence date was brought forward...

Sandra

Letter home, March 1996

'Termination of life,' says the judge, almost imperceptibly. I have been sentenced to death.

The next few minutes are a blur. I am in shock. *My parents will not be too happy about this,* I think to myself. *How can this man sentence me to die? Surely it is up to them whether I live or not? They have given me life and they should decide when it can be taken away.*

I look across the Thai Criminal Court and it is swimming with faces that I do not recognise. My legs buckle beneath me and my heart is racing. 'No,' I gasp, 'it's not possible.' My bones and flesh are exhausted.

I can see Robert's face but he refuses to look back in my direction. It is 28 February 1996, the day someone has decreed that my life will be taken and the day Robert has been found 'not guilty'. I have waited three years for this day and when I hear he has been acquitted I stand, dumbfounded. The expression of disbelief on his face shows he is as stunned by the verdict as I am.

From behind me I hear a voice. 'No,' she shouts. It is the voice of a reporter. 'No,' she says again. 'The judge reduced it to life, then cut it to again to 25 years for trafficking.' Her voice trails away...

Twenty-five years! *Thank God!* I barely hear a word of what the judge is saying and I am desperately relieved he has not upheld the death penalty for me. The court has lifted the charges against Robert and I whisper to myself, 'That is so unfair.' Robert refuses to look at me.

I am taken from court to where crowds of reporters stand outside waiting for a picture or a quote. 'It's not fair,' I say, 'it's not fair. It's really so unfair. I feel terrible for my parents. Robert is the one who lied. I told the truth all through my trial. How can I get 25 years and he gets set free?'

For the last few years I had been attending court and now I had finally been sentenced. But I was still confused. Was I supposed to be 25 times more evil than Robert? Yes, I was guilty, but so was Robert; and he would be leaving Thailand an innocent man. It was a farce.

Although I was distraught my lawyer, Khun Tawitchai, had promised me the minimum sentence when I met him in Lard Yao a few years earlier and now he had delivered. At least someone was true to their word. There had been so many lawyers showing up at prison with all kinds of promises – 'I'll get you bail', 'I know the judge', or 'I'll get you six years for this' – that I didn't know who to trust.

Khun Tawitchai, at least, was honest. 'I think I can get you the minimum sentence,' he said. 'If you get more than 25 years I won't charge you for my time.' He was barely in his twenties, had very recently finished university and spoke virtually no English. He had never dealt with a serious case before. I liked him immediately. We struck a deal that he would be paid after sentencing, but if I got sentenced to more than the minimum then he would have worked for nothing.

For two years he showed up at the prison before every court appearance, never missed a hearing and came to see me the day after every court hearing. At the beginning of the trial I had been accused of carrying 102 grams of pure heroin, which I denied, rather than the original 89 grams. Anything above 100 grams and the law calls for the death penalty or life imprisonment. During the opening stages of the trial it was revealed that a British Embassy employee had tipped the Thai authorities to look out for Robert at the airport. The prosecution had finished its evidence in 1994 and the trial had been adjourned to allow defence documents to be translated into Thai.

In January 1995 I had finished testifying and was no longer required in court. I had to wait for Robert to finish his testimony and for the outcome of our trial. According to newspaper reports following the verdicts, Jean Sharpe, of the British Embassy, said she was 'glad' for Robert and his family at his acquittal, although she confirmed that drugs liaison officers attached to the British Embassy had alerted the Thai authorities to his alleged activities. By the end Khun Tawitchai had earned his £1,000 fee. My dad duly paid up. The ironies escaped neither of us, and once again I wished I had just asked my parents for the airfare home in 1993.

The procedure in Thailand when someone on a serious charge is found 'not guilty' is for the prosecutor to appeal the verdict. The prosecutor is given 28 days to file the appeal and it normally takes at least another 12 months before the appeal court hear the case. I returned to Lard Yao believing that Robert would have to spend another year behind bars before he tasted his freedom.

Around this time there had been a plague of head lice in prison and everyone had been ordered to cut their hair short, to prevent it spreading. Normally, to have very short hair was a punishable offence because the tomboys were seen as troublemakers who didn't fit the prison description of orderly looking inmates.

I had already cut my long, blonde hair into a much more severe, cropped style and had started dyeing it black, which helped me blend in with the Thai prisoners. The day following my sentence I felt utterly lost and deflated. The only thing I seemed to be able to take control over was my hair. I had most of it shaved off and re-dyed it pitch black. Almost instantly I felt better equipped to deal with the coming decades. I counted them out: two more decades. It sounded barely possible.

'I cook for you, Sandee,' said someone. Or, 'I do your washing for you, Sandee.' My radical new look had an amazing effect on the Thai girls, who thought I had turned into a tomboy. They thought I was looking for a prison 'wife' and would have done almost anything for me in return for a bit of sex on a Sunday afternoon. I decided I'd better grow my hair long again; I preferred doing my own washing, thank you very much.

A few days later a guy I had never met before, from Scotland, showed up at Lard Yao to see me. He was hyperactive and he danced around the visiting room, shouting about how awful everything was.

'I've got a car outside,' he said, 'I could just drive you off in it.'

I couldn't quite figure why he had come up to see me. All of a sudden he pulled out a small camera and it started flashing. The mad Scot found himself surrounded by guards and he suddenly lost his bravado and looked scared, but he wasn't as worried as I was. I knew it would be me who would pay for his stupidity and I told him to give them the film from his camera.

'Will they put me in prison?' he shouted back at me as he was being ejected from the visiting room. I was told I would not be allowed any visits for the next month. The following week, though, I was called to the visiting room.

'Why were those reporters outside the gate yesterday?' asked a guard escorting me. I hadn't known there had been any reporters outside.

'You are a liar,' she said turning away.

I stood shaking my head. I had been called many things in Lard Yao but no one had called me a liar. My problem had always been telling the truth even when it meant I might end up looking foolish or get into trouble. I was shocked and when I walked back into the prison after the visit I felt lower than ever before. There was no real explanation for it. Who was this guard? She meant nothing to me yet she seemed to have a more profound effect than the rest of the guards combined.

Suddenly the military uniform she was wearing brought back memories of the military massacre I had witnessed in 1992. It was a brutal realisation and the weight of my sentence hit me. These people had total control over my life and I was scared. Like a dark cloud, the crush of depression descended. Finally they had won; they had beaten me.

There is a famously memorable scene in *Midnight Express* when Billy, the young smuggler, loses his senses completely and attacks Rifkin in a frenzy of violence. The scene culminates with Billy biting the tongue out of Rifkin's head. It is a brutal scene, but essential because Billy has finally snapped. The Turkish prison has finally beaten him. He has lost his mind. That morning I felt like Billy Hayes. My spirit had been broken and privately I admitted defeat.

For the first and only time in Lard Yao I sat behind the toilets all afternoon and cried. It was as if all the things I'd ever known and learned no longer made sense, and I sank deeper and deeper into the gloom. I don't know how long I was there, in this terrible black vortex, and I don't know how I got out but I had never experienced anything quite like it.

There was no appeal from the prosecutor and one month after the verdicts Robert went home. He was driven out of Klong Prem Prison in a police pick-up truck and taken to a nearby police station to sign release formalities. While he had been in jail, he had been given a 15-month suspended sentence for possession of heroin, but he appealed the conviction and had it overturned at the appeal hearing.

Years later, when I read about Robert's release, I discovered that he had said that the certainty of his innocence had given him the strength to survive. He refuted all my allegations and claimed he had never known me. While his acquittal had stung me at the time, I soon realised Robert's 'not guilty' verdict made absolutely no difference to my own situation. I was still guilty. I pushed Robert out of my mind and gave him very little thought again.

Prime Minister John Major arrived in Thailand on 29 February 1996 (the day after I was sentenced) for an international summit. He said he had no plans to intervene on my behalf, while British officials said that it was not possible for them to make any utterances or involve themselves in matters that were for the Thai authorities.

The Foreign Office had already stated they wouldn't intervene on my behalf, yet it was still difficult to accept given Major's previous position. What I couldn't understand was why Major had helped Karyn Smith and Patricia Cahill but refused to do the same for me. He had written to the Thai authorities on their behalf, and he did not question their convictions but asked for mercy on humanitarian grounds. Why was I so different?

At the beginning of 1996 the number of women in Lard Yao went up to roughly 2,800 and the overcrowding problem became immense. Around March the temperatures regularly rise above 100°F and, in this searing heat, squashed together, tempers erupted easily. Most inmates tried counting the hours until shower time when they could escape the heat under cool water.

One Saturday morning we got up to find the water tanks in the room bone dry and I ran straight out of the room to try to grab a shower before anyone else. No luck, the tanks there were dry also. The prison stayed this way until Monday morning.

No one washed themselves, or their clothes and cutlery, or brushed their teeth. Likewise, babies and children did not wash and the toilets became blocked with solid waste. Even the sewer was dry; piles of dirty pans stacked up in the kitchens. That weekend the smell was overpowering and we all lived in our own, drying filth.

Fortunately, on the first day of the 'dry time' I had managed to get hold of a bucketful of water and I sat guarding it all day; I wanted a wash before getting locked in for the night. I agreed to share the water with another woman and at 4 o'clock she went for a brief wash. I watched as the handle on the bucket broke, and the contents fell to the ground, spilling across the concrete. There was not enough water left to scrape across our teeth.

Someone realised on Monday that the water valve outside the gate had been turned off and by lunchtime the problem was resolved. By now everyone was desperate for a wash. As water gushed through the pipes into the tanks and out of the shower-heads, a group of Nigerians ran to the tanks and urinated all over the ground. No one wanted to walk barefoot across their urine; they had ensured a space for themselves by a tank of water.

On 9 June 1996 the King of Thailand granted an amnesty to celebrate his Golden Jubilee and I was given a reprieve of just over three years, an eighth off my total sentence. Drug cases had been included in the amnesty for the first time in years but the reductions were so small they hardly counted. Everyone who had been preparing themselves for release sank further into depression.

The size of my reduction reflected the fact I had only just been sentenced and had not had time to take any of the prison amnesty classes. The woman who slept on the floor next to me, who had chopped her husband up into eight pieces and thrown him in the river, had her 25-year sentence cut down to 12 years. Around 290 Thai prisoners were released, along with three foreigners from the men's section of Klong Prem Prison.

A Buddhist monk who had murdered a British tourist expressed gratitude for the reduction of his death sentence to life imprisonment by the king. Yodchart Suephoo, who became a monk after hiding a prison conviction for rape, had killed Johanne Masheder, a girl from Chester, in December 1995, when she visited a temple popular with tourists. Johanne was pushed down a steep drop in a cave on the temple compound, and then beaten to death with a rock. Her partly burned remains were discovered a month later. I was in such fine company, but according to Thai opinion my crime had been one against the whole of humanity, not just one person, and I was thus less deserving of the king's leniency than murderers.

I accepted my small reduction with the vice of stubborn pride. I would deal with it, just as everyone else would have to deal with their tiny reductions.

There was less and less space for women to sit on in the mornings and we washed, got ourselves ready, ate breakfast and tried to live a normal life, squashed together on top of each other. Kerry, an Australian girl, had been in Lard Yao for almost 10 years and every morning she would sit with her Thai friends. Once, while they were eating breakfast, a Nigerian stood over them, scraping her tongue with a prison-made knife. Kerry and her mates tried to ignore the scraping but when the Nigerian began combing her pubic hair over their rice, the Thai girls asked Kerry to get her to stop.

'If she was Thai we would speak to her,' said one of the girls, 'but she is not. You are a foreigner so you must ask her to be polite.'

Kerry asked the Nigerian to comb her pubic hair elsewhere.

'Fuck off,' said the Nigerian.

Losing face in front of your friends in prison is avoided at all costs so Kerry confronted the Nigerian woman and a fight broke out. The rules in Thailand were usually clear. Fight a Thai and you fight them all, but fight a non-Thai and you are left on your own.

Because of Kerry's standing amongst the Thais she was considered as Thai as any foreigner can be. When the fight erupted loads of Thais jumped up to give her a hand.

The other Nigerians joined in and a pitched battle ensued. A voice boomed over the tannoy. It was a guard calling all the Thai girls to help their 'sisters'. From all over the prison came Thais carrying sticks, stones, knives and machetes and they beat the Africans to a pulp. Deng had two large sticks in her hand and she cornered Anna, the Nigerian who had been at court when I had been taken there from the police station.

'Take a stick to defend yourself,' she ordered Anna.

'No, I don't want to fight.'

'Take the stick or you die,' Deng screamed.

'But I don't want to fight.' Anna was almost in tears. Finally she took the stick from Deng.

As soon as Anna had taken hold of it, Deng screamed out, 'Good, now you have a stick it is fair.' She proceeded to pound Anna's face to a pulp. The whole prison, it seemed, was fighting; someone had broken glass from a jar hanging out of her face, while another looked as if she might lose her arm. The blood, thick and red, covered the concrete and surrounding area.

This was more than the guards had counted on. The situation had escalated from a fight into a riot and the guards, fearing a mass break-out, called the riot squad from the men's prison, which arrived shortly to quell the rioters. Those not involved in the fighting moved away as quickly as possible or looted what they could from unattended bags.

Me? I just sat on the stairs, watching in amazement. Nothing like this had happened before and it wasn't my fight so I stayed on the sidelines. I knew how the Thais fought when they were protecting one of their own. I saw the riot squad arriving with shields, batons and truncheons, and I walked away from the bloodbath. It didn't matter why I was in prison; all I cared about was survival.

*

Some time later, I was moved from the remand room where I had slept for over three years into Pyleen, the building for prisoners sentenced to less than 25 years. Although the room was larger, and a better place to sleep than where I had been living, there were over 180 women there. The women there were more settled; they knew their sentence and had accepted it.

Stepping over the rows of bodies one evening to go to the toilet, I saw a tiny girl lying on the floor covered in blood. *Shit*, I thought, *she's been stabbed*, and I shook her awake. She had the eyes of a frightened doe.

She had not been stabbed but was lying in a pool of her own menstrual blood. I asked some of the Thais if they would lend me a sanitary towel. 'Oh, yes, Sandee, I give for you,' said a number of girls, but when I told them the towel was for the young girl they refused. Nolay was a hilltribe girl who came from the mountains in the north of Thailand, on the border with Burma and Laos, and spoke hardly any Thai. She was also very poor. That night I couldn't do anything but the next day I had a visit and gave my visitor a long list of things to collect for me. I waited for the young girl and later that night I gave her the bag of stuff. She dropped to her knees in front of me and put her hands up to her nose in thanks. I could see she was crying. The little mountain girl hugged the bag. I watched her as she slept with her arms and legs wrapped around the bag all night. She never let go of it once.

Nolay felt she had to repay me and every night in the room she made me 'friendship' bands and gave me two-hour long massages. Her name was Nolay and the prison had given her the surname Mai Me Namsakoon, which curiously means 'no have surname'. She guessed she was aged between 24 and 28. She had arrived from the mountains with a man she knew who had given her a two-inch drinking straw full of heroin to hold. Upon their arrival in Chiang Mai, the man had gone to the police and told them what Nolay was carrying and she had been arrested.

For a fifth of a gram of heroin, Nolay was charged with

trafficking and because she had no money, and could not afford a lawyer, she received a prison sentence of 21 and one-third years. She had been arrested with her baby but the police took him away and she never heard anything about him again. With no money, no baby, no surname and no family who knew where she was, Nolay did her best to survive Lard Yao. I bought her new uniforms, supplied her toiletries, took her to get her hair cut and invited her to come and eat with me twice a day. Eventually, when it was time for me to leave Lard Yao, Nolay clung to my waist and cried like a child.

Six months after I left, Nolay got sick and swelled up like a balloon. Her hair fell out, she turned yellow and died. As the body bag was driven out of the gates the authorities in attendance called out to her, 'Nolay No Have Surname, release yourself.'

Many of the convicted mothers in prison have been arrested on drug-related charges. Thai people know that if they are convicted of a drugs charge they will probably never see the outside world again, so their children are brought up either by the family or in a state-run children's home. Either way, many of the women in Lard Yao never see their children again.

If a woman was pregnant when she was arrested, the baby would be born in the prison, often in the chair where the 'intimate' strip searches were carried out, but possibly in the hospital wing. Young children and babies arrested with their mothers can stay in Lard Yao until they are three years old. If no one comes to take them, such children are sent to a state-run orphanage, and the mothers will never see them again. There are many sad sights in Lard Yao, but watching a child being taken away from its mother and walked out of the gate was one of the saddest.

The children are kept in the building euphemistically called the 'nursery' and are tended to by Thai prisoners, whilst their mothers are working in the factories. Some of these workers were brutal women who often took a sadistic pleasure in harassing their charges. One day I went there to donate something and saw a toddler tied by her ankle to a pillar. The nursery women had made a rope and tied the toddler to it because she kept crying. She had ugly rattan welts all over her legs. The women whipped the children with two-foot-long rattan sticks.

Because overcrowding is a problem, babies and toddlers sleep on the floor, with their mother wrapped around their bodies, trying to keep away from the person squashed next to them. Skin conditions and sickness are common. For the first three years of their lives they never see cars, or shops, or men, or anything most people consider normal. They receive an authentic prison experience before they are old enough to walk.

The library was a small, shelved room next to one of the main offices and, like the bakery, it was another of the prison showpieces. With no newspapers and no access to the media, most people developed a passion for reading books. I read everything from the instructions on a tube of toothpaste to *Papillon*, by Henri Charrière. There was an excellent collection of books donated by fellow and former inmates, over many years. Mostly I read about imprisonment and crime stories, but would escape with travel books and spy tales. I was in Lard Yao for over six months before I could concentrate on reading anything as demanding as a book. My mind was in such a whirl that anything that didn't demand immediate attention was dismissed. I watched others jealously as they disappeared into a good book, hoping that I might rekindle my own appetite for reading. Eventually I did and every evening I began escaping into Brian Keenan's *An Evil Cradling*, his account of his ordeal in Lebanon, where he was held hostage for years by terrorists. In comparison with what he had gone through I realised that I had nothing to moan about. I was not a hostage; I deserved to be where I was. His book gave me a great deal of strength and without it I doubt I would have been able to endure what lay ahead.

The woman working in the library came looking for me one day, telling me to take out as many books as I could store because the library was going to be closed for a while. There was no reason. It closed for months. 'It is not tidy,' was the common excuse. 'It needs organising to make it look orderly.' When it finally reopened most of the good books had gone. A few old romance paperbacks sat neatly on a few shelves and a pile of Bibles remained. The rumours circulated that the books had been taken by a group of American missionaries who sold them in one of the second-hand bookshops in the city. 'It's not good for you to think too much,' someone told us. 'It gives you new ideas.'

During my time in Lard Yao, hundreds of prisoners became mentally ill due to the stress placed upon them, but there had to be something seriously wrong with a prisoner before she was allowed basic hospital care. Winnie was a beautiful, charismatic, 23-year-old Eritrean, who looked like a model. She had a quiet, polite demeanour and those who didn't hate her immediately for her beauty took to her instantly. A year after her arrest, Winnie received a 40-year sentence. She had no embassy, no family, no friends and no money. The man who had claimed he loved her, the man whose drugs she had been carrying, had abandoned her and no one came to see her while she was inside. Rarely did she receive any letters. Emotionally, she began deteriorating and continued doing so until it was impossible to hold a normal conversation with her. Rapidly, she lost her stunning good looks and in their place appeared the gaze of a Lard Yao lunatic. Winnie was close to losing her mind and is not expected to survive her sentence. The common denominator with most of these stories? Men. Most, if not all, the women on drugs charges in Lard Yao had been recruited or duped by a man. Few, if any, of the women worked for themselves.

⋆

My sleeping space in Pyleen was a few inches bigger than my space over the previous years. The 'mother of the room' shoved me over and told a scrawny young girl to sleep in between my neighbour and me. Lui Lee and I looked in horror at what lay in between us; the girl was wild, filthy and rather large. Her name was Ghoonk, meaning 'shrimp'.

The following morning I decided to clean her up. I got her straggly hair washed and cut, bought her pyjamas and a bag of toiletries – if she was going to sleep next to me all night I wanted her to be reasonably clean.

Ghoonk was 18 years old and in many ways reminded me of myself at that age. She was one of Thailand's many street orphans and had been living under a bridge in Bangkok. She was serving a short sentence for possession of heroin after developing a habit on the street. She couldn't read or write so each evening we would have classes. She began calling me *mare* – mother.

There was also a separate class held most mornings for illiterate Thais, and Ghoonk, although under some duress, attended daily. Back in the room, after 'class', she would tell me to lie down. 'I'll wash your hair, mum.' I lay down while she scratched my back and my head with her fingernails.

Two blind kittens were dumped in a box on the bakery step and Ghoonk took care of them. After a few weeks the kittens were in great health and she would come running out of the room calling for them, 'Dam-Dam-Dam, Sua-Sua-Sua.' She loved them. Ghoonk was bright, and amazing and absorbing to watch. Holding a rat by the tail she would run around terrorizing others; she spent most days scrubbing the concrete around the wash area, and was always laughing. Nothing in Lard Yao fazed her.

Six months after I was shoved over to make her a space on the floor, Ghoonk was put on a list of names to be transferred out to a smaller prison in the provinces. As the guard called her name at five in the morning, she broke down. Her body shook uncontrollably as she cried. When she refused to leave the room, two guards came in, prised her away from me and I never saw nor heard about her again. It's not a moral story, just a sad one.

In Lard Yao most of the prisoners were uneducated but there were also others whose education far surpassed that of many of the officers. They could barely grasp how their social position had suddenly changed now that they were amongst some of the most leprous and cancerous individuals in Bangkok. Many of them had committed fraud or minor drug or victimless offences that would have merited non-custodial sentences in the UK.

One very bright woman, however, was there for murdering three of her husbands by hammering nails through their heads. In each of the cases, she claimed his life insurance. She had been a keen gardener and all three husbands had been buried in her garden. Before she could claim the third husband's life cover, the police dug him up and charged her with multiple murder. She received the death penalty, but had it reduced to life imprisonment eight years after being arrested. Like the cannibal before her, she had a job to suit her crime. She was Lard Yao's head gardener.

What does prison do to a person after a number of years? You become aggressive, brooding, angry, vengeful, spiteful, profane and frustrated. Any adjective, really, that describes hostility. Hostility and aggression bred like bacilli in Lard Yao and I was amazed at how volatile I had become.

A French woman arrived in the prison on a drug possession charge and received a five-year sentence. Five years in Lard Yao is the equivalent of a weekend break and 'the Slug', as she became known, got none of the sympathy she thought she deserved. For over 20 years the Slug had lived with a raging heroin habit and now, in middle age, her whole body was a mass of green, infected craters. She was sly, selfish, manipulating and devious. For some reason Moo, the woman who worked in the hospital, felt sorry for her and spent hours massaging and preparing special food for her. She also stole medication for her.

This continued for weeks until a guard noticed the medication was going missing. Moo informed the Slug she could no longer take care of her. In turn, the Slug went straight to the prison office, telling the guards that Moo had been giving her sleeping pills and antidepressants. Immediately, Moo was put into the *soi* for the next three months.

How could the Slug do this? Daily, I grew more and more irritated. Every time I saw her, I let her know in no uncertain terms how I felt. When I was sitting up a flight of stairs one day, the Slug walked passed me, avoiding eye contact, but as soon as she was at the top, she looked down and said simply: 'You are a fucking dog.'

It took me about two seconds to grab hold of her. I wanted to kill her. It really felt like I wanted her dead. I hit her, hard and fast, and her nose began bleeding. I almost threw her over the balcony but my rage subsided almost as quickly as it had appeared and I left her. It never bothered me at all that, yet again, I had just fought with another woman. In prison you become the thing you abhor. Fighting was normal. Fighting was acceptable.

Too many convicts succumbed to illness and disease in Lard Yao, the predictable result of dreadful conditions and even worse hygiene. Most drugs can be purchased inside the prison and, if someone was ill they could apply to see a man they called 'the doctor'. It was a loose term. He came in most weeks and would quite happily write out prescriptions for the sick prisoner.

Once you had a prescription you would send it out with a visitor to buy the medication for you. Hopefully your visitor would return to the prison with the medication and hand it in at the gate. Then you had to wait until the medication was issued by the hospital and you could then start taking it. From getting ill to getting the medication to treat it normally took several weeks. Sometimes you could buy the medication directly from a 'friend' in Lard Yao. Pills were common inside and anyone with money usually kept a large bag of antibiotics and painkillers. I always had a bag myself but I never managed to keep its contents very long. There always seemed to be someone close to me who needed them more than I did, and it didn't take long for word to get around that I was the sucker for anyone with a hard luck story, illness or infection.

One morning, while I waited for the hoisting of the national flag, I saw a group of girls standing around another girl squatting on the ground. Her head was down and she held the side of her neck with her hands. The girl's friends were collecting something from the back of that girl's neck and appeared to be throwing leaves into the bushes. I went over to look.

A large hole had exploded on the top of what looked like a tennis ball under her skin and, as the girls applied pressure, a thick stream of pea-green puss and blood shot out. The girl's friends gathered leaves to try and gather up the puss as it gushed out in a heavy stream. The poor girl squatted and screamed in pain. I almost threw up. When Thais talk about boils they do not mean spots.

The girl with the boil on her neck came to me three times a day for over a week and I gave her my antibiotics. She had no money and never received a visit. She was nicknamed 'Boil on the Neck'. I was glad to give her something to help the infection, which did clear up eventually.

Illegal drugs were available in Lard Yao but were not as common as most people imagine simply because they were expensive. The guards made a lot of money bringing masses of things like snuff into the prison, buying bags of it outside at four baht per bag and selling it in the prison for anything up to 1,000 baht. There were few women who could afford to pay the high prices for snuff, never mind anything else, so drug-taking was at a surprising minimum.

As I mentioned earlier, in July 1996, Patricia Hussain was away from Lard Yao for five weeks. Before she left, she received a letter from England telling her that her seven-year-old son had been 'collected' from school by two men and driven around Manchester for a few hours before being brought home. This was someone's way of telling Patricia that if she went ahead and testified against the drug barons, they had access to her son, so she should think twice about what she was planning to do. She went anyway.

'It's not revenge, Sandra,' she said. 'If any of those blokes had sent ten quid to my kids or even written to me after I was arrested I'd keep my mouth shut, but they acted as though they had never known me.' Did 30 men go to prison for the sake of a tenner? That's how she made it sound.

In October 1996 the Queen and the Duke of Edinburgh paid a state visit to King Bhumibol and Queen Sirikit. Secretly, I hoped that the Queen would approach the King of Thailand in a way that no other person could and exert some influence on my case. All I wanted to do was go home. I would hopefully be able to transfer at the beginning of 1997 but I prayed for more than that. In dreams I saw myself being flown home on Her Majesty's private plane. Her visit came and went and I remained where I was.

On my completion of the mandatory four years in Bangkok, a representative from the British Embassy came to the prison one day and asked me if I wanted to transfer home. Did I want to? What on earth did they think? Four years had finally gone by and I was desperate to get home. 'Yes, I definitely want to go!' I really didn't think I would get to this stage. Part of me believed I might be either dead or insane. Well, at least I wasn't dead.

The woman brought a single form with her, rolled it into a tube and pushed it through the bars. 'Sign on the dotted line,' she said, with a smile. It was the easiest thing I have ever done in my life. Quickly, I signed and she confirmed that my parents had sent over the money for my air ticket. 'The rest,' she said, 'is just formalities.'

Under the terms of the prisoner exchange treaty between Thailand and Britain, prisoners with a sentence less than life are eligible to return to a British jail after serving four years in Thailand. Those serving life have to wait eight years. The same decision would apply if Thai prisoners were in jail in Britain; they would be able to apply for a transfer to Thailand, although no one had ever heard of a Thai prisoner transferring from the UK.

I was told I would probably have to serve half my remaining sentence before being eligible for parole. Tony Blair looked set to become the next Prime Minister and, under a Labour Government, I really didn't believe they would make me serve half of the huge sentence remaining. *No*, I thought, *I'll be OK once I get back on home soil.*

I had already seen Americans return home under transfer treaties and they were all released within just a few months of being transferred. Most European countries reduced the sentence upon transfer and even the Australians, who don't have a treaty, support prisoner pardons, once the prisoner has served around the same time they would have been sentenced to had they been arrested in Australia.

The decision to send me home to finish my sentence was announced by the Thai Justice Ministry permanent secretary Kukiat Sunthornbura on 6 March. The move was essentially a humanitarian one, rather than being lenient towards drug offenders. I had no idea how long it would take before I actually transferred, but I was ecstatic knowing that I would be leaving Lard Yao.

On 17 April 1997, a Thai court granted me a transfer to Britain, where I would serve the rest of my 25-year sentence. I could not believe it. I was simply stunned. I would be transferring from Bangkok to Holloway Prison within the next eight to 10 weeks. Part of me still doubted if the day would actually arrive.

I was bursting inside. I was leaving this place, this horrible prison that had changed me so much.

*

At the beginning of May someone from the embassy told me that I would be leaving on 4 June. I sat and counted the days. 'Oh my God, that's just five weeks to go.'

The embassy woman looked at me and smiled, but advised caution. 'It could be a long five weeks, Sandra,' she said, 'so try to stay as calm about it as you can.'

Five weeks? A long time? No way! It's going to fly by. I think I was the happiest person in Lard Yao.

I had been sentenced for over a year and it was time to submit an application to the king for a royal pardon. My parents paid for the lawyer to make the submission, and a month after my sentencing they had arranged for one of the best lawyers in Thailand to organise it for me. When I was called out to the lawyers' room, my legal representative sat waiting for me. He was the lawyer who had defended Robert; he had now come to gather the details to go on my pardon application. He sat there, smiling, as if it was the most natural thing in the world to be working with the person he worked against for three years. To be fair, he was very professional and moved as quickly as he could to get the application in before I left Bangkok. There were many ironies in Bangkok and this was one of them.

Every week for three years I had scrubbed the bakery with a couple of the other girls but on my last cleaning day, Old Mother Penis was there to oversee the cleaning process. Because of this, many of the other girls who worked in the bakery decided it would be a good idea to help out to keep her happy. I decided I didn't need to bother with the scrubbing. I left the others to show off their skills.

There were so many kittens in Lard Yao that I spent the afternoon catching cats and taking them to the hospital, where I injected them with some feline contraceptive I had had sent in. Old Mother Penis went crazy and started throwing everything she could lay her hands on at me, and calling me a 'full of shit, lazy wanker of a European'. The barrage of abuse continued. 'You let Thai people clean your mess up. You work here, you eat Thai rice, you should help them work!' I thought she was going to burst.

After years of working in that stifling heat and filth, I could no longer keep quiet and told her that I thought she was a foul-mouthed, ignorant, corrupt swamp-reptile and no wonder her husband spent all his money and spare time in the brothels. Naturally, I lost my job in the bakery, but she lost a great deal of credibility in front of all the bakery girls and I walked away delighted to be leaving that horror story of a woman behind. It was a great relief being able to tell that slave-driver what I thought of her, but she sent me off to the office for my punishment. Over the following weeks she did her best to do what she could to make my life a misery. It didn't work; nothing could dampen my spirits now.

The guard asked me what sort of punishment I wanted for being rude to Old Mother Penis. Stopping my mail was no use because I would be out of Lard Yao soon. Two Thais were standing outside in the sun so I suggested I join them for the afternoon, as my punishment. It was boiling hot but knowing that I was leaving I was suddenly determined to go back to the UK with a suntan. I stood there with two girls who'd been caught in a short-time hotel. That afternoon I got other prisoners to chuck us blocks of ice and we stood there, sucking massive ice cubes, having a laugh and pretending we were on holiday. Lard Yao no longer mattered.

Being kicked out of the bakery meant that I had nowhere to go during the day times so I spent the following weeks sitting under the washing lines. I gave away most of my possessions; my bucket and my scrubbing brush, all my stamps and clothes apart from one change of clothes. I gave away noodles, bags of chillies and dried fish. I got rid of my shower bowl and most of my toiletries. I kept one small pillow for sleeping. My life was devoid of 'things' but it made my leaving feel more real.

Dear Mum and Dad

I've done my time. I'm coming home. I am so relieved! This will be my last letter to you from Bangkok. I can't believe my turn has finally come and I am coming home at last. What an amazing birthday present to be finally leaving Lard Yao. Everything will seem so easy after being here for so long. I am so excited and I don't know whether I am laughing or crying. This past four years has been a long time and I thought it would never pass. Without your help I don't think it would have passed. Thank you. Without you both I really don't know if I could have made it through…

See you soon

Sandra

Letter home, May 1997

I turned 32 at the end of May and organised a 'feast' to celebrate my last birthday in Thailand. But my teeth had been so bad for the previous couple of years that I could no longer eat anything harder than boiled rice. The girls made wonderful spicy dishes but I couldn't eat any of them.

Those last few weeks were, in their own way, sad times. As soon as I heard I was leaving I wanted everyone to leave with me, I wanted them all to come along. The women I had known and the women I had not known, the ones I had liked and the ones I had loathed; I wanted them all to leave too. Over the years I had watched so many people exit the prison and wondered whether my turn would ever come; now that it was imminent I didn't want to go alone. I also knew how it felt to watch someone leave and I really didn't want anyone to watch me go.

I could hardly bear the thought of leaving my cat, little Upstairs. He had been born in Lard Yao and this was his home. Who would prepare his sardines and rice twice a day and stand guard over him as he ate? Who would scratch the scabs off his tummy, as I had done for so long? He had been my only loyal friend since Karyn had left. He was the only thing I missed from The Lard Yao

Correctional Institute. I said goodbye to him and it broke my heart to leave him behind. He died about a year later, still only a young cat.

The morning I was due to leave arrived without ceremony. A group of reporters gathered outside the gate and I was held inside until mid-afternoon because the prison hated media coverage. I had longed to walk through the gates that led outside, but a van was brought into the prison instead and guards surrounded me.

'Sandra,' said the prison commander, as I left, 'if you lie about my prison or any of my officers you will get bad karma. Do you understand what I am talking about?'

I told her that 'yes', I did understand, and that I didn't need to lie about her prison because it was already bad enough. The prison officials were desperate to have the last word.

A Thai television company arrived and I was told to sit down in front of a camera. I gave an interview in Thai, which went out on the evening news that night all over Thailand. Ahead of my departure, reporters shouted questions at me as I left Thailand.

'I feel good,' I replied, 'but they won't let me speak to you.' That was it; there was nothing else to say. It was good to leave.

On Wednesday 4 June, I flew out of Thailand en route to Britain to serve the remainder of my 25-year sentence. Guarded by four British prison officers, I left on a British Airways flight, to arrive at Heathrow Airport the following morning.

I flew back with three other Britons who were also serving long sentences for trafficking heroin. Kevin had been sentenced to 25 years, Andy and Peter had both been sentenced to life, but their sentences had been commuted to 40 years by the 1996 amnesty. All three were aged under 40. Kevin had been friends with Robert inside and completely ignored me. Peter and I were handcuffed together from immigration on to the plane. We said little to each other. We were both in shock and both a bit scared of the grunting officers escorting us. Our passports were stamped: 'Deported

Thailand 4 June 1997. Convicted of trafficking in narcotics' followed by the relevant terms and dates.

We swooped down over London. The buildings were a familiar battleship-grey, mirroring the sky. My heart pounded. The captain's voice rasped over the tannoy, 'Prepare for landing.'

I had prepared for four years, four months and four days.

ELEVEN

Kangaroos

Drug smuggler Sandra Gregory was last night spending her first night in a British jail after being transferred from Thailand to complete her 25-year sentence. The 32-year-old teacher was taken straight to London's Holloway Prison, where she will be assessed before transferring to another UK jail... Last night she was getting used to being behind bars in Britain.

6 June 1997, *The Herald*

The three men travelling alongside me were taken off the plane first. Then it was my turn. Two huge policemen, wearing bullet-proof jackets and leather gun holsters, entered the cabin. 'Don't give us any hassle and we won't bother you,' barked one, 'and don't speak to the press outside either.'

I couldn't get over the size of these men; they were massive, hairy and gruff. During the previous few years the only men I had seen were either visitors or Thais and the Thai men were usually quiet and much smaller than me.

I was due to go to Holloway Prison, but it was so early in the morning that their reception staff had yet to come on duty so I was taken instead to Wandsworth Prison, along with the other three. Because Wandsworth is a prison for men, I could not be locked in a cell, so I was placed in a small, windowless room with cracked, flaking emulsion.

'Fucking hell, we had a fucking ball...' said a voice.

'Those fucking Thais...' said another. 'The fucking women will fuck you sideways...'

The voices were aggressive, loud and rude. It was the conversations of the guards who had travelled to Bangkok to collect us. The shouting continued and I felt like an unsavoury piece of meat. I sat listening to the crude voices around me, hoping that I had made the right decision in transferring back.

I was removed from Wandsworth at around 8 o'clock in the morning and as I left I caught a glimpse of the men I had transferred home with. They were locked together in a cell, looking as shocked by their surroundings as I was. Peter waved to me and wished me luck. I waved back. I would need it.

The prison van rumbled on. It was impossible for me to stop smiling as we drove through London; it was clean and orderly, historic and wonderfully familiar. I felt like a day-tripper.

They were still in the process of releasing some women when we arrived at Holloway, so we waited outside until they had finished. I marvelled at the array of bizarre-looking women and even the clothes they were wearing. Nose studs and rings and tattoos; everyone had them. Most of the women wore their hair cropped short. Jeans hung loosely from their waists. Everyone had tiny shirts.

I felt stupid. There I was in my tropical, cream-coloured linen suit and suntan. Two guards stood outside the van smoking.

'You know, love, you'll need to be strong in there,' the female guard said to me. 'When I signed up for this job I got them to put a clause in my contract saying I'd never be posted to Holloway. I told them I'd resign if they tried to make me work with this lot. I've worked some of the toughest nicks in the country but I'd never work in Holloway.'

My chest heaved. It felt like I was breathing underwater.

The male guard stood there smirking. 'Little girl,' he said, staring right at me, 'they're gonna eat you alive in there.'

*

Once inside the prison I was transfixed. It seemed so calm. All I remember saying is, 'Oh, wow!' There was hot water coming straight out of the wall! I had forgotten about proper plumbing; everything seemed so modern. People were talking in fast, snappy rhythms, joking sarcastically with each other. I felt like a foreigner. I *was* a foreigner.

'You can't have mirrors in here,' said the guard who searched me, 'you can't have spray perfume. You can't have *that* either. You could hurt someone with *that*. What is *that* anyway?' Just about everything in the carrier bag I had brought with me except my book of photographs and some mascara was confiscated.

Are you suicidal? No. Have you got a drug addiction? No. Do you need a doctor? No. Are you suffering from emotional problems? No. Do you self-harm? No.

'Look,' said the officer, 'you can't say "no" to everything.'

I was so unconcerned by anything they said and quite overjoyed at how pleasant everything seemed compared with Lard Yao that I stood there grinning like a village idiot. Immediately they sent me to the medical unit, which is more or less for psychiatric cases and people with serious illnesses.

I was given a prison number – BJ 4218 – and the reception officer escorted me downstairs. We passed through the prison and she pointed to a shelf-full of material. It was exactly the same as the material we wore on remand in Lard Yao: coarse, brown cotton.

'No way,' I said. 'There's no way we have to wear that, surely? Not here?'

'Don't be so stupid,' she answered. 'That's what you're going to put on your bed.'

One woman sat in a corner of the medical unit, rocking, squirming and twitching; another paced her cell, talking to the walls and shouting at the shadows. Most of them were covered in red welts and swollen scars. I wasn't checked by a doctor so I can only assume they thought I was a bit potty.

My first night in Holloway I bought a £2 telephone card and called my parents. 'How do you do this again?' I made the mistake of asking one of the other inmates. She realised I had not spoken to them for four years, since September 1993, so she shouted to all her friends to listen in to the conversation.

I dialled the number, shaking, the handset pressed against my face. My mum answered and my dad was on the other line.

'It's me.'

For a minute or two that's all I managed. I couldn't get anything past the lump in my throat. Their voices wavered and I could feel them both trembling with delight. I could almost touch them. There was also a strange sense of pain. I was ecstatic for sure. But it was so much more than that.

My mum told me she had booked a visit and would be down to see me the following day. But I wasn't ready to see anyone and didn't want her to see me in there.

'If you do come, Mum,' I said, 'don't look at anyone else; just look at me. Don't look at the other women, they're a bit weird-looking.'

The following day she arrived. Most of the other women in the visiting room looked quite normal, probably a lot more normal than I did. It was me who was the freak in Holloway. There were no bars to separate my mum and me, and for the first time in years I walked across an open room and hugged her properly. We squeezed each other tightly. For years I had been picturing her. She looked beautiful but traumatised and scared.

I was kept in the medical unit for two weeks and the amount of space in my cell overwhelmed me at first. 'How many people share in here?' I asked the guard. She just laughed and bolted the door. This wasn't possible. I had a huge cell all to myself! Even my bed looked far too big for one.

Other women called out of the windows to their friends or screamed through the hatches for a light and I sat, stunned, listening to all the new noise. The prison was electric. Yet, for the first few weeks I felt quite lonely. My new surroundings were very stark and all the heavy doors were locked shut. There would be no strolling through the prison in Holloway like I had been used to in Lard Yao.

I was freezing and I missed sharing with hundreds of other women, and missed having someone to talk to. Most of the time I just wrapped myself in one of the green prison blankets.

When the wing was unlocked I quickly noticed that none of the inmates knelt down when they spoke to the officers. How should I act with them? I really couldn't figure out the etiquette at all, so I did my best to avoid them. This continued for months and many of the guards thought I was an arrogant cow. But I was so used to the system in Lard Yao that it took time to adapt. For years I had spoken Thai; now I had to speak English. It was then I realised I no longer felt truly British.

10 June 1997

Dear Mum and Dad

I can't believe how quickly mail comes through here and the number of letters we are allowed to send out. It's great. I think I was in shock when I saw you, I found it hard to speak... the food here has had a terrible effect on my stomach and I didn't think I would make it through the hour-long visit. It was embarrassing having to see you here. I am so sorry for all that I have put you through. I don't want Granny and Pa-Pa to see me in here, or in any other prison. I can't even bring myself to telephone them...

Sandra

After my two weeks on the medical wing, I was moved upstairs into the main prison. What a shock. Thankfully the authorities had given me a fortnight to settle in the relative quiet of the medical unit...

Up on 'normal location', I was surrounded by sheer madness

and chaos; everything appeared crazy, as if the place had been bred for mayhem. Holloway was home to the biggest bunch of nut-cases, psychos, robbers, thieves, druggies, gang members, whackos and dysfunctional lunatics I had come across. The noise was unbelievable. Music blared, there was continual shouting from wing to wing, women argued and fought with each other. The constant rattle of keys on chains sounded more like chainsaws humming and the bolting and slamming of iron doors never ceased.

The routine of the prisoners was alien and confusing. It was both thrilling yet awful, shocking but somehow comforting. I tried hard to fit into this new world of walls and weirdos. I wanted to understand these people and the strange lingo they all spoke. I hadn't expected to feel such an alien when I came home, but this was not the 'home' I had remembered. Graffiti covered all the walls of the dormitory I now shared with three other women, and the air was grey with fag smoke. Candles made out of sanitary towels were stuck to the ceiling, leaving black burns all over. Blobs of toothpaste were shrivelled everywhere. It's used as glue to hold pictures on the walls because it sets so hard; every white blob was a reminder of those prisoners who had come before.

This was Beirut. It was loud, harsh and aggressive. I did my best to avoid having too much to do with anyone; the shock of Holloway was overwhelming.

'Swing a line,' someone shouted. 'We're rolling tonight.' Or, 'There's a kanger coming.'

Prison jargon baffled me. It took me forever to work out that 'kanger' was slang for an officer or guard, as in 'the kangaroos', the 'screws'. At night I would just sit in my dorm watching and listening to the three women alongside me, trying to figure out the language, the routine and how the prison ran.

The plusses began to outweigh the shock: I had newspapers to read, a radio to listen to and access to the telephone. Slowly, suspiciously, I came round to my new environment. In Lard Yao we had been allowed very little; no board games, cards or ball games. No telephone calls, newspapers, no radios, television, personal stereos or anything electrical. No one was allowed jewellery or watches, or personal clothing. There was no smoking, no gym or educational facilities. There were no chaplains, probation, personal officers, ombudsman or anyone else to make the misery of the place a little easier. Holloway, with all these amenities, began to seem fairly normal.

One afternoon a woman set herself on fire and suffered third degree burns as a result. When she was returned from hospital four months later, the prison authorities charged her with 'damaging Her Majesty's property', and she lost her evening association with other prisoners for a week.

'Shut the door, Gregory,' said the senior officer on the landing, a Glaswegian, calling me into her office. She sat down at her desk while I stood over her. What do you do in front of an officer? Should I kneel on the floor? Should I stand where I was or sit in the empty chair? I panicked. I felt awkward standing over someone in her position, a sign of insolence in Lard Yao. I sat down.

'Who the fuck told you to sit down?' she screamed. 'Who do you think you are, you arrogant fuck? Stand up in my fucking office!'

My attitude, she proceeded to tell me, was unacceptable and belligerent. Even my cell was a mess. It had taken me weeks to realise we had to make the beds each morning. My blanket was my first in more than four years. What did she expect? Christ, she was an aggressive cow. My legs trembled.

To be fair to the governors and many of the officers in Holloway, most of them treated me as fairly as the regulations allowed. Soon the chaos began to make sense. Mandatory drug tests, cell searches, the new terminology and prison protocol became a part of my life in much the same way as Lard Yao had got into my blood.

'It can do what?' I said to the woman on the education block when I saw my first computer. I began to feel a part of this strange new England where inmates were encouraged to learn. Work in the library kept me busy for a while before I got a job in the gym, and I worked there seven days a week, training constantly. I was fit! It was incredible. Inside, the gym was the best job to have.

The gym staff explained the workings of the prison: the rules and, generally, how the penal system in the UK worked. The staff's approach and general attitude can either make or break a prisoner and, with their help, I settled down and complied with everything that was expected of me.

Long-term inmates (LTIs) were permitted a bird and cage so immediately I requested a parrot. 'No,' was the response so I applied for a pair of lovebirds, the second smallest species of parrot. The prison agreed. I still had a long time to serve and the birds would be perfect company. Syd and Flo arrived on 31 August 1997, the day that Princess Diana died.

The two yellow, somewhat wild lovebirds took over the single cell I had recently been placed in and they had the run of the place. They would fly around at all times of day and night, devouring all manner of things with their massive beaks, at every opportunity. Occasionally they fought and drew blood. I began to think I'd made a mistake. Couldn't I get anything right? Still, I loved them anyway.

There was another girl on my wing with birds. Her name was Sharon Carr.

'Every night I see the devil in my dreams, sometimes even in my mirror, but I realise it was just me,' Sharon confided in her diary after the killing of 18-year-old Katie Rackliffe. Sharon was aged 12 when she murdered. She was 17 when she was sentenced to be detained at Her Majesty's pleasure, in 1997. The murdered girl had been stabbed at least 29 times.

In the years after the killing, Sharon kept a diary and wrote poems and notes about the killing. In one note, she wrote: 'I am a killer. Killing is my business – and business is good.' She was already serving a sentence for a knife attack on a 13-year-old committed two years to the day after Katie Rackliffe's murder.

One day Sharon asked me if she could borrow Syd because she wanted to try him with her female to see if they would mate. I was still quite trusting at that time and I lent her both of the birds. I didn't want them separated.

'There's blood, Sandra,' Sharon told me when I returned that afternoon to pick them up.

Blood? For fuck's sake. When I got them back to my cell they were traumatized and bloody. Flo held her right leg up and neither bird would come out of the box, lined with sanitary towels, in which they both slept. Flo's leg was broken and a guard took her to a vet. Syd didn't leave the box for over a week.

Much later I heard that Sharon had held a cockfighting session with my birds. Flo never stood on her right leg again.

Holloway never ceased to amaze me. Or scare me. Women generally do not rape each other, but it is not totally unheard of. In Lard Yao, rape was something that happened in the *soi* but in the UK women 'de-crutch' each other if they think someone is holding a package of drugs. One day a group of women heard that a girl in Holloway had a package of drugs 'crutched' and they wanted it. They waited until evening association and got the girl in a dormitory alone.

Two women stood by the door, making sure no one came in and the others held the girl down. They ripped the package from inside her but didn't leave it at that; they raped her with lumps of wood and left her in such a state that the ambulance crew had to come onto the wing with a stretcher. Rape amongst women is one of the most shocking things I heard about, but was rarely an act of pleasure or torture. It's usually more about drugs.

*

Heather was a bright, obsessive and possessive woman, and when I refused her advances she turned nasty and tried her very best to make trouble for me. She began spreading rumours about me telling a group of Jamaican girls – Yardies – that I was a grass. In prison, the last thing you want to be known as is a 'grass'.

Patricia Hussain, the Manchester girl with me in Lard Yao, had testified against some Jamaican men she had been working for and Heather told the Yardies that it had been me that had grassed on their men. The situation got very tense and I was always watching my back. The Yardies were out to get me.

I bought a large, silver ring with a big moonstone in it from a girl, and I planned to use it if the Yardies decided to take me on. (Usually, when fights started, they took place in the changing rooms, and I wanted to be prepared.) Then I just waited. Rings with large stones are classed as weapons in prison for precisely that reason. One day, when I was called to reception for something, I can't remember what, the guard saw the ring and pulled it off my finger. She stuck it in a bag.

'You can send that out with the next person who comes to visit.'

Next on my visiting list was my mum, who was going off on holiday for five weeks and had come to see me before she went away, so I sent the ring out to her.

Years before my dad had bought her a big, silver ring with a moonstone and, as a child, I had marvelled at the size of it. When my mum saw the ring I was forced to send out, she slipped her own ring off and passed it over the table to me in the visiting room. 'Take it,' she said, 'and wear it while I'm away.'

I didn't want it. I didn't want any part of her or my family in prison with me. I tried to explain to her but she insisted. Ever so carefully I slipped the silver ring onto my finger, hoping none of the guards were watching. It didn't look right on my skinny fingers, far too cumbersome, but she wanted me to take it.

When I was a young girl, she told me, I always got hysterical whenever she left me. She would give me something of her own and tell me to look after it until she returned. It always calmed me and she could leave without getting upset. My mum smiled and clasped my hands tightly. 'Take it. I'll be back soon.'

I left her ring in my cell, next to the bed, because I didn't want to wear it on the landings and it also kept slipping from my fingers. One day I got a room spin – a cell search – and the only thing the guards found was my mum's ring.

'What's this?' said the guard, holding it between her fat fingers. My heart sank. 'Oh God, no. Please don't take that. Take anything but that ring.'

She wanted to know where I had got it from so I told her. 'Oh,' she said, her face twitching, 'smuggled contraband.'

The ring was duly confiscated and taken to security and when my mother got back from her holiday I told her what had happened. She sounded a little upset. She wrote to Holloway asking for it to be returned and they told her she had to prove it was hers. After protracted correspondence it was returned.

For the remainder of my time in Holloway I was seated at the 'observation table' in the visiting room, whenever someone came to see me. The Jamaican girls quickly realised I was not the girl from Thailand who had grassed on their men and the whole situation was defused.

Months passed and I became one of the prisoners who had been in Holloway the longest. My first New Year in a British prison passed, and I grew accustomed to the lifestyle. The food was stodgy and bland, I slept awkwardly, I disliked most of the other women, I couldn't understand the workings of the system and the guards were a pain in the arse. I was now a fully paid-up member of Her Majesty's Long-Serving, Bored-out-of-My-Mind Offenders Club.

Observing the relationships that took place between staff and prisoners relieved part of my boredom. Affairs were common in Holloway and I remember asking one girl, who had been having sex with an officer for months, how she managed to get away with it.

'We meet in a certain place every fucking week and we do it there. It's foolproof really; nobody comes by there except one of the governors!'

Normally, at lunchtime, I was unlocked before anyone else so that I could set up the equipment in the gym for the afternoon session. One day, walking down a landing, while most of the others were locked up, I heard shouting coming from a cell. I looked through the cell-door hatch and saw two people inside – an inmate and a member of staff. The inmate shouted at me: 'Go and get Officer X', the guard who had forgotten to get them out.

I went to the office and told the officer that Jo in cell number seven was asking to be unlocked. The guard jumped up, dashed to the cell and unlocked it. The two people inside were dressing themselves and I asked Jo what she was doing. 'Having a shag,' she replied, 'what does it look like?'

I applied for a job outside the prison gate, sweeping up and fixing the small garden. 'No.' The authorities told me I was too political, too high-profile and my sentence was too long for me to be considered anything other than a serious security risk. Me? A security risk? What the hell did they think I was going to do? Tie my bed sheets together and escape through the front disguised as a prison chaplain? Someone had been watching too many movies. That was when I realised how seriously they viewed me as a prisoner. The length of my sentence in Lard Yao had been so normal as to render itself uneventful. Now I was top of the pile, almost Category A security. It was ludicrous.

One day at the end of April 1998, I was not unlocked after the lunchtime lock-in, as was the norm. *What's happening here?* I thought.

An officer stopped by. 'You're going to Foston Hall tomorrow.'

Later that afternoon, one of the gym officers took me down to the gym. He looked a little concerned.

'This is a security move, Sandra,' he said, in reference to my move. He continued, 'I don't know what it's about but security have either got it in for you, or the gym staff have, and you're out of here.'

TWELVE

Making Trouble

Dear Mum and Dad

My mind won't settle, I've had the same problem for days and I think it's from having to swallow so much negative emotion all the time. If I make a fuss about anything though, they will ship me out to God only knows where. I think it would be better to be doing what they think I'm doing rather than them simply thinking I am up to something. I have become a product of the system... survival is a lonely process.

Sandra

Letter home, June 1998

When I first arrived in Holloway, someone warned me not to get too settled in any prison because the authorities have a way of snatching your life away from under you, when you least expect it. It's just a way to remind you where you are and who is in control. Was this simply paranoia, fear and loneliness talking? I didn't believe them until I was transferred from Holloway to Foston Hall in Derbyshire, in April 1998.

One day everything was going fine and the next I was in handcuffs, being driven to yet another prison. The only brisk snippet of information I had been given was from the baffled gym officer at Holloway. This was 'a security move, Sandra'.

I was placed in a cell roughly the size of a large cupboard alongside two teenage girls. There was no running water and no toilet.

It was designed to disempower. 'You might be able to sort them two out for us,' said the guard as she was leaving.

Piss off, I thought. I might have no idea why I had been brought to Foston Hall but I wasn't planning on sorting out any of their problems. As the cell was so small and the three of us were banged up for roughly 20 hours each day, I had to ask someone to take care of Syd and Flo; I couldn't bear to see them caged up all day alongside me.

I couldn't seem to stop crying. *How had I imagined for one minute that the British prison authorities would like me? Why had I been brought here? What had I done?* My mind buzzed as I tried to fathom the logic behind my sudden move. I was just another package for their warehouse.

I put in request and complaint forms by the handful, and applied to see the governor, board of visitors and anyone else I could think of. I needed to know why I had been taken there under such tight security. A few days after my arrival an officer told me the reason. 'You were suspected of being too familiar with a member of staff in Holloway and they wanted you moved out.'

That was it. I couldn't believe it. After months of trying to work out how exactly I should be with the British prison officers, I had obviously got it completely wrong. Maybe I should have dropped to my knees every time I wanted to speak to one of them. Maybe I should have avoided speaking to any of them. The whole thing seemed ludicrous. I mean, I knew I'd never had great taste in men, but this was bizarre; there was certainly no one in Holloway I would have considered getting 'too familiar' with. When I thought about all the shagging and affairs that had gone on in Holloway and security knew nothing about them…

Within a couple of weeks there was some improvement and I was moved out of my cell. I had been told the authorities were worried I might 'swing' (commit suicide). I was moved into a single cell with a bathroom and large window.

The prison was built in the grounds of an old manor house and the wings were made like Swiss chalets. I looked out onto an open field and felt the wooden floor vibrate under my feet; such a strange feeling after so many years of concrete. I would sit for hours at night, mesmerised by the wide-open space in front of me. In the daytime, herons flew into the grounds and poked around in the grass while birds filled the trees. But as pretty as it was, it was still prison.

We were given matching curtains and bedcovers, but were 'nicked' if we placed a bottle of milk outside the window to keep it cold. It was the simple things that reminded us where we were. The officers knew exactly how many pieces of bread we should get at breakfast, but could never respond to anything out of the ordinary, like sentence-planning queries. Outsiders might think it was a soft option and that prisoners must suffer while inside but I hated Foston Hall. It didn't look like a normal prison, it pretended to be too nice for that.

Foston Hall was where I first realised that it is not the conditions that make a prison. No matter how comfortable an establishment, it is the staff's attitude that can either make or break the psychological well-being of a prisoner. It is the staff who have all the power in a prison and if a guard wishes to make a prisoner's life a misery they can do so, quite easily. Sadly this does happen and the prisoner can do little to protect themselves. It is unwise to make an allegation against a prison officer and virtually impossible to prove 'unprofessional' behaviour. Power can corrupt and, as I found, quite often does.

Having access to nice things like showers and newspapers does little to help ease the isolation and frustration. I so often felt as though I was drowning in confusion and chaos, at the hands of Her Majesty's Prison Service. The conditions in Lard Yao had been awful but the psychological effects of the British prison service were far worse than what I had experienced in Bangkok.

*

Compulsory for all sentenced prisoners was the 'daytime activity' and the choice in Foston Hall was full-time work or attending daily education classes. I chose the latter. I had done word processing and numerous gym courses in Holloway. In Foston Hall, I sat in on anything: pottery, art, computing. I took maths and English exams, and signed up with the Open University, taking a foundation course in social science. Anything educational was a welcome relief from the tedium of prison life and the teachers coming in from outside every day brought with them a sobering sanity.

At this time I befriended a young offender by the name of Sylvie and we used to hold 'toast ceremonies' most evenings before we got locked in for the night.

We sat around, laughing and telling stories. 'You know that teacher, Mrs X?' she asked me.

'Yeah.'

'Well, she saw you today and said to me that people like you make her sick. People like you drive around in their flash cars laughing at heroin addicts like me. You're the ones making big money out of drugs and don't give a damn for all the problems you cause. She said you're the reason me and thousands of other people in this country are heroin addicts.'

I was stunned but I pretended to Sylvie that I didn't care what the teacher had said. The truth is I did care. That evening, over toast, in the confines of Foston Hall, everything made tragic sense. And there was nothing I could do about it. Nothing at all.

Every morning and every night I prayed for some news about my pardon. The waiting was endless and intolerable. On the morning of 20 May 1998, a report came over the radio telling the world how Prime Minister Tony Blair had intervened in the case of the so-called 'Saudi Nurses' and that they were now due for imminent release.

Lucille McLauchlan and Deborah Parry were jailed in 1996 for allegedly killing an Australian colleague, Yvonne Gilford, in a hospital in Dhahran, Saudi Arabia. Now King Fahd bin Abdul Aziz had issued an order commuting their sentence to the period they had already spent in jail and had ordered their release.

I could feel myself withering. Had I committed a crime so much more heinous that I was not worthy of such government support? One month earlier, the Prime Minister had visited Saudi Arabia and it was widely speculated that he had paved the way for the release of the two. It was a diplomatic coup on a grand scale.

My moods twisted and deepened into despair. In Foston Hall I was a one-off; most of the other inmates were nearing the end of their sentences and preparing to go home. Some of them were already attending 'home leaves', while others were preparing for parole or waiting to go to an open prison. I was serving by far the longest sentence and was nowhere near the end of it. With so many people applying for day releases and home leaves, I wondered whether it would be worth my while doing the same.

'You're having a fucking laugh aren't you, Gregory?' laughed one of the officers. 'They won't let you out with your bird [sentence]. You're too high-profile.' They wouldn't even give me the form to apply.

It was early June in the education department and one of the teachers arrived with most of that day's newspapers for her current affairs class. She took me into an office before her class and showed me what she had read that morning. The headline in *The Times*, dated 12 June 1998, grabbed my attention – MAN CLEARED OF DRUG SMUGGLING FINED OVER HEROIN.

Robert Lock, the man cleared of drug smuggling when his co-defendant Sandra Gregory was jailed for 25 years in Thailand, has been fined by magistrates after admitting possessing heroin. Lock, 32, spent three years in a Bangkok jail before being cleared and allowed back to Britain. He had denied trying to smuggle heroin while Gregory, 32, pleaded guilty, claiming that Lock had paid her to carry heroin out of Thailand.

Now Lock has appeared before magistrates at Cambridge and pleaded guilty to possession of heroin. He was fined £100 and ordered to pay £69 costs. The court heard that Lock, of Cambridge, had been followed by a plain-clothes police officer in the city on April 9 after leaving an address known to be used for the supply of drugs. Police stopped him and searched his Ford Fiesta. He was later searched, and a single foil wrap containing 0.2 grams of heroin was found in his jacket pocket. Lock, who represented himself in court, said: 'I am sorry for any trouble I have caused. It was a one-off affair.'

The *Mirror* newspaper carried a similar story, although much shorter, but in it there was a quote from my mother: 'Sandra was telling the truth.'

An iceberg from my past had broken off and drifted away but now he was in my life again, staring back at me from a newspaper. 'There you go,' said one of the teachers in the education department, 'you were telling the truth after all. Now everyone will believe you.'

What difference did it make to my life now? Even if Robert had been found guilty, I would still have been here. I was still guilty. People expected me to hate Robert and to feel smug about his misfortune, but I didn't. How could I hate him? I didn't particularly like him but if I hated anyone I should have hated myself, for having taken him up on his stupid offer.

Joyce, the woman in the cell next to mine, was a rather eccentric Canadian who wore home-made clothes. A lot of her time was spent writing letters to Charlie Bronson, 'Britain's most dangerous inmate'.

We spent our time moaning together about the usual stuff – the prison itself, the guards, the legal system, the other inmates and, ludicrously, how fat we were. We decided to fast. At the end of the first day we felt in control of a very small part of our lives so we decided to go without food for another day, and then a third.

We began fasting for three days just about every week for weeks on end. Being able to control something as basic as food – or lack of it – brought with it a sense of control and management. We decided to do our fast for 'world justice', something we had read about in a newspaper.

One afternoon I was taken to see the governor to request a visit to see my grandfather, who was ill. As I sat outside her office I told the guard that I was in the middle of my 'world justice' fast. She thought I was on hunger strike and that afternoon, after being told I did not 'fit the criteria to see my grandfather', four officers appeared in my cell, demanding to see a clean food plate 'three times a day.'

I found this hilarious. *Fuck them*, I thought. I had spent so much time rebelling in my mind that now it was my turn to make the rules. The fasting continued throughout my three-month stay in Foston Hall.

If I had committed my crime in the UK instead of Thailand, I would have been sentenced to between 18 months and two and a half years in prison and would have been released after serving half of that. It was irritating to hear other prisoners moan about the severity of their sentences. One woman was arrested in the UK with exactly the same amount of heroin as I had been caught with and she was constantly harping on about how unfair it all was. It never felt appropriate to keep going on about my 25 years. But it was tempting.

Maxine was serving just four years and I had little to do with her until I came across her crying. Maxine had always come over as a tough cookie and capable of doing her time, so I asked her what was up.

'My Mum died of ovarian cancer at 36,' she said, 'and I've just been diagnosed with the same sort of cancer.' Maxine was 34. Dying at that age would have been awful but to die at 34 in prison would have been a nightmare.

'You've got two choices,' I told her. 'You either tear up a sheet and hang yourself tonight, or fight it. What do you reckon?'

Maxine had family outside prison and was due for release within a few months.

'You take my 25 years and I'll take your cancer,' I said. 'Would you swap?'

She thought about it for two seconds. 'No way. I couldn't do a 25 stretch. I'll stick with what I've got. I'm going to beat this.' Less than six months later Maxine died.

Someone was shouting. I could hear voices echoing around the wing. It was nearing the end of July and I was about to go up to the education department when all the girls started running back to their cells. 'They're doing a search,' they shouted to each other.

I had nothing illegal in my cell so I didn't bother running back. The guards could carry out a search if they wanted. The guards came through the wing.

'You had better sit down,' one of them said. 'You're leaving today.'

Why? *Why?* No one answered.

I was strip-searched and my stuff thrown into bags. I was taken through to reception and an officer sat down next to me. 'Gregory,' she barked, 'you're being taken to Durham today.' That was it, no explanations, nothing. But I guessed they weren't taking me on a sightseeing trip.

Since my arrival back in the UK, Durham was the one place I'd prayed never to be taken to. Within the prison system Durham is used as a threat to all the prisoners. 'We'll send you to Durham if you're not good,' was the regular refrain to troublemakers.

Durham had been my immediate allocation from the Home Office when I had first transferred back to the UK, because of the length of sentence I was serving, but Governor Leonard in Holloway had blocked the proposed move. 'It's not for you, Sandra,' he said. 'Durham will kill someone like you.'

I felt sick, and my insides hadn't felt that way since I was stopped at the airport years earlier. I couldn't answer the guard who told me where I was being taken. I just looked straight ahead.

'Do you understand what I have just said?' she snapped.

I turned to her, the venom rising in my throat. 'Are you implying that I no longer understand my own language?' I was furious. The guard sucked her teeth and then smiled, satisfied that they were getting rid of another so-called troublemaker from Foston Hall.

How could they do this to me? I had done nothing wrong. I had been here for just three months. Why was I being taken to Durham? I tried to remain calm. I had managed to get through the last five and a half years. Now came the real test.

THIRTEEN

House of Horror

Dear Mum and Dad,

I don't want to frighten you, but God knows it frightens me! Finding myself in the infamous maximum security institution, amongst the 'Roses', has shattered any illusions I had about the British system… I am here with 44 nutty-looking females and surrounded by guards who just stand around watching us all the time. The cell I am in is freezing, and the toilet is in the middle of the room and in full view of anyone wanting to look through the flap in the door. It is all a bit surreal really, and I can't believe I am here. All the 20-foot fences have a razor wire frill on the top and security sensors on them, so that the alarms go off if a fence is touched. Even the sparrows no longer land on them. Tell Granny and Pa-Pa that all is fine.

Sandra

Letter from Durham, 31 July 1998

More than 120 years after she was hanged in Durham Jail, the prisoner Mary Ann Cotton remains Britain's worst female serial killer. Despite the apparent niceties of Victorian society, they did little to contain her less than puritanical urges and, although convicted of six murders in 1873, Cotton is widely believed to have sent more than 20 victims to an early grave. No convict in Durham Maximum Security Prison, in north-east England, is there for singing too loudly in church.

Four hours after leaving Foston Hall I arrived outside Durham Jail with my escorts. A large, blue gate opened like a whale's mouth and the prison van drove through. Packs of snarling Alsatian dogs and their vicious-looking handlers greeted me. What was this all about? I looked around: grey brick walls with grey, barred windows; heavy metal fences; double rolls of razor wire; security cameras; wires to prevent helicopters landing; guards; truncheons and chains. Every inch of it was high security.

The guards I was handcuffed to said nothing to me, as if a simple conversation might reveal a hidden escape route. As far as they were concerned, they had a seriously dangerous prisoner to guard and nothing, not a whisper, would flow between us. Them and us, that's all it was. That's all it would ever be.

They led me handcuffed through to the infamous H-Wing, a tiny fenced-off island of women who are classed as potentially dangerous, amid a larger men's prison. We passed through 20-foot fences, steel doors and metal detectors. No keys opened any of the doors I was confronted with so far in Durham. Everything had to be monitored and electronically operated from the security tower. Keys were power and keys were a potential to escape. The fewer keys in prison, at least in Durham, the fewer attempts to escape. Keys also kept officers out of trouble. If someone bungled a lock-up then it could be traced back to a specific officer who was in charge of a particular set of keys.

'Get your clothes off,' shouted a tough sounding Scots officer, with chewed fingernails and bleached hair. Then she glared at me. 'What do you think of Durham?'

'I could do with going to the loo.'

'Right, lassie, you can go later.'

Entering Durham Jail was like checking into a very bad hotel. There were four floors separated by heavy wire nets to catch falling bodies – either those who are pushed or those who are attempting to commit suicide – metal staircases and rows and rows of steel cell doors. Even the noises from inside of it, garbled and dark, sounded like prison: voices, shouting, music, keys rattling, boots on metal floors, slamming doors and the soft chatter of security over walkie-talkie radios that all the guards carried filled the air. And it smelled of detergent and inmates' urine. It was such a shock to find myself all of a sudden in this shit-hole that it took a while for me to settle. Much to my amazement, the walls were bubble-gum pink. It's supposed to help female prisoners calm down. There is little, or no, legislating for stupid ideas when it comes to prison psychology.

By now I was desperate for the loo. A huge, fat woman sat on the floor in a red prison tracksuit and I asked her where the toilet was. Her body was a patchwork of heavy scar tissue. Scars over scars had created welts all over her arms and neck and, judging by their depth and width, I guessed they extended further than where I could see. A pudding-basin hair cut exposed red, droopy eyes, and yellow fingers scratched at newly opened cuts. She mumbled something and I followed to where she had pointed.

When I returned, the Scottish guard had sent Syd and Flo, my lovebirds, off somewhere, and I could hear them calling. Everything in H-wing echoed. They were almost as distressed as I was. The few things I had in the plastic bags from Foston Hall were being thoroughly searched.

'You can't have *that* here,' someone said pointing at the offending object. 'And you can't have *this* here.' Tweezers, nail clippers and a map of Britain were taken from the bag. I was then ordered to my cell by the Scots guard, known as Scottie.

Dragging my torn plastic bags along the floor in the direction of the calls of my birds, I headed to the cell. When I looked at the bags I realised the guard had not searched them all and one remained unopened. Everything you have in prison is written down on your 'property card', and if your cell is searched and they find something that isn't on your card, you get 'nicked'. In the middle of the highest security jail in England, the silly cow had overlooked one bag. I didn't want any more problems, so I went back and told her what she had not done. She was embarrassed in front of her colleague that she had not done a thorough job, and that an inmate had pointed it out to her.

I had a few units left on a phone card and I called my mum.

'I've only got a minute,' I said, 'so sit down. I'm in Durham.'

'What? Now? Oh my God, Sandra! Why have you been taken there?'

'I don't know, Mum, but I'll call you when I get another phone card.'

My birds had been left in a cold, dark cell and I assumed that was where I should go. There was no discernible heat and the walls were filthy with age and blood splatters. The paper-thin mattress was dirty with yet more blood and urine. I sat down on the bed, rocked back and forth and cried. *Don't sit here and cry, Sandra*, I said to myself. *Get your head together and sort this out*. The door slammed shut at quarter to five. The average time a prisoner spends in her cell never really changed. It was usually between 14 and 18 hours, depending on the day of the week.

H-wing in Durham housed, and still houses, some of Britain's most dangerous female convicts. I had now been classed as a high-risk prisoner and was, therefore, considered to pose one of the greatest risks of escape and danger to the general public. As a result, I was subject to the most stringent security measures. From the minute I arrived in Durham I knew life was going to be tough. By the time I left, it had just about finished me off. There was very little to laugh about in there and most of the people I met were, to be gracious, a little freaky, while others were downright hellish.

Few female serial killers can lay claim to the level of fear inspired by Myra Hindley. Moors murderers Ian Brady and Hindley were both serving indefinite life sentences, and remained two of Britain's most demonised figures. Their attacks on five small children, whom they disposed of on Manchester's bleak

Saddleworth Moor in the 1960s, scandalised the nation and continue to cause outrage.

Fortunately for me, Hindley was moved from Durham some months before my arrival. That pleased me no end. I doubt whether my sanity could have withstood meeting her on the same landing, never mind that I would have been placed in a similar category for my crime. Myra Hindley is a name that resonates from my own childhood and a constant reminder not to stray too far from home. 'Remember Myra Hindley,' adults would warn, if I were ever tempted to go off onto the South Downs. Now I lived in her shadows.

Hindley was moved to HMP Highpoint in Suffolk, after having spent decades on H-wing, but her legacy remained like a tombstone. There were two constants in Durham. One was hidden away on a wall deep within the bowels of the prison – it was the heavy metal lever once used to open the trapdoor when prisoners were hanged in the prison grounds. The other was Hindley.

There was the most awful feeling that she lingered beside you in lunch queues or in the laundry. Hindley *was* Durham Prison.

Perhaps the most notorious British serial killers of recent history are Fred and Rosemary West, whose names are synonymous with some of the most depraved acts ever detailed in court. I was in Lard Yao when nine bodies were exhumed from under their home in the now infamous 25 Cromwell Street, Gloucester, south-west England, after the investigation was launched into their activities. One of the bodies was that of their own 16-year-old daughter, Heather. Another body, that of Rose West's eight-year-old stepdaughter Charmaine, was found in a former coal cellar at the couple's former home in Midland Road, Gloucester. It appeared the Wests' horrendous indulgence was a joint passion for sexual depravity and death.

Never in my wildest imaginings had it crossed my mind that I might end up in the same prison, on the same landing as Rose West. I had survived those long years in Lard Yao with the belief that coming home to a British prison would be as good as coming home. Now I was in the company of Rose West. It was simply beyond my comprehension. In the British system, prisoners are classified according to the sentence they are serving, not the crime they have committed.

Fred West committed suicide in Winson Green Prison in Birmingham, on New Year's Day 1995, before being brought to face charges of murdering 12 people, including his first wife and eldest daughter. Rose West was convicted of 10 murders at Winchester Crown Court in November 1995 and began serving life in Holloway Prison in north London, before being transferred to Durham for the rest of her 'natural' life.

A few days after my arrival on H-wing someone said to me, 'Have you seen Rose West yet?'

I hadn't really thought about her at that time. 'No,' I replied, 'not yet.'

Some hours later I spotted her walking around the wing and she looked exactly the same as she had in all the pictures I had seen of her in magazines and newspapers. The sweater, the short hair, the large glasses; I was transfixed. '*Oh, my God,*' I thought, 'that's *Rose West*.'

She seemed to scuttle around the place, not walk, as if she was always making plans for something and her manner of walking helped keep her occupied. She also appeared blinkered, as if she found it impossible to see anything else around her. Later I realised that Rose actually doesn't see much that goes on around her at all. There were many times I would be standing right next to her and she just didn't see me.

The sight of her brought me out in a chill. *Jesus*, I thought, *why am I here? These women are child-killers, murderers, serial killers, arsonists, terrorists, paedophiles and all manner of beasts. And West. She's a fucking monster.* I looked at her again, as she scuttled into a corner, and decided never to speak to her. Even though there were only 44 of us on that wing I would not speak to her – how could I, knowing what she had done to so many young women?

A few days later I had a visit from home. The routine was always the same; we had to go through to the workshop before we went for visits. Standing in line, I turned to the person behind me and asked them whether I'd need a sweater in the visiting room. Most people imagine that prisons are cold, miserable places but Durham was usually quite hot. I didn't know if it would be warm in there.

'I wouldn't really know,' came the voice of the woman standing behind me, 'I'm not often in there.'

It was Rose West. The hairs rose on the back of my neck while my stomach twisted at the thought of her standing right behind me, talking to me. Breathing on me. *How can I possibly be talking to this woman?* I turned away without smiling or acknowledging her response...

The most unsettling thing was that it didn't take me long to realise that although Rose West was regarded by most people outside of prison as the most abominable creation, from where I stood, she was not the worst, not by a long shot; she is just the one everyone knows about. And in Durham she was a whole lot easier to live around than many others. One day, after watching Rose over some time, and listening to what others told me about her, I gave her an egg, and in so doing created a different relationship. She was never quite what I would call a friend, but we did speak at length over a period of months.

I tried, on the whole, to be optimistic. Perhaps Durham might even be a valuable learning experience. Daily, I would tell myself that I wouldn't be here long so I would use it as an observation point. I would observe the system and the people here to pass the time and look at it from a sociological perspective.

In reality I sat around sinking deeper and deeper into depression. I could hardly believe the crimes some of these people had carried out, yet there I was, sitting next to them, eating breakfast, showering and working alongside them. Two women I met were each serving life sentences for imprisoning and abusing a 14-year-old girl for five days, and I sat with one of those women every morning before we went through to the workshop to paint pottery.

During the five days they had tied her down to a bed, raped and battered her, pulled her toenails out with a pair of pliers, burnt her with cigarettes and force-fed her disinfectant. On the sixth evening they took her to a remote spot, poured petrol over her and set her on fire. Burns victims don't usually die straight away though, and the youngster was no exception. It was while in intensive care that she gave the names of those who had tortured her and they were caught. She died a few days later.

Then there was DA, who imagined herself as some sort of special-forces specialist. She had a 'thing' about older men. She had already served a prison sentence as a teenager, for the manslaughter of an elderly man. DA was on H-wing serving two life sentences for stabbing two pensioners through the side of the neck with rusty screwdrivers. She was one girl who gave me the creeps constantly.

Everything about her oozed evil. There was a spate of cell fires on the wing and no one was ever caught for them. According to the rumours, DA had been setting them all off; it made her feel important. She enjoyed the fact that women on the wing could have been smoked or burnt to death. Week after week she would pirouette with glee as another cell was gutted and closed off. DA was determined someone would die in a fire.

2 August 1998

Dear Mum and Dad

I honestly have no idea why I am here, but I got a cutting from The Times *newspaper this morning and they seem to have been told all about my move. How can the press know why I am here when I don't? If they really do think that I was planning an escape then chances are I'm going to be here forever… I have no idea how these people think or how they come up with their conclusions, but I suspect that a lot of it is just a charade. Trying to help Sylvie has me classed as a security risk… it's all madness. But maybe I am the mad one. I should never have come back. I should have stayed in Thailand.*

Sandra

I asked anyone in a uniform who had the time to listen, why I was there. After several days a governor informed me that there had been security information reports against me since I had arrived from Thailand, and the decision had eventually been taken to move me after false fire alarms had been set off in Foston Hall.

'But, they don't really think it was me who set off the alarms, do they?' I asked. My response was pathetic.

'No, they don't, Sandra. It's a bit more complicated than that, I'm afraid.' That was it. No explanation, no discussion.

It took me over three months to find out why I was in Durham and I nearly collapsed when I got the information. I received a copy of a letter that a magistrate I know had received from her MP. The MP had written to a prison minister asking for information as to why I was in Durham. The letter stated that suspicions were raised that I had sent my passport out to my parents as soon as I got to Holloway. I had done so because in Lard Yao that was the first thing prisoners, especially non-Thais, are ordered to do; otherwise it is likely to go 'missing'.

I had also arrived in Britain 'with a quantity of foreign money', which was deemed enough to pose security risks. That quantity was a 10-dollar bill and 20 Dutch guilders, hardly enough money to flee to South America. Furthermore, I had also been considered a 'bad influence on younger inmates' and suspected of organising 'hooch' brewing in Foston Hall. The drink they had found had been in the cell of a friend of Sylvie's, the young girl I had eaten toast with and who I had tried to encourage to stop taking heroin.

The dossier continued. I had also been seen 'speaking to a man in the visiting room who had come to visit someone he didn't know'. The man in question was someone I had written to for years and he had agreed to give Sylvie his spare room when she got out of prison, rather than have her go into a hostel full of hookers and junkies. Sylvie had no family of her own and she had been brought up in foster homes. She was a bright girl and, after my own experiences, I desperately wanted her to get on in life away from the drugs. Naturally he had wanted to meet her before he opened his home to her and that was why he had visited.

In Foston Hall there had been a phone scam going on, which allowed prisoners 'reverse charge' calls. Ironically, I had always been too scared to attempt it. Liverpool Lindsey managed to blow the phone off the wall one day, trying out the scam, and I think I got the blame for that too. Then there were the fire alarm episodes. The officers had not managed to find out who had been responsible for setting them off.

Inevitably, when fire alarms go off the fire brigade are alerted. In a woman's prison, bringing the fire brigade in for a bunch of cooped-up, sex-starved women is like inviting the Chippendales to an Anne Summers party. Not a good idea. The fire brigade are heroes – sexy heroes – and a whole truckful of them with helmets and hoses at the ready is better than television for many women with nothing much else to look at in prison. And the firemen seemed to like the attention they were given when they arrived. The girls inside would put on a real show for the boys.

So this was why someone was setting off fire alarms in Foston Hall. For some reason, because the guards couldn't find out who it was, they used me as a scapegoat. One of the principal officers, a six-foot hulk of a woman, was in charge of the investigation into the alarms and saw me as an easy target. According to Lindsey, the Hulk had, a few weeks earlier, referred to me as an 'arrogant tart'. Hardly enough for me to hate her but I knew I wasn't her favourite inmate. In her report she said she believed I had found a place for Sylvie to stay once she was released and in return Sylvie had set the alarms off for me. She also said that during the fire evacuation I was planning to hop over the fence and disappear; hence my status as a threat to national security. What a joke!

I could accept the sentence that had been handed down to me by the Thai Government but I found all this hard to deal with. As ridiculous as it sounds, my move to Durham was totally unjust and I began to get seriously down. There was no avenue of appeal. I had been well and truly stitched up by some fat screw who had it in for me and there was nothing I could do about it.

Eventually I got to see governors and tried desperately to explain why I would never attempt to escape, that it was the most preposterous idea that I would scarper over a wall. Where the hell would I go? Hide out with my parents in rural Aberdeen? I was hardly Ronnie Biggs material. I told them I had committed my crime in Thailand in order to get home and I would never do anything that would keep me from home again. My reasoning and logic fell on deaf and amused ears.

'You were clever enough to orchestrate a large drug smuggling ring,' said one governor.

'But it was three ounces,' I told her.

'That's what you say, but I know different,' she replied, her face neither expressive nor inexpressive.

The stupid woman thought 89 grams was the same amount as 89 kilograms. She thought I had attempted to smuggle 89 sugar-bagfuls of heroin.

4 August 1998

Dear Mum and Dad

I used to always say that this ordeal was 'all character building stuff'. Well, now my character is built. They are now trying to demolish it. Being on H-wing is not as bad as trying to deal with the reason for being on H-wing. How can helping out a homeless

19-year-old have led to all this surveillance stuff? I may be a bit of a wreck if you come down. Life is feeling like a nightmare and I know I'm getting paranoid, but nothing here is logical.
Sandra

When I was first arrested and I sat in the dirty police cells, one of my greatest fears was that I might live for years without ever seeing the sky again. As stupid as it sounds, I just couldn't imagine not being able to see the clouds or be around anything natural. When I first entered Lard Yao there was a sense of relief when I saw grass and trees and the beautiful blue sky. But in Durham one of my greatest fears had materialised.

To all intents and purposes we were surviving in a modern dungeon; it was just so oppressive and claustrophobic. I had felt in Lard Yao that I was on the ward from the film *One Flew Over the Cuckoo's Nest*. I was wrong. Durham was far more like it. Most of the women had serious psychiatric disorders and many were very dangerous. Not merely deemed dangerous by the system, but actually dangerous. A lot of the inmates should have been kept in psychiatric units.

Dawn was nuts. Inside for arson, she would literally 'go off' with disturbing regularity. She was constantly being controlled and restrained by the guards and I got used to seeing her being bundled across the wing by four or five officers. Many nights we would be kept awake listening to the sounds of heavy thrashing, screaming and thudding echoing through the wing and, the next morning, Dawn would emerge from her cell looking like she'd been run over by a cattle truck.

She would stand, facing a wall, and bang her head against the bricks for hours. Later her forehead was a mass of glowing, red swelling. One day she threw herself off the stairs and was grabbed, in mid-air, by a guard who saved her from certain serious injury. In the process she nearly pulled him over the railings. H-wing was always colourful when Dawn was around.

H-wing is merely a wing of a prison, and everything needed to keep a prisoner secure is there; the cells, all the offices, a cell where the doctor came to issue mind-numbing medication, a tiny gym, two filing cabinets of books for a library and the servery where we ate our food.

Food in Durham came in two colours: pale and bland. Pale chips were cooked three hours before they were served up and pale pies were like something left over from an abattoir's toilet. There were always pots of porridge and pale bread. Pale food fed pale people. And the pale people grew increasingly tense at having to eat so much pale, crappy food. Even the prison doctor, whenever he entered H-wing, arrived with more than a hint of trepidation. He wore a suit and a pair of Nike trainers so he could leg it off the wing at speed when necessary.

Noise pollution in any prison is unbelievable but on H-wing it almost drove me insane. As soon as the cell door is opened it hits you, slap-bang in the face. Cell doors are clanked open like coffins. Prisoners clatter around, shouting; they go for breakfast, arguing, calling out to their friends; guards bark orders from the ground floor to the fourth floor (the echo made a better intercom than an electronic one did); radios blare; stiff keys are turned in locks, while the security chatter in walkie-talkies echoes. Boots stomp on metal floors. It is constant and incessant and utterly numbing.

All the prisoners lived on top of each other within foot-thick-plus walls of stone. Despite a difference in construction material, they reminded me of the gerbil cage my brother had made for my pets one Christmas. They also brought to mind the experiments scientists perform on rats in laboratories, where they allow the population to grow to see what happens when too many are placed in a confined area for too long. The results are devastating in a lab, and equally devastating when it is people who are forced to live so close together for a prolonged period of time. Here, reality was skewed.

How do people behave in prison? Well, it didn't take long to realise that groups, both prisoners and officers, were bad, often leading to brutality and rarely leading to passivity. Brutality counts on the certainty that time will heal bruises.

Boredom drives prisoners to ever more pornographic and degrading treatment of themselves and other prisoners. Prisoners suffered from emotional disturbance, uncontrollable crying and uncoordinated fury. Simple things like gossip turned vicious with sometimes-terrible consequences. There were frequent bouts of terrible self-mutilation; frenzied lesbian circles and violence were the norm. An arbitrary division of oppressors and oppressed exists before long, within a framework of punishments and privileges.

Years ago British prisons were full of inmates smoking cannabis and, according to prison lore, many of the officers used to turn a blind eye to it all. Many of them said that when the inmates were smoking cannabis the wings were calm and relatively quiet and overall a landing full of stoned prisoners made their jobs a whole lot easier.

In 1996 all prisons in England and Wales were told to start carrying out mandatory drug tests (MDTs) and a prisoner had to provide a urine sample, every four weeks, at least. The penalties for a positive drug test are severe, regardless of the drug being used. Cannabis traces stay within a person's system for up to 28 days, while traces of heroin are washed out in just a couple of days.

Post-1996 most prisoners stopped smoking cannabis and turned to heroin, because the chances of them giving a positive test were greatly reduced. If someone got a package of heroin on a Friday, smoked it all over the weekend and didn't get a test until Wednesday they would be in the clear. But if they had been smoking cannabis for two days they would not be clear for about a month.

I have met women who came into prison having taken nothing more than a bit of hash in the evenings but who developed a taste for heroin inside. Upon their release they joined the ranks of heroin addicts. Tobacco and phone cards were once the main commodities in prison; now it is heroin. While a lump of hash lasts a prisoner a fair length of time, a small wrap of heroin doesn't last very long and the frenzy people get into trying to get more of the stuff is horrendous. Heroin in prison is expensive and many inmates develop huge debts, which they cannot pay off, and the violence that has resulted from the use of heroin in prisons is terrible. Durham was no different.

For months I appealed the move to Durham. I wrote to Home Office ministers and the ombudsman, and spoke to security officers, governors and guards, but none of them would listen to me. Every one of them was convinced I had been up to something in Foston Hall and the frustration drove me round the bend. Self-harming and suicide attempts are commonplace on H-wing and I began wishing I were brave enough to have a go.

One woman left an almost tangible legacy. She had been so determined to kill herself that one night after lock-in she lay face down on the floor with her knees bent and her feet up behind her back. She had ripped a sheet into a rope and tied one end around her ankles and put the other end around her neck. Then she slowly pulled her legs straight and suffocated herself. They said it probably took at least 10 minutes for that woman to die. Every minute she must have wondered if she was doing the right thing. At the time she probably was.

I started looking at doorknobs and anything else I could hang myself from; I just didn't want to do all this any more. They were killing me. I felt as though I was being microwaved from the inside out.

I had carried a card for years that was printed with the words: 'The truth defends itself. Only lies need defending all the time.' In Durham I threw the card away because I no longer believed those stupid words. Maybe the truthful approach was not the best way to get through life. Despite my stupid mistake, I didn't want to live a dishonest life, but maybe it would be easier for me if I did.

While the cell area of Durham resembled a cupboard, out on the wing we fared little better, as there was nowhere to go and little to do. Everybody watched everybody else and mostly I just sat looking at my surroundings, amazed that a place like this still existed.

The exercise yard for H-wing inhabitants was a triangular area of tarmac, roughly 20 paces by 11 paces by 14 paces. Penned in by two parallel fences and two walls of the prison, between the fences a dog and his handler would pace backwards and forwards whenever we were out there for our 20 minutes of fresh air. If the weather was deemed 'inclement' then no one got out that day at all.

Boredom set in. When boredom set in, self-mutilation was not far behind. It was not a major issue on H-wing – it was a competition. Women would use anything they could find to open their flesh. Some bent a phone card in half to produce a sharp enough edge to slice through muscle; others rubbed their arm with a new scouring pad for a few hours. You'd be amazed how much skin comes away.

One woman broke a plate during lunch one day and opened her throat from just inside the jugular to just inside on the other side with the sharp edge. The following afternoon her friend did the same. A few days later the first woman slashed her arms open from elbow to wrist and the same afternoon the friend gouged out such a groove on the inside of her leg that the doctor thought he would have to amputate. Self-harming is very common among women prisoners; it is usually to do with control, so those who do such things normally know what they are doing, and don't usually die. The madness of H-wing was infectious. Many times I thought, *I am in a fucking nuthouse.*

A woman I had always considered one of the better-adjusted individuals filled two flasks with boiling water and, behind a closed door, took off her shirt and poured the lot over herself. Her skin melted away in sheets.

That was the sort of thing that happened regularly and people just got on with their lives. Everyone stopped caring. I stopped caring. I couldn't give a rat's arse who was winning the mutilation marathon. *Fuck them, fuck them all.* The staff stopped caring, because the madness had become normal. They would, of course, go through all the motions, fill in the forms, sound conciliatory, but really, deep down, no one cared. No one gave it a second thought. Ripped flesh? Pass me a teabag. Gouged eyes? What's on the telly? Sliced from tit to tendon? One lump or two?

The two women who had been ripping themselves to bits later slit their throats and no one really cared. All it meant to us was that we all got locked in because the guards had to take them out to hospital; we were overtime and money. The paperwork, said the officers, was 'a bastard'.

I was on the telephone one day and a woman fell to the ground at my feet, jerking and convulsing in an epileptic fit. Thick, runny blood was pouring out from somewhere on her face, and I just moved over slightly and carried on with my conversation. I actually felt like kicking her for interrupting me. *Don't take a fit in front of me, in fact, don't take one at all because we'll all just be locked in for the night, thank you.*

I had lost all sympathy, and I no longer cared. Blood and fits and fires and self-harming and women sliced in two were simply slight inconveniences. *Your Honour, this is prison life.* They trimmed your fat to the heart in Durham.

14 October 1998

Dear Mum and Dad

Today I began a two-week stretch of solitary confinement, I shall be locked in 23 hours a day for the next 14 days, and so I won't be able to phone you. A lass set fire to her cell and then bit an officer on the chest the other day and she got three days behind her door.

So, I hear you wondering what my crime is... well, worse than arson or assault, I've got a bad back... I really don't care any more though...

Sandra

I found myself in solitary confinement. My crime? I had trapped a nerve in my back while competing in a triathlon for charity in Holloway and the injury had flared up when I got to Durham. I had been limping for nearly a year but the doctor in Durham said the job I had been given on the wing (I was a painter and I was turning the place from bubble-gum pink to pale green), was supposedly making the back problem worse. The doctor ordered that I be placed on 'cell-rest'. So, I began a two-week stretch of solitary, which meant being locked up for 23 hours every day, for the next 14 days.

Dear Mum and Dad

In here alone I find my mood swings extreme. I don't want them to ever open the door again. I would prefer to do the rest of my time totally alone, just emerging for a wash and a flask of hot water.

Solitary was a relief and I felt as though I had been granted a holiday. I no longer needed to come out of the cell, and no longer had to do anything because there was nothing to do. No one could speak to me and I didn't have to speak with anyone. I sat in that cell for two weeks, retreating into my own world with my two lovebirds. The birds were the only things I cared about.

When I finally got off solitary I had to pretend that I was OK, but I was desperately unhappy that I had to be with other prisoners. The rule in prison is not to let anyone know how you are really feeling and the best way of doing that is to laugh and pretend you are fine. The Thais were right, I suppose, crying does make you feel worse and self-pity does no good, so you may as well smile.

November 1998
Dear Mum and Dad
These people are indeed mad... I am beyond anger... surrounded by evil; it is not the inmates I fear but the staff. Because I neither kick-off nor kiss-ass they don't seem to know what I'm about. They are trying to kill me, slowly from the soul outwards. My head is totally shattered... I'd be up for a lobotomy if they were still allowed to perform them.
Sandra

My mum and dad thought I was going to kill myself because I giggled when I phoned them. I had tried to keep my head together and not let my parents know how bad I was feeling there, but they figured things out for themselves and were almost expecting an official letter arriving to tell them I had been found hanging. They resolved to do something about my imprisonment.

We had all believed that the Foreign Office would agree to support my pardon when the time came to submit it, but when I got to the UK and asked for official support I was sent an official letter saying they could not because there were no 'compassionate or humanitarian' grounds to do so.

Up until this point my parents had taken the advice of the government and kept their profiles low. For years they had barely said two words to the media but after the response from the Foreign Office they lost their faith in the hitherto-great British establishment. Did I mind if they 'went public'? they asked me. I most certainly did mind. The last thing I wanted was my family parading themselves in public for my cause: I wanted them to just get on with their own lives.

My parents had firmly believed that the British government would support two upstanding, law-abiding members of middle-class society in their times of need. When this was denied them, they resolved to come out fighting.

The Foreign Office had supported so many others; I wrote to Prime Minister Tony Blair asking him why all the others had been helped and why would he not help my parents. My lawyer and Liberal Democrat MP Malcolm Bruce had had a meeting with Baroness Symons. The government refused to give in to quiet negotiations. Essentially they told us all to fuck off.

My dad always made go-carts, seesaws and sledges when we were children, and built and mended things around our house. After more than five years of adhering to government advice, he decided to fix things himself. He had had enough. Although it would have pained them to admit it, they knew I deserved to be in prison, but the idea of my having to serve at least 11 more years and possibly almost 20 was just too much for them.

So my mum and dad decided to go public. One day my mum told me that I should try and watch the early morning programme, *Kilroy*, on television. Every morning, at 9.00 am, for a week, I watched *Kilroy*. When the show they were appearing on finally came on, I almost died. They were right there, airing all their dirty laundry on the BBC, trying to help their stupid daughter. Another time, shortly after *Kilroy*, the door of my cell banged loudly and a guard told me to turn on *GMTV*, and there they were again. This time they were being filmed from their own living-room. I hated it. It was as though they were there in Durham with me, keeping vigil.

Soon they were in newspapers and posing for the cameras. Gradually, the momentum gathered. They did radio interviews, magazines, television and as many papers as would grant them column inches. They wrote thousands of letters to MPs, MSPs, MEPs, church ministers, bishops and archbishops. Not only did they campaign, costing them thousands of pounds, but they continued to send parcels and clothes in to me as well. Despite my reservations about the campaign, it seemed to be having some effect. The media had taken notice. Gradually the politicians were looking at my case. Secretly, I kept my fingers crossed.

One bank holiday afternoon, I was pulled into the office and told I was 'self-opinionated' and would no longer be considered 'a well-behaved inmate'. I lost all the usual prison privileges including the one good thing about being on H-wing – the television. I felt nothing but contempt for the prison authorities.

There is constant banter in prison and many of the officers often throw their weight around under the guise of humour. I developed the tendency to give back as good as they gave, but my sense of humour had now got me downgraded.

So many of the women in Durham were genuinely bad people, but in order to be accepted by others they projected themselves in a sociable manner, feigning concern for others and trying hard to appear genuine. My mind began working overtime. If the officers could slate me when I meant no harm, then I was convinced the evil prisoners could take them in. I had visions of all these nasty cons being allowed to leave prison and my grandfather being stabbed through the neck with a rusty screwdriver, my mother being tied up and battered, my niece being abducted and abused. It was crazy! My mind was no longer working normally, I was no longer thinking in a rational manner. I was paranoid.

By October my mood swings were extreme. Alone, I seemed to be fine. But when the door opened and other prisoners or guards spoke with me I would get angry or upset. Quietly I sank into a deep depression. On H-wing, no one noticed. No one wanted to.

Despite some of the crimes many prisoners had committed or been involved in, I didn't hate them all, they weren't all so bad, but I did hate the system. Likewise, not all the officers were so bad either. Some were genuinely good people, who treated the inmates with respect, trying hard to fight their own battles against the system in which they worked. The good ones, of course, were few and far between.

There never seemed to be any light at the end of the tunnel and if things carried on the way they were I was sure I'd never reach the end. At this time I was still facing at least another three and a half years before being eligible for parole. I would be almost 40 if I was granted parole and released. It would be Christmas Eve 2003 and I would have served 11 years in prison.

Constantly I was told 'There is no guarantee of parole no matter how good your prison behaviour. First application on a drugs charge is usually declined.' And I had four parole dates – one in 2003, others in 2004, 2005 and 2006 – and this security move to Durham would certainly go against me if I made it through to parole. My release date was at the end of 2007 and the licence would expire in June 2009. The end of the sentence was listed as being 10 November 2014. I would have no family of my own and all my good years would be behind me.

But I never wanted to be treated differently or given special privileges; all I asked for was that I was treated fairly. At this stage, with my mental health in tatters, I felt that I had suffered enough. In any other prison I would have been OK, but this place was killing me. Letters from friends and my family tried to keep my spirits up but even these were not enough. I couldn't connect with people outside any longer but didn't want to go on about my own situation all the time. I was losing touch with the real world and losing touch with reality. H-wing represented the whole world to me and I imagined people everywhere to be the same as those I was living with.

So many times I wished I had never transferred back from Thailand. Over there it had been bad but the way the place had run the prisoners had to organise their own lives. There was always something to keep you occupied. Even the stressful elements became quite stimulating. I'd learnt to look out for myself, knowing that if I didn't no one else would do it for me. In Durham I was simply a cog in the lousy system of so-called reform.

Rehabilitation? What exactly is meant by this term? I know the literal meaning but I doubted if anyone in Durham did.

In Durham there was such an impending sense of isolation and frustration, with virtually no control over my own life, that it caused great psychological hardship, and proved virtually impossible to deal with. In Bangkok, while the conditions were pitiful, coupled with the physical brutality and distance from home, at least there was a sense that I was someone.

Durham was so much harder to endure than Bangkok. Although being able to see my family, being able to use the telephone and having access to newspapers and radio brought their own rewards, other than the walls to focus on, there were points in Durham where I was on the verge of collapsing with insanity. In Lard Yao I was treated no better and no worse than anyone else, yet here I seemed to find myself singled out and subjected to scrutiny for no reason. All I wanted to do was get through my time. I didn't want to rock the boat and wanted nothing from the system. I never expected or wanted to be treated differently, and I just couldn't understand why I had come home to be treated with such suspicion?

Intimidation and bullying are as commonplace in prisons as mugs of weak tea. But when that intimidation comes from an officer you are in serious trouble. When I found myself subjected to the antics of a guard it was impossible to win. Report an officer for any indiscretion and they will all be on your case. Try to defend yourself verbally and you will find yourself on adjudication, charged with something ridiculous.

Constantly, prisoners are subjected to monitoring and counting, rub-down searches and wanding – being checked for metal objects with a black-stick type of metal detector. There are cameras everywhere, so every single movement is monitored, recorded, noted and analysed; and conclusions, invariably, are drawn from them. Is the prisoner acting normally? Is the prisoner a risk? Is the prisoner depressed? Is the prisoner suspicious? Is the prisoner plotting? Is the prisoner likely to? On and on, questions and counter-questions, but never anything direct.

We were watched constantly and the guards noted their observations in daily records. One guard noted that I had 'looked at her funny on the stairs'. It was first thing in the morning and I was off to collect some milk, and I doubt I even saw her. After being told I was self-opinionated, I realised that they misunderstood me and I couldn't speak to anyone; I was too scared to speak in case my words were misinterpreted and I began again to withdraw. I couldn't see the point in speaking and wanted to just crawl into a hole and disappear. I couldn't win with them, so I gave up. Most guards do their job just because they need the money. The rest are usually just sickos who have managed to sneak through the selection process.

Maybe I was as bad as the others. As the months ticked by I began believing I was worthless and evil. Maybe that was the purpose of punishment. Break down the spirit and compliance will follow.

I knew it wouldn't be a holiday camp and knew I didn't deserve one after what I had done but I hadn't expected it to be like this. It got to the stage where I no longer wanted to call home to my family and I didn't want anyone to come and visit me. I felt like a fraud; I was not the person I had thought I had been. I was now as bad as all the other reptiles. Was suicide an option? Constantly. Yet it didn't seem like an option as much as a beautiful promise.

Prison cells are specifically designed so that suicide is as difficult as possible but where there is a will there is always a way. Cells in Durham are about 10 feet long by about six feet wide, with a small sectioned off area (in some of the cells) with a sink and toilet. The ceilings are low and there are no fixtures from which a prisoner could hang something. All the iron beds are clamped to the wall with metal brackets so that they don't move. It used to be common for people to stand the bed up on one end and attach a rope to the top and hang themselves from there. A bed standing on its end is about six feet high, so there's plenty of space for an average-sized woman to dangle from.

There are doorknobs on the sectioned-off area and inmates have been known to tie a short rope around the doorknob, sit on the floor, tie the other end around their necks and hang that way. I'm not sure that I actually wanted to die; more that I no longer wanted to live. My saving grace was that I am too much of a coward and was never brave enough to hang from anything. I was even embarrassed in case I failed. If a prisoner tries and fails, everyone knows because they have a red mark around their neck. Can you imagine? Too embarrassed to commit suicide.

We nicknamed one woman 'Knit One, Purl One', because she loved knitting. Before she had come to prison she had also liked to abuse her daughters. She and her husband had taken pleasure in hanging their daughters up by their ankles, over a bed, from a hook in the ceiling and had systematically sexually abused them with table legs and sadomasochistic devices. Knit One, Purl One and her husband had videoed their acts for years and kept the videos on a bedroom shelf. A neighbour had asked to borrow a movie one day and Knit One, Purl One had lent them the wrong video. The neighbours took the horrendous video to the police and the couple were arrested. She got 12 years for what she had done to her daughters, and when I was on H-wing with her she was applying for access with those girls. Social services were even bringing the children up to see their mother.

I couldn't put myself into the same equation as those people who were sent to H-wing. I wasn't a first-stage lifer, vulnerable prisoner, troublemaker, Category A prisoner or 'danger to society'. I was none of those. I didn't think I was danger to anyone or a threat to national security. I could barely tread on a spider.

A male member of her family had abused Mary until the age of four. She was taken into care for the rest of her childhood, while the man remained within the family and carried on abusing the female children around him, so at age 22 Mary went to see the man with a carving knife in her hand. She looked him in the eye and told him he was about to die and promptly stabbed him once, straight through the heart. She told me she had not done it because of what he had done to her, but because he had continued with his perversions and she saw no sign that he was intending to stop. She is currently serving a life sentence for premeditated murder.

Whenever anyone went anywhere in the prison they would be escorted by two officers and a guard with a dog. Rarely was anyone taken off H-wing, but if they had to go to the dentist, for example, which was up at the medical unit inside the men's section, they were given an escort. The parade of guards and dogs would bring the men up to their cell windows to watch and shout at the spectacle being escorted.

The hierarchy in Durham was obvious. The governors and the officers were the bosses. The male prisoners were next in line. They had extremely low status, but they had more than the women. Monkeys in the zoo, that's what we were. We were nothing. Prison life creates its own hierarchies and women were at the bottom of the pile.

FOURTEEN

Jailbirds

Dear Mum and Dad

Here is like a slow torture, kept alive to suffer. They get most upset though if anyone tries to end their suffering and go to great lengths to prevent anyone doing so…

Sandra

Letter home, January 1999

Night became morning and then night again. Then morning. Then night. I found myself staring at things in my cell for minutes or hours; never quite sure how much time had passed. I had no strategy for dealing with time. Some days I would confront it head on and other days more covertly. Either way it almost drove me insane.

There are many consequences of putting women in cells, under strict supervision and even stricter control of their movements. Everything in a female prisoner's life becomes dependent on someone else – often a man – and that is difficult to come to terms with. Invariably, most women who have ended up in prison have done so as a result of their involvement with a man.

The self-esteem of the women in Durham was almost zero. We were fed, clothed, told when and where and how to say 'yes' and 'no'. We were required to walk when ordered, sit when ordered, and stand when ordered. The natural spirit of independence is usurped and the prisoner becomes dangerously like a child, invariably a volatile one. In most cases, women in prison have their natural roles reversed. It is a radical, anonymous cleansing.

When this happens, inmates attempt to put some degree of control back into their lives. I was no different. Amidst all this chaos of feeling completely and utterly insecure about my future ability to cope with my sentence, I gradually developed a friendship with a security-cleared, male member of the prison staff. I will call him Chris. We became close friends.

Chris was interesting, fun and, surprisingly, completely normal with a great many feelings and opinions. When the opportunity presented itself, we talked and talked about everything from current affairs to our various ideologies and he seemed to care about the things that mattered most to me.

He also believed me when I told him about my transfer to H-wing and how unjustified I thought it was. This was wonderful. For the first time in years, I thought that maybe they were all wrong about me, and maybe I wasn't really so very bad after all. Chris restored some of my faith in human nature and, at the same time, re-established a sense of normality in my prison life. I had fairly regular contact with him and, after a while, he wasn't simply a member of the prison staff, but a friend. Each time I saw him we spoke about how I was coping with prison life, both physically and emotionally, and he listened attentively and reassuringly. He told me about his life outside, shared his interests and dreams with me and I would return to my cell after seeing him, already looking forward to our next conversation.

At this time I was so down and depressed that I could barely remember the last time I had an interest in living. It was still difficult to rise in the mornings, and I couldn't be bothered going for hot water for coffee, something that I previously had done almost religiously. My letter-writing had grown infrequent; rarely did I make telephone calls. I just couldn't muster the enthusiasm to do anything.

Chris and I managed to be alone together rather often. In

prison which, at the best of times, is not a normal environment, a female and male should never be able to be alone together for any length of time. In Durham Maximum Security Prison it should have been totally out of the question.

What kinds of idiots are running this place? I thought to myself, when we once again managed to organise time by ourselves. One afternoon our relationship went a step beyond talking together and before I knew what was happening we were having sex.

It certainly wasn't planned but I had a good idea what the consequences would have been if we had been found out. I won't go into the details of the where and the when but we began seeing other and the sex continued. This unique and rather special relationship lasted for over five months.

To be honest, I couldn't believe it and every time I saw him I was even more astonished that it was actually happening, almost under the very eyes of the system that scrutinised my every move. I didn't care. What else could they do to me?

I hadn't purposely tried to get one over on the system and yet that is exactly what I was doing. Right there in the middle of the highest security prison in England, where £20 million had been spent beefing up security, I was having an affair under all their noses. No one knew; not a soul guessed what was happening.

Affairs between staff and inmates in prison are quite commonplace, although not so many were happening on H-wing. In most cases prisoners are aware of them, but tend to pretend that nothing is happening – they don't want to know because they don't want to grass on anyone. For a lot of the prisoners if someone has found a piece of happiness, even through sex, then it's none of their business. The officers don't want to know either because they will have to file a report about a colleague that basically means making another enemy (in prison prisoners and staff want as few enemies as possible) and becoming buried under a stack of official paperwork. The basic laws of duty fall under the spell of the basic law of entropy.

Chris and I got on well together and our relationship, of course, was good fun but it was also more than this; I felt real again. It had been years since I had last had sex but that was never the issue, the sex was peripheral. We were friends, and I loved having a secret, because it gave me back something to call my own. Our relationship and our secret were more powerful than the actual sex. And I was the one who was orchestrating it, except for its timing.

In prison, the first rule is that if you want something to remain a secret, a real secret, then you cannot afford to tell a single soul; no matter how much you think you can trust them. If you tell your best friend today, and they're not your best friend tomorrow – something that happens with regular monotony – they won't have your friendship, but they've still got your secret. So I told no one, either inside prison or out. The only two people who knew about this were Chris and myself.

Having been shipped from Holloway to Foston Hall as a result of being accused of having 'an unsuitable relationship with a member of staff', the irony of what was happening did not escape me. It was exhilarating and being in a place like Durham and doing something completely taboo added to this sensation.

Following one of the first times it happened, I was told to go to reception. *Oh, my God,* I thought, *someone knows something. How did they find out?* But, of course, no one knew a thing and, in this instance, I was simply going to reception to have my photograph taken, following the introduction of key fobs with each inmate's picture, name and number on them. Looking vaguely ridiculous and wearing a broad grin, the picture was duly taken. I've still got that key fob and every time I look at the photograph I'm sure the secret still shows.

On a number of occasions we were almost caught when someone came into the room. Yet Chris always remained cool while I, meanwhile, was shaking to the marrow with fear.

I did actually like Chris and I wasn't simply having this relationship with him because I could, or because of the power trip.

Outside of prison we may well have had a decent go at a relationship, but inside we simply got on well and enjoyed it until it proved impossible to continue with it.

Around Christmas 1998 panic set in. There was no sign of my period and I thought I was pregnant. I couldn't believe it. Was I pregnant? *In here? In Durham Prison? God, no, please, it can't be true!* I was scared out of my wits. I could barely imagine the reaction – not to mention the headlines – if it had been discovered that I was having sex with a member of Durham's staff.

Nervously I paced my cell, taking half steps forward and then hesitating. Wondering whether I was pregnant was absolute torture and I couldn't eat or sleep. '*Jesus*,' I thought, '*if you're out there, do something*.' I couldn't have a baby born in prison. I mean, what would I tell the rest of the prisoners, and what would I do if I really were carrying a child?

All around me the usual signs of Durham life continued. My situation seemed completely improbable, yet it was true. Most true stories, I suppose, are those that seem so far off-the-wall that they must be true. My head was spinning. What was I going to say to the prison doctor?

'Hello, doctor, I think I'm going to have a baby.'

'Fine, OK. How long have you been in prison?'

'Um, well... about six years.'

Finally I got the opportunity to tell Chris of my suspicions and I thought he was going to collapse. He looked about as freaked out as I felt.

'Look,' I said, pacing the room, 'you don't need to worry. If I am pregnant they won't know it's you. I wouldn't allow them to carry out any DNA tests or anything like that.'

He looked dazed. Despite this we continued seeing each other, hoping that it was just an oversight on my part and that my period was simply later than normal. The panic continued for weeks and, in prison, weeks are very long at the best of times. Every day passed more slowly than the last. I think I even began thinking of names. There wasn't a minute that went by when I wasn't thinking about it. I lost weight dramatically.

In the meantime the rest of the girls were getting on with their sentence and I was trying my best to act normal. Most of the time I felt sick and I imagined that it might be morning sickness. Our predicament continued over Christmas that year and Chris was away from work some of that time, which made the waiting even longer. It was a dreadful Christmas.

When he returned we spoke about how foolish we were and all of the things both of us had to lose. After what seemed like an eternity, my period arrived and I was ecstatic. He was relieved. Both of us breathed an enormous sigh of relief.

We realised that continuing seeing each other wasn't a good idea at all; in fact it was downright stupid, although I can't say that I regret it. We saw less and less of each other until we stopped seeing each other alone altogether. Durham was such a difficult, horrendous place to be in that I needed something to remind me of the real world. Chris had done that for me. Even now it's hard to believe it happened. But it did and, looking back, I wonder whether perhaps, in some small way, Chris saved my life. Or at least my sanity.

For several months before Christmas someone had been setting fires off all over the wing; black smoke billowed constantly from someone's cell. Even though the whole place was built from concrete and steel, it was very scary being locked behind a door when flames crackled close by. When we were not locked in our cells or at work, the doors remained open and there was no way of closing the door if you were going for a shower, so anyone could enter your cell when you weren't around.

On Christmas morning we were unlocked at 9.30 and, as I emerged onto the wing around 10, I looked around as plumes of smoke filtered across the landing. Rose West's cell had been set on fire and the blaze had developed ferociously. There was shouting and screaming and orders being barked; we were promptly locked back in our cells. The whole wing was locked in for the whole of Christmas Day, Boxing Day and the day after that.

Rose wasn't in her cell at the time of the fire but Jack, her beautiful blue-and-yellow budgie, hadn't been so fortunate. Although he survived he was covered in black soot, stunned and more than a little choked. It was awful to see that poor bird carried out of that cell in such a state.

Everything in Rose's cell was turned into a black, charred mess. Her stereo had melted along with all her tapes, all her clothes were burnt, and even the plaster had fried on the walls. I doubt the arsonist was trying to kill her but they knew it would cause considerable damage. While the fire burned, Rose was collecting her breakfast, three floors down from her cell.

Her routine had made her an easy target. Rose would be up and dressed and out of her cell first thing in the morning. She is very orderly and fastidious and always seems to be busy. She cleans constantly, washes, organises things and makes tea as soon as the cell door opens. She gets hot water, milk and her cornflakes, and then fixes herself neatly before moving onto the next chore. Rose created her own regular routine of bustle, as if to compensate for the way in which her life was controlled, whilst appearing oblivious to the chaos around her.

In prison you get to know people, their routines, what they prefer to wear, how they like to be spoken to and what makes them stand out; the whole process is like seeing someone constantly stripped bare, undressed and naked in front of you. I noticed this about Rose and most of the others. Then I realised everyone looked at me in exactly the same manner.

After the fire, Rose was put in the segregation block because that was the only vacant cell. Somewhat ironically Rose's cell had been secured with yellow, police-crime-scene tape. Now she was the victim. No one got to use the telephone.

I was amazed to discover that Rose loved budgies. I hadn't imagined her capable of loving feelings, but Rose doted on Jack. Sometimes he even sat on my shoulder and chewed my earring. Now he was black with smoke, trapped in someone else's fire, inside a prison cell that held Rosemary West. A real jailbird.

After the fire Rose gave Jack away. She was traumatised by the event and I actually felt quite sorry for her. She had nothing at all in there apart from that bird. There was no life for her to live inside and there never would be outside. I felt sick that someone could go out of their way to cause someone else grief, first thing on Christmas morning. Durham suddenly seemed such a dreadfully sad place to be. And I was stuck in the middle of it all.

The fire had upset Rose terribly and much more profoundly than any of us really understood. No doubt many people will be delighted at the thought she was upset – they might even criticise me for feeling the way I felt, but in prison inmates are as you find them on the landings, or at breakfast, in the queue for the toilet or in recreation. Whoever they have been or whatever they may have done before coming suddenly becomes less important.

Writing about Rose West is difficult because to put a human element into her story seems almost disrespectful to those that died. I spent a long time on the same wing as her and could see that she did have feelings, although initially my response was almost paralysed by my knowledge of the events from her past. As the months passed in Durham, people-watching became the only activity worth spending time on. Rose West liked to sew and, before the fire, had a cell full of frilly pillows and doilies. She cleaned incessantly and liked what she always described as 'a decent cup of tea'. She liked to cook shepherd's pie or a pasta dish – always something simple and ordinary; nothing with spices or anything like that. I think she probably felt safer that way. By all accounts the men who worked in the kitchen had been putting disgusting body excretions and sharp objects in her food.

In Durham we had access to a small kitchen and in there, whenever possible, I would make the fudge my mother had taught me to make as a child. One day I found myself transfixed as Rose, who was making some pasta, automatically turned the handles of the saucepans inwards and away from the edge of the cooker. I had been taught to do that at Girl Guides in Hollingbourne; it was for safety, an action mostly to prevent young children and babies from burning or scalding themselves. It was strange to witness Rose West, the woman charged with killing all those kids, carrying out a little act like that. It was heartbreaking. Who was she? I'm still trying to figure that one out.

'Sandra,' said Rose one day, 'do you know how many loaves of bread it takes to feed eight kids and lodgers?' She always seemed concerned. I used to find that rather odd, given what she was in prison for.

Rose rarely got a visit but when she did the dogs were brought out and there was a massive security operation just for her. Rose was not allowed to use the same visiting room as the rest of the prisoners, because she was vulnerable to attack, so she was taken to another part of the prison. One of the first questions asked by anyone visiting me in Durham was about Rose and what she was really like. In the visiting room I would notice people looking around at the other prisoners, hoping to catch a glimpse of her. She is one of only a few women whose names are whispered instead of spoken.

Anytime Rose was taken off H-wing and into the open grounds, the local police were informed. Three officers usually accompanied her, and two dog handlers, while all the security systems in the prison were alerted. The male prisoners watched her while she was being paraded under guard and they screamed and bawled as she passed. Rose walked with her head down, trying to appear oblivious to anything that was going on around her.

Early one afternoon, before the fire, the guards came to deliver her to the visiting area. Because such a large operation has to be carried out before they unlock the rest of the wing, their appearance had caught her by surprise. When they opened the door, Jack flew out and she had no time to get the bird back to the cell before her visit. I spent the afternoon with Sue, another inmate, trying to catch him.

We tried everything to get that bird back but nothing seemed to work. Rose returned around four and Jack was still high up on the bars near the ceiling of H-wing, chirruping and laughing at us. Rose did not look happy.

'Rose,' I said, 'I can't get Jack back. I've been trying all afternoon.'

'Right!' she shouted, 'I've had enough of this. Jack, get in that cage, it's teatime. Get in that cage.'

Instantly Jack flew down from his perch, over my head and into his cage. I was amazed. Rose just laughed.

Initially you perceive people for their case and your judgements are made accordingly. My impressions of Rose were challenged constantly.

It was the same with Rena. She was in her early twenties and as cute as a button to look at. She also possessed that elusive spark of a bright young woman who is ready to meet life head-on. But there was another side to her. After years of neglect and torture her three-year-old son was found dead, tied up in her bedroom, as she slept with her boyfriend. The baby had numerous broken bones and his battered body was dehydrated, malnourished, covered in cigarette burns and black with bruises. Rena was serving a 10-year sentence.

The case was shocking. Everyone in the prison, as you can imagine, treated her dreadfully. Inevitably I was forced to speak with her. If you are housed in the same facility, your path will eventually cross with that of someone you have no intention of ever conversing with. Most of the time your feelings towards that person are formed by the case in question. The curious thing with Rena was that her personality never really tallied with her actions.

She had an acceptable face. Sometimes we even laughed together. It was the same with Rose.

She never actually said to me that she was innocent, but when she talked about Fred I would just sit there and think to myself, I can't believe what I'm hearing. She was spouting all this stuff about the trial, about her treatment during the trial and what a psychopath he was.

'Sandra,' she would say, her voice lifting, 'He [Fred] was a fucking psychopath. Do you know what a psychopath is?'

'No, Rose,' I replied, 'I don't think I do, but I think you're going to tell me.'

'Do you know why he fucking hung himself?'

'No. To protect you, I suppose. Or he wanted to take the easy way out?'

She was foaming at the mouth by now. This is what she did when she was excited.

'No, no, no,' she screamed, 'none of those. I'll tell you why, because all their lives they are planning the ultimate fucking murder. Do you know what the ultimate murder is?'

'No, Rose,' I replied, nervously, 'I don't.'

'Their own. Their own murder. That's the ultimate murder for a fucking psychopath. He planned all his life to kill himself. When it came down to it, he carried out the ultimate murder and hung himself. Not for me. For himself.'

I was stunned by her conversation, the chill of it and the matter-of-fact common sense of it. It seemed quite a profound analysis from an uneducated woman.

I am still not at all sure whether Rose West is mad, sad, or just down right bad. Never once did she speak highly of Fred West, but perhaps my own mind was so frazzled that I could no longer think rationally. What does go through my mind, now that I have met her, is whether or not she received a fair trial. I am not saying I believe she is innocent – far from it – but I don't know whether she knew for sure what West was doing in the cellar of their house.

'Why was it only Rose who was arrested,' she constantly asked, 'when that house was full of people for years? Why weren't any of the lodgers ever arrested as well? If I'm supposed to have known what he was doing why wasn't any one else supposed to have known?'

Until very recently her lawyer was preparing a fresh attempt to clear her name. However, Rose decided that she would resist the temptation to appeal, knowing that if she ever were released she would never be accepted back into society...

After months of feeling it was impossible to continue I calmed down, accepted being on H-wing and accepted I was no different from many of the other women being held there. Home Office ministers, prison ministers and prison staff had all told me there was no chance of me getting a transfer out for at least three years so I had no choice but to deal with it.

'Gregory,' barked one of the screws one afternoon, after I'd been called down to the wing office, 'you've been placed on a 20–52 order.'

In layman's terms, this basically meant I was now considered a potential suicide risk. If I hadn't known the consequences of that I would have found it hilarious. I was now feeling OK about things and yet now they were putting me on a 15-minute suicide watch!

For the following week I had officers coming to look in my cell at 15-minute intervals and a file followed me everywhere I went. Written into that file went any observations regarding mood swings, behavioural traits, and changes in attitude, communication problems and any comments I happened to make.

Guards came by and sat with me, while others enquired about my birds, my family, my friends and prison life. A certain shame hung over me. I didn't like their attention and felt that most of them were insincere, but I was no longer feeling the way I had been feeling previously. Why had they not noticed then?

During this time, late one Sunday night, Sue and I stood at our cell windows, watching an ambulance crew walk into the men's prison. Shortly afterwards the governor came in and then they called the prison chaplain. An hour after the ambulance crew had arrived, they took out a young man on a stretcher covered by a sheet. He was 26 years old and had served 16 months on remand. His cellmate had woken to find him hanging from the top bunk. Obviously the suicide-watchers had neglected their duties.

Every night, during my 20–52, officers appeared in my cell, turned the light on and woke me up to see if I was alive.

'If I'm dead, can't you deal with it in the morning?' I'd shout. 'Why do you have to know now?'

A suicide watch is enough to encourage anyone with even the remotest suicidal tendencies to just go ahead and do it.

'Bang, bang, bang.' Depending on the occasion, officers would appear every day early in the morning and do their LBB checks – locks, bolts and bars. They would bang on all the bars of the cell to make sure they hadn't been sawed through during the night. Then they would thump on all the walls. Fists thudded against steel and bricks. They checked all the bars, then they checked to see if there had been any security violations; they looked under the bed and thumped any pictures stuck on the wall.

Every day they would come in and thump around, sometimes even twice a day. If they came early on a weekend morning, I tried hard to ignore them and would usually get a poke in the side to make sure I was still there and not just a bag of pillows. Most of the officers, I think, watched too many bad prison movies.

There were so many difficult people in this prison, and the events that took place on an almost daily basis were shocking, frightening and, occasionally, funny. I don't want to identify all the women I came across in Durham, who caused certain things to happen, but their stories give a flavour of the kind of place Durham is.

L never said much about her case or why she was serving a life sentence, but her heavy eyes and general air of despair told their own stories. Once, I remember, we were walking together in the exercise yard and she was rambling on about how much she was looking forward to her visit at the weekend. Politely, I asked who was coming to see her.

'Just some Christians,' she replied. She proceeded to tell me how she had brought some lads round to her house and together they had killed her father.

'He must have been a bad guy, your dad, eh?' I asked, a little shocked.

'No, not really,' she smiled, 'it just kind of happened.'

Often in prison stories there's really no point to them at all. They're just too crazy to explain. That's why these people are here.

Durham became more than a synonym for horror to me; it became a category of it.

Another time two prisoners were arguing over something, and one screamed at the other, 'At least I didn't kill my own children.' One of them had stabbed her husband to death, and the other had poisoned her two young children. Can you imagine, two women using the deaths of two children to win an argument about their own morality? Before long their voices faded. Even horror turns to dust.

Zeena went to Asia and bought a matchbox full of arsenic and poured it in a samosa that she had cooked for her abusive husband. He had been making advances on her 14-year-old daughter so, rather than have her daughter go through the abuse she had herself suffered, she poisoned him. She is serving life for premeditated murder.

Then there was Jane who had stabbed her boyfriend's wife. She had been sleeping with this man for several months and, in a frenzied attack, she had stabbed the woman over 30 times, in front of their two young children. Just a few months after she arrived on the wing, she decided to turn into a Christian. A short time later she was confirmed and organised a 'party' for everyone on the wing. I declined the invitation although one tabloid newspaper, the following Sunday, included an article about me having gone to the party virtually hand in hand with Rosemary West. Rose hadn't gone either.

Tiny Tears and Winnie had both taken 'hits' out on their husbands. Both men had been murdered because the wives had preferred the new men in their lives and they didn't want to share the proceeds of the marriage out between them.

Do these stories matter? Are they even true? In prison, especially in Durham, the answers are never meant to be easy. A lot of the time there's no point; they're just stories. But they'll probably stick with you for another 20 years.

Not all the women I met in Durham were mad, bad or evil. When I first met Sue May I thought she was just one of the many nutty jailbirds I'd come across so many times over the years. Sue constantly went out to exercise, whatever the weather, wearing a pair of cycling shorts and carrying a bag of bread to feed the sparrows.

This mad old jailbird, I thought to myself, *going out in shorts to feed the birds*. A number of times I walked around the yard with her. Sue's a talker and every day she'd tell me about her case, the way the police had handled it and how her lawyer had not offered any defence at her trial. She was innocent of the crime she'd been accused of, she said, and I took absolutely no notice of any of it because you hear these stories all the time inside. I sometimes used to think I was the only guilty person in prison.

After a while I thought about the things Sue was saying. I'd question her at length, trying to catch her out with something she had said earlier. But her stories always added up. Out of the blue, I'd quiz her on some small detail, pretending I was a little confused, but the responses always flowed without her having to think about it and always linked in perfectly with something she had said earlier.

On 12 March 1992 Sue discovered the body of her aunt, Hilda Marchbank, a frail 89-year-old woman, in her aunt's house, which had been ransacked. Immediately a neighbour called the police. Eighteen days later, Sue was arrested and charged with murder. For several years, Sue had been her principal carer, visiting several times a day to provide meals and clean up.

The police initially claimed Sue had killed her aunt for money; it was later shown, however, that Sue had been given power of attorney over her aunt's affairs some years previously, so the police dropped that claim, arguing, instead, that the two women had rowed. There were clear indications of an attempted burglary at the house but the police failed to pursue this.

Typically, her inexperienced lawyer did not present evidence that would help her to the jury, and much evidence against her went unchallenged. An unidentified male footprint was found in the wardrobe and unidentified fibres were found on Hilda's hand. Similarly, an unidentified red car was seen parked outside the old woman's home for 15 minutes at a time when the murder could have taken place. Incredibly, a man with a record for burglary informed his wife of Hilda's murder one hour before Sue discovered the body. The jury knew none of this.

There is no evidence to prove Sue guilty beyond a reasonable doubt. Sue had no history of violence of any kind and she had no motive to kill her aunt. It didn't take very long for me to realise she was serving a life sentence for a crime she hadn't committed and, the more I listened, the more my faith in the British system of justice shattered. Was it possible that the police in this country could be as corrupt as they are in other countries? Before Sue's story I would never have believed it. Sue will never be released unless she admits guilt and shows remorse, something that she will never be able to do.

I cannot possibly do Sue May's case justice in this book, the details need a book of their own. But I defy anyone to read about her case and still say that they think she murdered her aunt. I have no idea how Sue manages to cope with the massive injustice she has lived with for a decade. Sue lost her appeal in London on Friday 7 December 2001.

My grandfather had not been well for a long time. On the day before New Year's Eve 1998, I telephoned home and my dad told me that he was in hospital but they had been to see him and he was fine. Fine! How the hell can he be fine, I wanted to know, if he's in hospital? The following day, at 4 o'clock in the morning, a guard came banging on the cell door.

'Get up,' he shouted, 'get up.' Bang, bang, bang.

'What's the noise about?

'Out. You're going out today,' was all that the guard said.

Christ, where the hell was I going? At 5 o'clock I was taken out of the prison in a Category-A bullet-proof van, flanked by five prison officers wearing bullet-proof vests, and driven to the Victoria Hospital in Dundee, Scotland. An armed police escort led the way. No sooner had I walked in to the room where my grandfather lay than I had to walk straight out again. I knew he was dying.

I was wearing prison handcuffs and one of the guards asked me if I wanted to wear a chain instead. I did. I returned to the room wearing a cuff with a four-foot chain attached to a guard. It was awful. I had not seen Pa-Pa for almost 10 years.

The nurse woke him and he looked at me and, to my amazement, went back to sleep. She woke him again and this time he cried.

'Oh my God, Sandra, it's you!' he wheezed, 'I thought it was your mother. I can't believe you're here.'

He looked at the cuffs, with a quizzical expression on his face. He thought it was modern jewellery.

After half an hour my mum, dad and grandmother walked into the room. The whole place froze. No one had told them I would be there and it was the first time my family had been together for almost a decade. It was awful and wonderful at the same time. I was terrified. There they were, all the people I loved most in the world, and I was in chains. Our body contact was minimal.

The doctor called us all out of the room, telling us there was nothing else they could do for Pa-Pa and he had very little time to live. We were devastated. I had only an hour and a half with him yet, by the end of our time together, he seemed to have picked up. The lines lifted from his forehead and he seemed to breath a little easier.

It was time to go. 'But I've just got here,' I wanted to say. Rules are rules though, so I just kissed Pa-Pa on the forehead and, as I was being led away, I desperately wanted to throw a tantrum; I wanted someone to stop all this. I was out of prison. Why couldn't they just leave me here? I wanted my dad to stop them taking me back.

But of course he couldn't. I turned away, just walked off, chained to a guard. I was then placed in double cuffs. I looked at my father and, for the first time in my life, I saw an almost spiteful resentment towards authority bursting from within him.

'How can you let the IRA out for Christmas,' he spat at them, 'and chain her up like an animal?'

I smiled to myself. He didn't need to say anything, but he did. He put an arm round my shoulder with his words and all of a sudden the ground around me was more solid.

Before I left, a nurse came to me and said, 'You've just saved an old man's life, Sandra.'

We celebrated Pa-Pa's ninetieth birthday a few months ago, and the fire is still burning within him.

Although I was always expecting the worst in Durham, out of the blue – after endless hours of high-level discussions, being placed on suicide watch and sending hundreds of letters to all the official prison bodies – I was being transferred out. I could not believe it. I barely knew whether to laugh or cry. Someone, somewhere had decided to drag me out of the dark and into somewhere with a little more light. I had spent 15 months on H-wing.

Now I was being transferred to Cookham Wood Prison in Rochester, Kent. It was October 1999. All of a sudden, they couldn't wait to get me out of Durham; something had happened to expedite my transfer although I never did manage to find found out exactly what it was. There was a slight hitch, I told them. I still had to take my end-of-course Open University exam and if I didn't I would have wasted the whole year's coursework. So I was allowed to complete it. My stuff was packed for me while I sat the three-hour exam and then I returned to my cell. It was the way I had found it over a year before: cold, bare and impersonal. What poor soul was going to take my bunk?

The following morning I queued for a small pot of milk before giving it to Sue. She was crying. I think I was too. It was difficult to leave her in that dire, disgusting place. Sue supported me when I couldn't move with depression and I tried to support her when her own depression had rendered her almost rigid. Now I was leaving her, now I was leaving Durham. But she accepted my leaving with grace.

If ever a place was a working metaphor for some of the worst things in life then Durham was it. I said my goodbyes, and then my good riddance.

As I was taken from H-wing I dared not look back, fearful that one look might mean I would one day return. I was driven out of Durham in a Group Four security sweatbox. The big, blue gates swung open and I closed my eyes. 'Don't look back, Sandra,' I whispered, 'don't ever look back.'

FIFTEEN

'So Long, Farewell...'

Dear Mum and Dad

I seem to spend my life in a perpetual state of exhaustion. Please don't order any papers for me, everything can wait until I know what's what and if I am still here next year I will deal with these things then... this Pardon is certainly taking its time, I really don't expect to get it now. It would be nice to know one way or another though, living like this is doing me in...

Sandra

Letter home, April 2000

A recommendation from the British government would be likely to improve her chances of a successful appeal. But the Independent *has learnt that, after two and a half years of deliberation, Foreign Office officials have decided to abandon the former English teacher to her fate. In a letter to Gregory's parents, the Foreign Office minister Baroness Scotland says the case lacks the 'compassionate grounds' to justify government interference.*

Independent, 20 December 1999

As in Durham, the shadow of Myra Hindley hung over Cookham Wood Prison in Kent. She had stayed here for several years before being transferred, but still I could feel her lurking around the place like an imperious fog. It was 600 miles and two days' drive from my parents' home in Aberdeenshire.

Yet no matter where they decided to send me, it was only the walls that changed. Prison was simply a repeat of the previous day, over and over and over, as I struggled to find something approaching meaning or purpose through punishment. Wing life was always precarious and I rarely had any answers as it continued swallowing me up.

All my hopes lay with the Royal Pardon, but the chances of receiving one appeared to recede daily. After negotiating the intricacies of Thai bureaucracy, my application had been at the king's office for around six months. My chances of an early release would undoubtedly have been enhanced greatly if the British government had given it support, but they had refused to do so on several occasions.

Christmas and New Year passed me by once more. I was near the end of the seventh year of my sentence and still I had little idea when my appeal would be considered. I was told it might have been before Christmas, and then I was told it might be in the New Year. Someone else told me it might be another six months. The uncertainty was incredibly frustrating. On Boxing Day, a friend who had served over six years took a huge overdose and I understood perfectly what had driven her to do it.

By now prison – with all its ghosts, both the living and dead – was posing questions of such certain intensity that I was utterly exhausted by it; I was tired of the befuddling soap-opera sagas of everyday life and tired of living like a confused animal.

The British government maintained that it was not policy to support clemency appeals for British nationals under foreign jurisdictions, other than in exceptional cases. This usually meant cases involving the terminal illness of the prisoner or a next of kin. UK practice, however, seemed to differ a great deal from the practice of other governments worldwide and did not even seem to be applied consistently by the UK government.

If I had been an Australian, I would have received automatic government support for my pardon. If I had been an American, my sentence would have been reduced to take account of time spent in Lard Yao Prison. The American system automatically multiplies Thai prison years by six, which would have meant my four years spent in Lard Yao would have been regarded as 24 years in the American system. I would have been eligible for parole immediately upon my return home and would by now have been deemed to have served the entire sentence without remission. The Dutch government reviews the sentence of those who are transferred from conviction under foreign jurisdiction back to Holland against the domestic equivalent sentence.

Patricia Hussain's appeal was apparently supported by UK's Customs and Excise. I could not understand how that was consistent with the government's stated policy. The reason seemed to be that she gave evidence leading to the conviction of other drug dealers. While I would never grudge Patricia for one minute the reduction of her sentence, I didn't feel that it was fair. When my parents asked the Foreign Office for an explanation, a spokeswoman of the consular division said, in a letter: 'Consular confidentiality precludes my commenting on Patricia Hussain's situation.' I still wonder how the difference can be justified.

Throughout the previous year, my parents had sought and won support for my application for clemency from a wide cross-section of people. They received the backing of the Church of Scotland, the Roman Catholic Church in Scotland and the Episcopal Church of Scotland. They had the support of 35 Anglican and Roman Catholic bishops, including one archbishop. There were 57 Members of Parliament from all parties, including former cabinet ministers, who signed a motion calling on the government to support my appeal to the King of Thailand, and more than 30 Members of the Scottish Parliament backed a similar motion, while many others had given public or private support. All these people and organisations support the need for tough penalties, especially for drug-traffickers, but for them that has never meant that the normal rules of justice could be set aside.

My mother held a candle-lit vigil outside Downing Street on 5 February 2000, to mark the beginning of my eighth year in prison. She stood in the cold for three hours with a group of supporters while I stayed locked in my cell, less than 40 miles away. My father, meanwhile, was rising at five in the morning to give radio and television interviews. Finally, I called them and asked them to stop. This whole clemency bid was a charade.

I always wondered how much the lack of British government support for my appeal to the King of Thailand continued to prejudice my chances. Respectfully, all I wanted was the government to make it clear to the king that there was widespread support in the UK for my sentence to be reviewed and reduced.

I hoped the government would convey to the king that their lack of support was more an issue of general policy, and did not mean that they did not believe there might be a strong case for clemency. Rightly, I should be punished, but surely it was time for mitigating circumstances to be fully considered? The punishment, more than anything, seemed disproportionate. At the same time, Kosovo war criminals who had been convicted of systematic, cold-blooded mass murder were getting lighter sentences than mine. I was paying dearly for my crime, but I didn't want to be made a scapegoat for those who were not.

After months of fighting my high-security status through all the available official channels, I gave up trying to convince them I was not a threat to national security. I no longer cared. One evening the governor walked past me on the landing.

'Good evening,' he said.

'No, George, it is not a bloody good evening at all. I am sick of this shit and these fucking idiots who run the show. All these allegations against me came from one female, Officer fucking Bulldog, in Foston Hall, and I'm tired of it.'

The governor stopped me short. 'I know her.' That was all that he said.

I kept rambling. 'Isn't she the most disgusting excuse for a woman?'

He nodded. I had finally said something that hit a mark.

The following week I was working outside in the garden, the lowest-security job in the prison. It was wonderful. I could feel the wind on my face for the first time in ages. Part of me felt free. I think the governor understood.

Every day, every single hour of those days since my plea for clemency was presented to the Thai king, I had been praying for the pardon to come through. I would pray overtly, telling God that I would do anything that he wanted if he could see to it that I could be free to spend time with my family; I would pray secretly, avowing that I had changed my ways and that all my arrogance and cockiness had gone and in its place was some kind of decency; I would pray by night and by day for intercession, for a sign, at least, that things were changing.

'Maybe this will be the day I'll hear something,' I repeated, every morning. Every time I saw a prison guard staggering towards me carrying a piece of paper, my heart missed a beat, thinking, this is it. I turned the radio on every morning, hoping to hear something, anything. I read my stars every week, scoured the headlines in newspapers, and scrutinised the body language of the guards.

Then there were days when I just wanted them to say, 'Gregory, your pardon has been rejected.' My life was on hold constantly and that was hugely problematic because I knew the rest of the prisoners and many of the guards thought, 'Who is this stupid cow, waiting for a pardon from the King of Thailand?'

If my pardon were rejected, I would still have to wait years before applying for an open prison. Should I concentrate on the next three and a half years until my parole date? Or should I plan for release? Or maybe I would get a reduction in sentence? I even stopped buying prison socks in case I was going to be set free. Nothing ever seemed to add up.

Working in the gardens, I saw the gate every day and I remember seeing one prisoner being released. She was taken to the gate and allowed to walk through it, just the same way I had imagined it would be for me one day too. She carried a black bin-liner full of clothes and held a bus pass in her trouser pocket. The guards just opened the gate and out she went. It was beautiful. She strolled, as if leaving prison was the most natural thing in the world, as if all the wasted muscle memory in her legs had clicked back to life and was saying to her, 'Relax, take it easy, just stroll. Don't let them see you rushing this. *Savour* it.' And she did. She simply strolled out of the prison into the real world. It was such a moving experience.

I never knew the girl, but I understood what she was feeling. The officer who had taken her to the gate just looked at me, and said, 'Well, what did you expect?' She just couldn't understand.

In April, the then Foreign Secretary Robin Cook failed to raise my case with the Thais on an official visit, when he met with Prime Minister Leekpai Chuan, and I knew then that the government was not going to change their minds about offering me support. The state visit came shortly before celebrations to mark the king becoming the country's longest-serving ruler – the sort of occasion where dramatic gestures were often commonplace.

I read that my father had said it was 'a total arrogance of power that Cook seemed able to ignore the churches, politicians and anyone else who believed that I had been sufficiently punished for what I did'. I loved him for that; standing up in public and saying these things against the government.

One day I was in the lifers' room when Butchy, a hard-faced girl who was serving only a few years, was in with her girlfriend. She shouldn't have been in the room but she wanted to watch something on the television. After a heated row about what channel we should watch, I sat down, hoping she would go away.

From behind she punched me on the side of my head and by

the time I realised I had been hit, another followed, then another and another. The blows crashed down on me and I jumped up, squaring up to her. My fists were clenched and I was ready to strike back, when I quickly realised that if I were caught fighting it would affect my parole, especially if I got a reduction of sentence with the pardon application. As it was, my earliest parole date was still over three years away but if I was lucky enough to be granted a reduction of sentence that parole date would come forward. Depending upon the result of my pardon I could be eligible for parole quite soon and I just couldn't afford to have anything negative on my record. I didn't hit her. I just stared at her. Then I opened the door: 'Get the fuck out of here.'

The whole prison knew I had taken a battering and Butchy gained a lot of kudos for her actions. Part of me found it unbearable to have let her off the hook. I wanted to batter her. But I couldn't. So I lived for a decision on my pardon application and I lived with numbers and reductions and terms and one-fifths and two-thirds and paroles and kings of Thailand and all kinds of craziness.

'You are to call your mother at 3 o'clock,' said the governor, one afternoon in the garden.

Surely it was good news. It couldn't be something tragic, I decided, because it is the chaplains who break unfortunate family news to prisoners. 'Call my mother?' I replied. 'Why do I want to call my mother?'

'Just be in the office at three.'

'Oh my God! It's my pardon, isn't it? Has it come through?'

'Not yet, it hasn't.'

At three I called home and my mum answered. I don't think she even said hello. I can't really remember everything that we said but I can *feel* it.

'The King of Thailand has granted you a full Royal Pardon, Sandra.' Her voice was quiet, compliant and dignified.

I said something stupid like, 'Oh wow! Oh far out!' It was all I could muster. It sounded too good to be true. My mum was silent and I knew she was crying.

My mum and dad had been informed, unofficially, on Thursday 20 July, by the Foreign Office, and the reaction of them both was one of stunned silence. Immediately, they telephoned the prison to break the news to the governors. The Foreign Office was called for confirmation, but the prison authorities could do nothing until they had some paperwork.

There are no words to adequately describe the elation I felt when I heard my mum telling me I had been pardoned. Part of me exploded with joy; the rest, I think, with absolute fear. I was afraid it might not be true.

For weeks before my pardon I had been desperately low and my moods had deepened. 'The sentence is too long,' I kept thinking, 'I can't do it anymore.' I couldn't be bothered going to the gym, or even watching movies. I lost interest in reading the papers and barely mustered the energy to write letters. Even visits from friends failed to inspire me.

My mum put down the telephone. Now the pressure was gone. It was as if the heaviest imaginable weight had been lifted from my belly. 'Oh my God,' I said out loud, 'I've been pardoned.' I ran back to the prison garden, where I had been weeding, and found T, a close friend.

'I've got a full pardon, T,' I screeched. 'My mum said I had been given a full pardon. I'm going to be free!'

The first thing I thought about was buying every prisoner in Cookham Wood a Mars bar, 150 of them. Although I was warned it could take seven days to translate the necessary documents, that night I began packing all my possessions and throwing things into piles for my friends. I lay awake all night listening to the residual clanking of keys and then the silence. I thanked God for his help.

The next day I tried to act normally. I still had to type an essay on the disposal of radioactive waste when a guard came by the education class. He threw a black bin-liner at me and said: 'You are leaving.' That's all. Nothing else. There was no sense in prolonging the details with mere words.

The whole room started applauding and as I turned around I saw Natalie crying on the other side of the room. A lump appeared in my throat. What could I say? I knew how she felt; we had watched so many women leave before us. Now it was my turn to leave.

My imminent release was viewed, at least in diplomatic circles in Bangkok, as a victory for quiet diplomacy, despite persistent UK government refusals to back pleas for clemency. I would like to think that people might understand that I was not freed on a whim but according to the rules of the Thai justice system.

It is a simple fact of Thai law that the king has executive power and it is he who decides whether someone deserves forgiveness or not. I don't think I got off lightly and I do think I deserved my punishment. I was dealt with according to the laws of Thailand and Britain, and had never said that I should receive a pardon; I simply applied for one. It was up to other people to judge whether I should get it or not.

The prison was buzzing with excitement. After lunch, when the guards unlocked everyone, all I could hear was applauding and banging on doors; even the officers, many of whom thought I was a stuck-up cow, were smiling.

Every time one of the women was released the inmates burst into a song from *The Sound of Music*. I had heard it hundreds of times. Now it was being sung for me. 'So long, farewell...' They sang through tears of joy and it seemed appropriate to end my sentence with a song instead of anger. It was a miracle, I was getting out. Some of my clothes were still spinning in the prison washing machine.

On 21 July 2000, at around 2.30 pm, I stood at the gates of Cookham Wood Prison, after serving a total of seven and a half years of a 25-year sentence. I was met by my mum. The sun was shining as I held my mother in my arms and we both cried. It was the most wonderful sensation of my life to hold her. I had £45, the stereo I had bought in Durham and two bags of books and clothes.

At the time of my release 1,293 Britons were being held in foreign prisons in 76 countries. More than half of all offences committed by British inmates abroad were drugs-related. There were 33 convicted Britons in Thai prisons, mostly on drug charges.

It was seven and a half years since I had sat in the customs room in Don Muang Airport, with an officer threatening to shoot me.

SIXTEEN

Holding the Keys

23 April 2001

The government in Thailand says it plans to hold more publicised executions in its efforts to control rising crime rates. On Wednesday, the media was summoned to Bangkok's toughest prison to watch the last moments of five condemned men, before they were shot by firing squad... Suranit Chaungyampin, advisor to the Prime Minister's office, said it was being done for psychological reasons... the condemned men had not even been told that they were going to die that afternoon – they were given just two hours' notice.'

BBC

It is 4 o'clock in the morning, a shaft of light has filtered into the room at my parents' cottage in Aberdeenshire, and I can hardly wait to step outside. Later, I hear the rumblings and morning sounds of my parents and, although I have barely slept, I don't get up immediately. My prison habits are still with me.

In Durham Prison, one year before my release, the evening officer had forgotten to lock the door of my cell and, several minutes after everyone was locked up for the night, I stepped out tentatively onto the landing, smiling at my daring, but wary of the trouble I might get into if I was caught. This is how I feel on my first morning of freedom for seven and a half years.

After a while I open the door and creep out from the room. Downstairs my dad, wrapped in his old, black dressing gown, is making tea. How long has it been since I have seen him wearing it? Ten years? No, longer. I am mesmerised. I stare as he fills the kettle with water. His legs are thinner than I remember and he takes a little more care as he pours.

While I have always imagined him as a younger man, he looks burdened by the weight of the last few years and I realise I have been responsible for so much. He turns around, catching me staring, and smiles. 'Tea, Sandra?' is all that he says. He doesn't need to say anything more. He knows. He just knows. And right there, in his old, black gown, I love him more than I have ever done in my life.

I laugh as I struggle to unlock the door of the house. Prisoners, of course, are not used to having a key in their hands and the memory of such a simple task needs to renew itself. I turn it this way and that until finally the door clicks and a sliver of fresh air touches my face.

Now I can feel the weight of the grass beneath my feet, I can sit and watch the birds and squirrels dancing in the trees and I can walk outside whenever I choose, even in the rain, or in the dark. There is nothing between the sky and me, and I put my hand out and almost touch it. It is surely a dream.

My release from prison was, in many ways, as much of a shock as being arrested. In prison I still knew who I was but outside my life has become a little more ambiguous. As an inmate I formed friendships and understood the common ground I had with people. Now this is gone. What could I possibly talk to anyone about apart from my prison experiences? Would I end up like the proverbial old soldier who tells the same war stories over and over to his grandchildren?

Most of my friends from the past have moved on, apart from one or two, yet even with them I am unsure if we are still friends or simply people hanging onto something that existed, almost in other life. Mark Holroyde remains the exception to this confusion. He has been such a loyal friend. My relationship with Shanty, the girl who introduced me to John, the guy I left for Thailand with, never lasted the course, for reasons that I will not go into, but I mourn the loss of her friendship.

One of my more incredible experiences, and one that suffers from no such confusion, was meeting up with my brother and his family. His little girl was more amazing than I had ever imagined possible and her admirable strength of character and remarkable beauty now sees her over her physical problems. For so many years she had been frozen in time as a baby, hidden behind the plastic case in the little book of photographs that I had carried. In my mind she remained a baby, wrapped in a warm blanket, but now she stands over four feet tall. Can I really have been away for so long?

My grandfather, thank God, survived also. Almost immediately after my release, I travelled to see Pa-Pa at his home in Dundee. It was wonderful to touch his hands, as fragile as autumn leaves, and to listen to that gravelly, Scottish burr. I loved being beside him. I loved the smell of his nearness and the fact that he had fought against the odds and stayed alive. My dear grandmother was still there, still looking like a spring chicken and at 83 still believing she was one. Never once did they condemn me for what I did.

My prison experience has made me appreciate so many things about my life, my country and, especially, it has shown me what wonderful parents I have. I always believed that I knew better than my parents, especially my dad; I always imagined that I had nothing to learn from them. How terribly wrong I was. My parents were my strength – are my strength – and they have been hounded by the press and have suffered terribly since my arrest; but they never gave up on me. They are the still centres of my storm.

How much did they suffer? Once, on a radio programme, I heard my mum being interviewed. When she heard of my arrest she just couldn't stop crying and eventually she had to stop going out of the house because she constantly broke down in tears. She gave up going to work, gave up her social life and stopped playing golf. What she did instead was, very early in the morning, go to the local swimming pool and cry openly, hoping that the water would hide her tears and that she would be able to cry it all out of her system. My mum only stopped going to the pool in July 2000, when I was released.

It is impossible ever to repay them for all they have done. What I have tried to do in this book is provide them with some kind of answer as to why I made this terrible decision. This isn't really a book about a drug smuggler. It's a book about love and the things people don't say when they should. It might only be some pieces of paper stuck together but it is the best I can do after all these years.

Perhaps one of the more emotional episodes following my release was returning to the house I left in West Yorkshire. Trying to get back there, where my story really began, has been like a slow-motion dream; the more I tried the less chance, it felt, I had of succeeding.

When I arrived outside the house it took a few seconds to compose myself before heading towards the building, nestling at the heart of a quiet road. The short walk from the car to the front door, after Holroyde had dropped me off, felt as though it had taken a lifetime. The last time I stood there, in front of the frozen hills and the endless, metallic sky, I was 25 years old, filled with excitement at the prospect of travelling to another country. It was 10 years later, and the hills and the sky remained unchanged, although I did not.

As I stood outside that door, I had a strange feeling that I no longer belonged. Once inside I discovered that most of my furnishings and belongings had been either sold or stolen. The house was filthy and smelled awful. Still, I was home at last.

No one wanted me to live there, especially my parents, who wanted me to move to Scotland. A few weeks after my first visit I returned to the house and gradually I could feel a little warmth returning, a little part of my old life coming back to me. So I have kept it, and I live here now. Part of me died in Lard Yao; perhaps being home might bring some of me back to life.

Robert Lock had made everything sound so easy. Yet I cannot put all the blame on him, although I can still barely fathom how I could have been so stupid. So I hope that Robert Lock has grown, as I have grown over the past 10 years, and I wish him well. If I had thought a little more profoundly and a little less selfishly about what I was going to do, it would never have happened.

For me, smuggling drugs was a way to get home, but I suspect that for many there are a range of feeble excuses. Most of those who agree to smuggle are, in the main, preyed on because of their youth, naivety and inexperience. Single women, in particular, are often targets for the well-dressed, attractive drug dealers. I have met people who have tried to smuggle in order to pay for medical care and surgery, to fund university, or simply to be able to buy a loved one something that they have always wanted. There are, of course, also those who do it for greed and selfishness. There are as many reasons for people smuggling drugs as there are people who do it.

The Thai government will continue to hand out stiff sentences and execute prisoners and, although I do not agree with much in their system of justice, I was a guest in their country and accept what they do, albeit with reservations. My only real complaint, now that the pain and suffering appears to be over, is that perhaps the sentences are a little too long.

I truly believe that little good comes from locking people up for years and years away from their families, without any real support, especially if they are to be released back into mainstream society. Some people will disagree. They are, of course, entitled to their opinion.

It is very easy to criticise the Thai system of punishment but, in many ways, the system in Britain is worse than it is in Thailand. Sometimes this is easy to forget.

Part of me is stunned by the direction my life has taken over the last decade but nothing has surprised me more than my acceptance for a university place. On days when all I could smell was the stench of rotten food and open sewers, I constantly asked myself, 'How did I get here?' Now, having been accepted to read for a geography degree from September 2002, the same question comes back to me. I was supposed to begin the course one year earlier but I decided to delay it for a year so that I could, in some small way, repay my pardon, by trying to give something back to society. Since my release I have given anti-drugs and travel-awareness talks at schools and conferences throughout Britain. It has been a humbling experience, offering what advice I can to young people who might one day find themselves in one of the most beautiful countries in the world and be tempted to do as I did.

With gap years having become so popular amongst young people I hope that they can learn something from my own experiences. Perhaps, just as they are about to take a bad man up on a bad offer, they might look back at the talk I gave them and remember what a fool I was. Maybe, just maybe, my experiences might have had some kind of value and resonance.

I have also been working with a doctor from the prison in Bangkok to raise money for a hospice. There is an old building in the prison that we hope can be converted into a quiet, clean place so that terminally ill patients can be taken there to die with dignity. To die alone and forgotten, in a noisy, hot and filthy room, is a horrific ordeal that no one should have to go through. So many times I thought that that would be my fate.

Curiously, while my acceptance at Oxford became public knowledge and was received with some criticism, I seemed to cause a mild furore in the media after being recruited as an adviser to Scotland's prisons inspector in a bid to improve conditions for inmates. Around July 2001, Clive Fairweather, then chief inspector of prisons in Scotland, asked me and two other ex-convicts to advise on reform, in the first programme of its kind in Britain.

My role saw me writing a report for the prison inspectorate on the benefits of electronic tagging as an alternative to custody. It was planned that I accompany the inspectorate team on their official inspection of a prison, but the media managed to put a stop to that and I stopped working with Mr Fairweather.

The fact that I was paid for two days' work appeared to upset a number of people, including some politicians and drug campaigners who questioned whether I should benefit from my crime. I accept that I have no relevant academic qualifications, apart from the experience I gained through prison; however, I do believe that it is only right that any assessment of prison reform should listen to evidence from those who have spent time inside and who have an intimate knowledge of the machinations of that system.

I believe it's time to look at alternatives to custody for those who are not a danger to the public. During my work on the tagging paper, I was impressed with the proposed reforms, which meant some offenders would be given the choice of a prison sentence or serving their time under curfew at home, while their whereabouts were monitored electronically. I do worry whether or not we are releasing better people back onto the streets after a period of incarceration.

Having been released from prison myself, I know what a shock to the system it is. I was one of the lucky ones who had somewhere to go and a family that were prepared to support me. So many more inmates are not as lucky and the cycle of crime continues. Over 95 per cent of the prison population in this country face release at some point. We'd better hope that someone somewhere is planning to improve their lot.

I have served a long and punishing sentence, which I deserved, much of it in one of the toughest foreign prisons in the world, and in some of the toughest that the UK has to offer. I truly hope that some of my experience in these environments can somehow be used to improve the penal system for those that will continue to enter it. Life in prison is not easy, nor is it meant to be, but in many instances there has to be a viable and more productive alternative.

The prison system at present is unacceptable and only getting worse. The chances to provide constructive opportunities for offenders have diminished. I hope there will be serious attempts to find solutions to the ever-increasing problems in British prisons.

Sometimes it all seems like a dream – not a nightmare – just a dream. I wish, of course, that the dream had never happened but that belongs to the past. But I can truthfully say that I am not bitter; I can't afford to be. I am 37 years old, and still, occasionally, I find myself dreaming this life away. I have no family of my own, and I suspect I never will have. I'm like the girl with the new identity, washed up on the tide somewhere, waiting to enter a new world, unaccustomed to the language and the protocol involved. But now I must deal with the future.

There remains, and I suspect that it always will, a part of me that is secretly happy that I was caught and that, curiously, I was given the time and the space to reflect on my life and on the lives of those around me. As a teenager, and as a young woman in my twenties, I harboured the notion that the world belonged to me, and me alone, and that I would take from it at will. During that time I forgot, as many of us are prone to do, that this is not the case and that, if anything, our world is simply loaned to us by others: God, family, friends, children and even strangers.

If I had never gone to Thailand and had never been caught for attempting to smuggle drugs, I might still have been living the life of a rather self-indulgent young woman who expected more and gave less in return. I doubt that my relationship with my mum and dad would be as honest, sincere and loving as it is now. For this, I am eternally grateful. I wanted my parents to forget they had a daughter; they didn't. And I love them for that too.

When I stood at the gates outside Cookham Wood Prison, I said that I was guilty of breaking the law in Thailand and that I took full responsibility for what I had done. I am glad that I said this. I still believe it. One of my regrets is that I cannot return to the country that I grew to love so much. Thailand embarrassed me and I embarrassed it. It also saved me. It is a beautiful country, with a wonderful culture and lovely people. It gave me many moments and continues to do so.

I have tried to be as honest as my conscience and the law allows and I hope that I have not done anyone in this book a disservice. My intentions are simply to say sorry to everyone involved, especially to the people of Thailand, and even the Thai prison system. I took an extraordinary risk for money and I ignored the price to be paid for smuggling drugs. I will live with the shame and consequences of what I did for the rest of my life.

As I write this, while the sun is shining outside my house, I realise that my experiences were actually some kind of privilege. I stare into this huge crystal ball of thoughts and dreams, nightmares and fears, and the wonderful thing is that I can see only myself, alive. I am seven years old, playing with my brother; I am a teenager annoying my parents as only I could have done; I am reckless and impulsive, trusting and selfish. I am a traveller, then a prisoner. Then, of course, I am free.

And yet… in the background I can still hear prison, the screaming, fighting, and the shouting. I will never be free of my past.

Epilogue

Two years after being released from prison I went to Oxford University to read geography, and after three years of intense studying I finished with a 2:1. My parents are, at last, proud of me.

Most of the time it feels as though the person who went to prison for drug trafficking is someone I once read about in a book. Then, out of the blue, I can be thrust back in time to that horrendous world of walls, with all the frustration and despair. I am eternally grateful for my second chance.

Catherine, one of the South African girls in Lard Yao, became ill in 2003. Her health deteriorated dramatically in just a few months and she was taken to the hospital building. There, she spent a week screaming in pain and begging for help. None came, and she died alone. All the other South African women remain in Lard Yao. They live in hope that a transfer agreement will be signed with the Thai authorities, so that they will be able to transfer home to a South African prison. And they all pray that they too may be granted a Royal Pardon.

Eritrean Winnie went quite mad. She sits all day, slumped in a corner, raising her head occasionally to ask, 'What time is the plane leaving?'

Sue May made legal history in April 2005, when the Home Office released her on parole 11 days before her tariff date. No other life-sentenced prisoner who has not pleaded guilty, has not shown remorse or addressed their offending behaviour has ever been released on or before their tariff date. Most serve many years longer than the recommended minimum term. Some are never released. I can't help but wonder whether *the system* also knows that Susan May did not murder her aunt. Sue continues to fight her case, and her anger and determination to clear her name becomes stronger with each passing year. The injustice she continues to suffer would destroy many people, but with Sue there is no sign of any bitterness. She has retained her sense of humour and sweet nature, but will continue to fight until she has succeeded in proving her innocence. I wish her justice.

The end of my story is a happy one. For many others it will not be so.

Sandra Gregory, September 2005

ACKNOWLEDGEMENTS

Sandra Gregory

I am sure that I would not have survived the long years in prison without all the true and very good friends who stuck by me, all the amazing people around the world who wrote to me, sent me parcels of chocolate, books, toiletries and cat food, and my family, who all supported me; they all, ultimately, kept me and my spirit alive. I was so very lucky in so many regards and during my years in prison, both in Thailand and in Britain, rarely felt truly alone. To all these people – I am eternally grateful for your friendship and the strength each of you gave me; thank you. I would not have survived the ordeal alone.

There are so many people I would like to thank personally for all their help and support but do not have the space here to do so. Gratitude is hard to express with mere words, but I know not how else to repay my debt to you all. Thank you all for your help and support and for all the letters you wrote to me and in support of me or on my behalf. Your friendship, prayers and encouragement gave me the courage to get through those years locked away.

I am grateful to so many people but would especially like to thank:

His Majesty The King of Thailand for forgiving me the crime I committed in his beautiful country and giving me back my life.

Olivia and Victoria for protecting certain persons.

Khun Tawitchai, my lawyer in Bangkok, who remained loyal and reliable for over three years and ensured me the minimum possible sentence for the crime I committed in his country. Good lawyers are hard to find, but he was surely one of them.

Jean Sharpe for being so much more to me than just an embassy representative and for the many times she 'fought my corner' in the 'early years'. And to all the other members of the consular staff at the British Embassy in Bangkok.

Prisoners Abroad, who were a continual emotional and financial support and offer a lifeline to any British person who finds themselves incarcerated abroad.

To Julie, who came religiously to visit me in Lard Yao. She shared my pain and helped me cope with the isolation and madness. God did indeed send you.

James and Mary Mackay and Matthew Rodger for having faith in me and winning the support of the Church of Scotland. Your confidence in me and continued friendship gave me hope and continue to do so.

All the MPs, MSPs (special thanks to Nora Radcliffe MSP), MEPs, councillors, church ministers, bishops and archbishops who supported me and pestered the British government on my behalf. Special thanks to Malcolm Bruce, Liberal Democrat MP, for his continual support and hard work throughout the years and for the Adjournment Debate he held in the House of Commons on my behalf. And, of course, to Martin Bell for supporting Malcolm that evening. Thank you both.

Warm thanks to everyone who became a member of the 'Friends of Sandra Gregory' support group based in my home town. Special thanks to Jackie Cox for speaking out on the record and for her support throughout the long years. Each of you shares a very special place in my memory.

Special thanks to Reverend Jim Jack for being so supportive towards my dear grandparents and for all your prayers. Thanks also to Stan and Eddie from Prison Fellowship.

Thank you, James, for being so much more than you were expected to be. You were as much of a treat as your 'treats'.

Thank you also to Sue May, who is about to enter her second decade behind bars. The support and friendship you showed me in Durham when I was crumbling under the weight of depression helped me survive the place more than you will ever know. How you survive the massive injustice dished out to you I will never know. Stay strong my friend; the truth will prevail in the end.

Enormous thanks to my best friend Holroyde for being such a special person, a treasured and loyal friend and for taking care of my house. For almost a decade you kept my life outside together for me and enabled me to come home. I love you.

Anthony McLellan, I thank you also, for helping me rebuild my life following release from prison and enabling me to do something I had always hoped to do. You have done far more for me than simply make it possible for me to share this experience with the young people of our country. Your faith in me, loyal friendship and sincerity re-established my faith in people and have enabled me to move on from my past. You're special too, Tony.

And, of course, huge thanks to my parents for not giving up on me. You were, and remain, my strength.

This book would almost certainly never have been written if Michael Tierney had not contacted me in June 2001 asking me if I fancied having a go at writing it. I know I was not an easy person to work with, but neither were you, M! My years in prison taught me to be suspicious and mistrustful of people and so often I doubted Michael; doubted his integrity, his capability and his level of honesty. Once again I was so very wrong. I am honoured to have had the privilege of working with Michael and must thank him for his immense patience, guidance and incredible depth of understanding during the months we worked on this. Thank you.

Many thanks also to Kath, Michael's lovely wife, for all her reassurances, her understanding and incredible patience throughout the writing of this book.

Michael Tierney

It is never easy being prodded, pushed and cajoled by a Glaswegian male at the best of times, so my thanks go to Sandra for allowing me to do so with annoying regularity. Her patience, despite our occasional 'divorce' during this project, is much appreciated. I hope I have not done you a disservice. Now enjoy Oxford.

At Vision thanks to Sheena Dewan, Stella Wood and the rest of the staff for appreciating that Sandra had something to say and for their thoughts and advice.

There are a number of people at *The Herald* newspaper, where I work, who are deserving of thanks. In the library, Angela Laurins, Sarah Stewart and Natalie Bushe helped my research; on the editorial floor, Kathleen Morgan, Hugh MacDonald, Cate Devine, Dawn Miller, Lorna Martin, Elaine Livingstone, Susan Swarbrick, Barclay McBain, Chris Starrs and Keith Sinclair for their encouragement. Also the staff at *The Herald* magazine. Outside the paper Ron McKenna, Jonathan Russell and Craig McGill for listening to my Friday night ramblings. Also Campbell Gunn. Thanks also to Brian Savage for our friendship.

Two weeks before the completed manuscript was due to be handed in my father, John, suffered a massive brain haemorrhage that almost killed him. The evening before it happened we spoke on the telephone about the book and I knew he was eager to see it finished. I spent the following two weeks working into the dark hours for him. Although he is still in hospital he, and my mother, Catherine, are with me always and I cannot ever thank them enough for what they do, and have done. They raised nine of us. I still don't know how. My love and thanks go to my wonderful brothers and sisters, Lorraine, Maureen, Iain, Fiona, Mark, Catherine, Vincent and Claire. Love as always to my nephews and nieces. *What we have, we hold.*

To the nursing staff and doctors at Stobhill Hospital and the Southern General Hospital, in Glasgow, you have my thanks. For anyone who took the time to say a prayer for Big JT and anyone else I have forgotten to mention, I am sorry. You are in my thoughts.

To Kathleen, my lovely wife, your patience knows no bounds. Thank you for everything and allowing me to be me. There is not enough thanks in the world for my daughter, Mahoney, and my son, Gabriel. They are perfect angels.